LISTEN TO THE STORIES

GARLAND GAY AND
LESBIAN STUDIES
(VOL. 6)

GARLAND REFERENCE LIBRARY
OF SOCIAL SCIENCE
(VOL. 741)

GARLAND
GAY AND LESBIAN STUDIES

General Editor: Wayne R. Dynes

LISTEN TO THE STORIES
Gay and Lesbian Catholics
Talk About Their Lives
and the Church

Raymond C. Holtz

GARLAND PUBLISHING, INC. • NEW YORK & LONDON
1991

Library of Congress Cataloging-in-Publication Data

Listen to the stories : gay and lesbian Catholics talk about their
lives and the Church / [compiled by] Raymond C. Holtz.
    p. cm. — (Garland reference library of social science ; vol.
741. Gay and lesbian studies ; vol. 6)
    ISBN 0-8153-0045-X (alk. paper)
    1. Catholic gays. 2. Homosexuality—Religious aspects—Catholic
Church. 3. Catholic Church—Doctrines. I. Holtz, Raymond C. II. Series.
Garland reference library of social science ; v. 741. III. Series:
Garland reference library of social science. Gay and lesbian
studies ; vol. 6.
BX1795.H66L57   1991
282'.08'664—dc20   90-24817
                                                              CIP

Printed on acid-free, 250-year-life paper
Manufactured in the United States of America

TO SYLVANA

For patience, fidelity, and support

CONTENTS

vii

SERIES EDITOR'S FOREWORD

In a half century our understanding of homosexual behavior has been transformed. During the 1940s psychiatric and medical approaches dominated the subject. When not simply characterized as social pathology, same-sex behavior still ranked as an aberration, something to be overcome. Hence the emphasis on therapy or "cures." Even then, though, change was in the air. The two Kinsey Reports of 1948 and 1953 not only revealed that the incidence of homosexual activity was much greater than previously thought but, by adopting neutral, nonjudgmental terminology, suggested that it lay within the normal range of human experience. This implicit assumption found confirmation in the research of a psychologist, Dr. Evelyn Hooker, who showed that using a random sample chosen from the general population—instead of the clinical sample routinely employed at that time—the performance of homosexual subjects on objective tests was indistinguishable from that of heterosexual ones. In retrospect, the most startling innovation was the founding of the homophile movement by Henry Hay and others in Los Angeles in 1950. Bedeviled by growing pains and the hostile climate engendered by the McCarthyite trend, the movement evolved slowly. In 1969, however, in a climate of social ferment conditioned by the Civil Rights movement and opposition to the Vietnam War, the homophile movement turned a corner, a development symbolized by the Stonewall Riots in New York City.

The ensuing decades saw not only a torrent of publications—so many that bibliographers can scarcely keep up with them—but also a decisive shift in the center of gravity. Major works that could not be ignored now appeared under the authorship of open, proud gay men and lesbians. No longer was gay life described as a remote, exotic phenomenon, but directly by those who had actually experienced it and who had no hesitation in saying so. "They" yielded to "we." In an effort to correct previous distortions, some of these writings erred on the side of advocacy. Today, however, thanks to the mingling of many voices, a balance is being struck that is moving rapidly toward consensus. Another shift was away from present-minded social science toward a new emphasis on cultural themes. Gay men and lesbians, it was increasingly recognized, had made immense contributions to the worlds of literature and drama, art and music, film and photography. Scholars could chart the role of the sexuality of many creative figures. Moreover, scrutiny of records from other cultures—Islam, China, and Japan, as well as a host of tribal cultures known from the field work of ethnographers—signaled the need for an understanding of same-sex behavior as a world-wide phenomenon. The new climate of acceptance revitalized the older approaches of sociology and psychology. Even those in the natural sciences, which insofar as they had addressed the subject at all, were hostile, reentered the arena with interesting though often still speculative contributions in the realms of sociobiology and constitutional biology.

Although the new research rightly seeks to overcome older negative approaches, questions of value persist. A survey of the history of the subject shows that in addition to ascertaining the facts of same-sex behavior and its cultural expression, it is essential to scrutinize attitudes toward it. All too often these have been disparaging—they have reflected facets of homophobia, the irrational dislike of sexual attraction between members of the same sex. While some scholars have contented themselves with tracing and recording the influence of these adversarial views, others have felt compelled to refute them. As in women's studies and black studies, this sense of a need to correct the record leads to a perceived departure from older ideals of dispassionate objectivity. Yet now that the more vehement expressions of outrage have passed, it is possible to see that a passion for justice is not incompatible with an objective search for truth.

Today the panorama of studies in the field is a rich one, and it is becoming richer still. In all likelihood, however, the subject of sexuality, linked as it is to so many other spheres of human aspiration, is inexhaustible.

The conception of this series is deliberately pluralistic. Some volumes collect representative papers or articles together with critical commentary by the editor to bring a current issue into focus. Other books are substantial monographs reconsidering major aspects of the field. Intersecting with these two categories are research manuals, sometimes overtly bibliographic and sometimes more discursive, which serve as critical tools for advancing work in the field.

Raymond Holtz is a Catholic priest who has been associated with several universities in teaching and campus ministry. He is currently engaged in parish work.

In view of the past record of Christian persecution of homosexual men and lesbian women, some will find it anomalous that today's gay people should seek to maintain ties with the churches. Most human beings, however, seem to have an unquenchable desire to understand their roots, be they religious or secular. In addition, some have strongly felt that homosexuality has a spiritual element, however difficult it may be to define precisely.

The recent history of relations between homosexual persons and the Roman Catholic Church has been complex. The path-breaking pontificate of John XXIII (1958–63) accomplished liberalization in several spheres, leading many to hope that the momentum of reform would continue. Out of this optimistic climate arose the Catholic gay group Dignity, founded in San Diego in 1969. This lay organization, which had over 7,000 members at its height, was in fact the model for affinity groups of homosexual persons seeking dialogue with their churches. It was followed by Integrity (Episcopal), Axios (Orthodox), Affinity (Mormon), and many others. At the same time, however, the position of the Vatican Curia shifted, as shown by the letter of Joseph Cardinal Ratzinger (see Appendix), and the Dignity chapters were denied use of church premises.

This book addresses the transformations of individual consciousness that accompanied these changes in the Church. The testimonies that make up the main part of the volume reflect the fact that for many Americans, religion—whatever its institutional framework—is a matter of personal concern and valuation. Some maintain a long-range perspective on a two-millennia-old tradition which allows them to hope for or expect a return by Rome to the path of reform, and encourages them to remain identified as Catholics; others have despaired of change and left the church of their ancestors. The stories gathered by Raymond Holtz reflect a broad spectrum of response by religious and lay people, by Catholics and ex-Catholics. Above all they are intensely *human* statements, and the drama they unfold is of universal interest.

Wayne R. Dynes

ACKNOWLEDGMENTS

I want to thank Daniel Burr for his patient and long-suffering work in editing these stories, and for his invaluable suggestions and ongoing support.

I also want to thank Professor Wayne Dynes for his enthusiastic support of this project and his suggestions for improving the manuscript. Thanks to Gary Kuris, publisher, for his continued commitment and support of my work.

In a very special way I want to thank all the people whose stories appear in this book. They have been an inspiration to me of personal integrity, good will, and tenacity in the face of much opposition and criticism.

INTRODUCTION

I am a Roman Catholic priest. The incentive for gathering the stories found in this book is the result of an experience I had reading *Once a Catholic*, edited by Peter Occhiogrosso. The book consists of a series of interviews with prominent authors, artists, movie producers, and others who share a Catholic background. I was fascinated by the strength of the Catholic roots of those raised by Catholic parents and educated in parochial schools. Many of these people have ended their affiliation with the church, yet they would identify themselves as Catholic when asked their religion. As I became engrossed in these stories, another group of Catholics came to my awareness. These are the people who still attempt to be part of the Catholic community yet feel alienated and discriminated against by the very people who are calling them to be faithful. They are the legions of gay and lesbian Catholics. Their stories need to be heard also.

I have been associated with gay men and lesbians for nearly twenty years, mostly in university settings. The important benefit of these associations for me has been the destruction of stereotypes of homosexual men and women. My experience during these twenty years, and especially during the period of interviewing people for this book, has shown me that the ten percent of the population who are constitutionally homosexual have created a vital culture of their own while successfully functioning in the mainstream of American life. They are the people we work with and ride next to on the commuter train, they serve us in banks, supermarkets, beauty salons, and churches. They are waiters, teachers, writers, singers, musicians, doctors, lawyers, and bankers. They have the title Doctor, Reverend, Sister, Father, and yes, Bishop. Their stories have something to teach us.

My methodology in approaching this project was to gather stories from a cross-section of about fifty Catholic gay men and lesbians. The

two criteria to qualify for an interview were a homosexual orientation
and a Catholic background. I attempted to have a geographical spread
that included New York, Washington, D.C., Chicago, Detroit, San
Antonio, Austin, Minneapolis, and San Francisco. A chief source for
contact was the national office of Dignity, which accounts for the many
references to the organization in these stories. Another source of contact
was the Conference of Catholic Lesbians. There were three areas I
asked each person to reflect on in telling his or her story: (1) family
background and religious education; (2) how and when each became
aware of his or her homosexuality; (3) where the person now stands
in relation to the church. Less than one-third of those interviewed asked
that their name be changed to protect their privacy. When this occurs,
it is indicated at the end of the story.

Recent events have caused major turmoil in the gay community
and serious questioning by many theologians and Scripture scholars.
The focal point of this turmoil is a document from the Vatican entitled
"Letter to the Bishops of the Catholic Church on the Pastoral Care of
Homosexual Persons." This document was released on October 31,
1986. It was signed by Joseph Cardinal Ratzinger, prefect of the
Congregation for the Doctrine of the Faith, with the approval of Pope
John Paul II. Many of the interviewees comment on the Ratzinger
letter.

The purpose of this book is not to offer a theological reflection
on this document, nor to dispute its conclusions. This has been done
by several commentators, the most recent being Jeannine Gramick and
Pat Furey in their book *The Vatican and Homosexuality*. My plea to
the reader, especially to bishops, priests, and all who are involved in
ministry, is to listen to the stories of gay and lesbian Catholics who
would like to remain Catholic but find themselves defined by church
officials as objectively disordered. It would seem appropriate that those
who make decisions about the morality of homosexual behavior would
take into account the experience of women and men who are Christian
Catholic homosexuals. Theologian Mary Hunt remarks that experience
needs to be taken seriously if we expect to do good theology. "In a
remarkably short time the particularity of experience has been taken
seriously. . . . But there is now a framework for saying that *particularity*
is important." To understand the particularity of homosexual experience,
one has to listen to the stories of homosexual men and women.

There are several stages that homosexual people go through on
their journey to wholeness and integrity. They experience anguish and
pain when they begin to become aware that they are different from the

mainstream of heterosexual society. Some unfortunates do not get past this stage and opt for the only solution they see, suicide. Many others come to an awareness and acceptance of their homosexual orientation after years of denial and wishing that it could be otherwise. They "come out"—they admit who they are, at least to themselves and a few intimate friends. This is usually an experience of freedom. Some feel exhilarated by their new-found revelation and freedom. They share it with the larger world. Others continue to hide this aspect of their lives from certain segments of their world, often because of their work or other pressures. We are told by the professionals that from a psychological point of view it is healthy to admit who one is, to affirm and celebrate one's identity. Those who are able to share their experience with others become positive role models and make it easier for others to "come out."

The people interviewed in this book have gone through the stages from denial to full acceptance of their sexuality. They are all self-affirming gays and lesbians. They hope that their experiences and the telling of their stories will encourage and strengthen others in their resolve to be who they are before God and their fellow humans. They are people who once found meaning and direction in the church of their childhood. Many have abandoned that church because it has made them feel less than human and guilty because of who they are. Many of them made renewed efforts to come back to that church and found new meaning when they could be recognized as gay and Catholic. However, that church, which was the source of succor in their past and hope in their struggle to be Catholic adults, is now making it more difficult for them to continue their life journey in conjunction with their spiritual heritage. James Zullo and James Whitehead predict in their chapter of *A Challenge to Love* that, "as the larger Christian community is instructed in the differing patterns of gay religious maturing, it will be exorcised of some of its homophobia. It will come closer, if belatedly and reluctantly, to its own ideal of Christ's radical mutuality: gay and lesbian Christians are more like heterosexual Christians than they are different." The need for the Christian community to understand the lives of gay people is greater now than it has ever been before.

The AIDS crisis has contributed to the homophobia that has long existed in our society, even though many gains have been achieved in the last twenty years. Twenty years ago the Stonewall incident in New York was the beginning of the movement among gay people for recognition and pride. Since then there have been advances and setbacks. From all indications the struggle for basic civil rights and recognition of gay people will continue. This is evidenced by the recognition given to gay issues by politicians. They are aware of the large constituency of gays in some cities and the economic power this group has. Although most people running for public office would rather keep the discussion in the back rooms, Jesse Jackson recognized publicly at the 1988 Democratic Convention that gays and lesbians are a part of the fabric of this nation that needs to be recognized. AIDS now threatens the very survival of gays and other members of our society. The plight of those who have AIDS demands a compassionate response from all religious groups, including the Catholic church.

A new awakening among Catholics has occurred since Vatican II. No longer do many feel that if they disagree with church officials, they have to leave the church. They have been made aware that they *are* the church. They will continue to identify themselves as Catholics even though they do not fully adhere to every detail of the traditional moral teaching of the church. This same experience has pervaded the community of gay Catholics. Even though they have been kicked out of Catholic churches, and even though they are called disordered by church officials, they will continue to be church, with or without permission of the Vatican. Mary Hunt insists on using the expression "to be church." "Until you can be something you are always outside of it. That is the sinister genius of Roman Catholicism: to prevent lesbian and gay people from being church, so that we are always reacting to something that we are not a part of in an integral way."

One of the questions the people interviewed in this book struggle with is, What do I do about my continuing affiliation with the Catholic church? All were raised and educated as Catholics. Several spent time in convents or monasteries. Some were ordained priests. No one easily discards the powerful imprinting that occurs with this kind of training and conditioning. When a decision is made to leave the Catholic church it is only after much deliberation and agony, forcing one to admit that there is no other choice if one is to maintain his or her integrity, sanity, and spiritual existence. At the same time, one hears an underlying wish that things could be different, that there would be a way they could continue affiliation with the church.

Many of those interviewed have had some contact with Dignity, a national organization of gay and lesbian Catholics. Dignity looms as a significant part of their faith journey. Where they once experienced the church as disdainful or rejecting, their experience in Dignity gave them a sense that it was possible to be both gay and Catholic. Many were content to be part of this organization because it put them back in touch with their religious roots. They found community and support within the organization. They were able to engage in the traditional liturgy of the Catholic church and not feel alienated or ashamed of who they were. Some found Dignity so important in their lives that they remained active members for many years. Others found that it allowed them to move from a state of alienation to some other form of religious expression. Some lesbians had temporary affiliation with Dignity, but experienced the alienation that many women feel, that of being second-class citizens in the church, sometimes even in Dignity. Their first argument with the church is that by being women, they are excluded, which is a prior exclusion to that they experience as lesbians. Most dioceses in the United States where a Dignity chapter existed either cooperated by allowing them space in which to worship and supplying a priest for their liturgies, or tolerated or ignored their presence with benign neglect. All of this changed with the letter from Rome in October, 1986.

The Ratzinger letter is significant because it redefines the basic status of homosexual people. Formerly, statements by various national groups of bishops have discussed homosexual orientation as being morally neutral. People discover that they are homosexual at some time in their lives. They are aware that they never made a deliberate choice to be that way. It is a given. The Ratzinger letter defines the homosexual condition differently. It says, "the inclination itself must be seen as an objective disorder." This statement has far reaching and disastrous implications. It was the rationale later in the letter for demanding of the bishops that: "All support should be withdrawn from any organizations which seek to undermine the teaching of the church, which are ambiguous about it or which neglect it entirely." Because of this letter, bishops around the country began to oust Dignity groups from the Catholic churches where they had been gathering for Mass.

This sudden shift in policy was not the result of new insights into the theology of sexual orientation, but obviously the result of authoritative decision. As several of the people interviewed commented, we are dealing with the issue of power and authority. Bill Knox remarks, "The current developments in the church, i.e., the Ratzinger letter, I see as an effort of a church that is struggling to regain power and authority, and in a sense almost becoming desperate." If this position is shared by others, which my experience tells me is true, then the very thing that the Vatican is trying to bolster, its authority, ends up being eroded. Mary Hunt considers the Ratzinger letter to be "theological pornography," and gives forceful reasons to substantiate her position.

Another source of consternation for gay Catholics is a statement in the letter that, "neither the church nor society at large should be surprised when other distorted notions and practices gain ground, and irrational and violent reactions increase." Karen Doherty remarks, "I think the potential for violence is going to show up. That was the worst part." Other people interviewed decried the violence that can occur as a result of this statement in the letter.

Some others experience the Ratzinger letter as providential, and in the long run beneficial for the gay movement. It forced the gay community to marshal its forces and become more "out," more vocal, and more demanding in pursuing basic rights and freedoms. Karen Doherty thinks that "It helped a lot of comfortable gay and lesbian Catholics to get off their fannies and start to see how things are." Jim Bussen, former national president of Dignity, reports that "the recent actions have changed the face of Dignity. The chapters that have been booted out and have decided to fight . . . have grown by leaps and bounds. . . . We are getting more activist people. They are people who want to be church." The risk, of course, that Catholic authorities run by dismissing gays from church property is that thousands of talented, service-oriented people will find a new home, a new church.

Many of these talented and creative people have become aware that their relationship with God is much more fundamental than the place where they worship. They experience their homosexual orientation as a gift from God. They are convinced that they have been created this way, and that all that God creates is good. They are able to see the positive resource that their homosexuality is, often experienced as sensitivity, compassion, and creativity. Tom Cunningham expresses this thought: "In looking back at my own life, there is no way I can say my being gay is not a gift from God. I know that it is not something of my own making. . . . I believe this . . . sensitivity is an integral part of my gayness and emotional disposition." James Abdo reflects that "Earlier, I would have wanted this removed from me, but it became clear to me that this was a tremendous source of my creativity, and my ability to invest in work and relationships." Toby Johnson discovered: "The realization that I was a gay man and that it was a wonderful thing. . . . I understood that to be one of the most beautiful parts of myself. My prayer life was involved with the people I was attracted to."

The lives of these people show evidence of a deep spirituality that was formed in the Catholic tradition. Part of this tradition is to maintain close ties with parents and other family members. These stories describe the loneliness of hiding and the fear of being rejected by parents who are loved and respected. They tell of efforts to be gentle and patient when disclosing the truth, of families who can accept a gay or lesbian member and those that cannot. Some of the interviewees have tested positive for the HIV virus. Others spend time and effort to care for people with AIDS. The response of the gay community to the AIDS crisis has been an inspiring model of what the church can be. Many of the interviewees, as is true in the general gay population, are involved in service-oriented work. Some who were ordained priests and some who were religious women and men consider the work that they are now doing as ministry, although not recognized as such by the church. Some are active in their parishes, and are accepted by the parish communities. Others would like to have what Dorothy Fisher wishes, that gays and lesbians in relationships be accepted in the ordinary parish community.

Although there are shades of anger among some of these people, there is also a wholesome attitude, a letting-go of oppressive structures and creating of new forms in which gay people can be self-affirming about their sexual orientation and at the same time express their religious and spiritual needs. When one listens to Bill Storey's account of the bishop telling him, "The church has nothing to learn from lay people," it points all the more strongly to the need for constructive work on the part of these talented men and women. For Toby Johnson, this is a plan to establish a monastery. For Mary Hunt, it is to continue to offer constructive methods to "be church." The Catholic tradition formed these people. Some have ended their affiliation with the church. Others continue to work for change from within. Their lives and their stories stand as a challenge to the idea that homosexual people are "disordered," that they are not healthy, creative, or spiritual human beings.

More than half of the people interviewed are living in committed monogamous relationships. Several have publicly-blessed unions, or marriages. They give every evidence of being stable and successful relationships. The prevailing myth that homosexual relationships are unstable, and that most gay men and women prefer a promiscuous lifestyle, is belied by many thousands of committed and enduring gay relationships around the country that most straight people do not see. Kosnick et al. in *Human Sexuality: New Directions in American Catholic Thought* state that: "The traditional Christian attitude toward homosexuality down the centuries makes the Church responsible at least indirectly for prejudice and discrimination that homosexuals suffer in society today. . . . Inadvertently, Catholic pastoral practice has promoted the incidence of promiscuity among homosexuals precisely by advising them against forming intimate or exclusive friendships." Healthy, self-affirming gays and lesbians have recognized the immorality of such pastoral advice, and have chosen the only moral and healthy path available to them, committed monogamous relationships. They experience in their lives and in their relationships the presence of those qualities that identify good moral values in regard to sexuality. According to Kosnick et al., these values are self-liberating, other-enriching, honest, faithful, life-serving, and joyous. In his interview, Jimmy Kennedy remarks, "We need to let others know that gay people can be happy and live fulfilled lives with wonderful relationships." Josephine Bruni states, "My marriage is the same as my parents' marriage." If church authorities could witness the many committed relationships and happy unions among homosexual people, perhaps they would experience these people as other than "disordered."

What is the hope for gay and lesbian Catholics? Will the church change its position on same-sex unions, or at least not condemn them? It seems unlikely that this will happen in the near future. It is likely that the mentality that spawned the Ratzinger letter will prevail. This feeling is echoed by several of the interviewees. Bill Knox remarks, "Many of the things that are happening now will have lasting effects, and will not disappear in our lifetime even if we got a new pope soon. The pain that is being thrust upon us will not soon disappear." Larry Sullivan feels that, "While we are waiting for the pendulum to swing back to some normalcy, there will be two or three generations of gay people who will be mangled and alienated." Bill Storey takes the strong position that "even if Ratzinger and company could change their tune . . . a return to the church is quite out of the question."

Others are more hopeful that some change will occur even though they don't expect it soon. Jim Bussen expects that "there will be a new age in the church. There will be a sexual revolution in the moral teaching of the church. I think the women's movement will be the major focal point in the future." Joe Izzo also focuses on the women's issue as the catalyst for change. "I think through the living example of Catholic women who are dedicated to Christian life, the powers of the church are going to be changed." This is because of a new sense of what it means to be church. Mary Hunt reminds us, "Don't expect that the church is going to be for you. The primary Christian responsibility is not to change the church but to *be* church." This is echoed by the experience of Karen Doherty: "I know who I am. I can call myself lesbian. I can call myself Catholic. I am comfortable with this. I don't need a bishop to tell me who I am or what I can do." Perhaps it will be the women's movement that will be the chief source of hope for the future of the institutional church.

I gained two strong impressions in the course of these interviews. The first was the spirit of cooperation that was evident from the beginning. When I identified myself and explained the project I was embarking upon, there was almost unanimous consent to be interviewed and a willingness to make it as convenient as possible for me. This was not done out of exhibitionism, because several of the people asked that their identity be disguised in order to protect their jobs or other people in their lives. It was done out of a desire to be heard. The second aspect that impressed me was the network that exists among gay people. There is a powerful and extensive contact system, not only within an individual city, but throughout the country. Many of these people were willing to make contact for me with friends or acquaintances in other parts of the United States. They want their story told.

As I reflect on this unusual willingness of gay Catholics to tell their stories, I should not be surprised. There are two strong motivations for this phenomenon. These people have deep roots in their Catholicism. Often a love-hate relationship with the church exists in their lives. In their stories they express their desire to maintain contact with the church that once nurtured them, yet they also tell of feeling repulsed by the behavior of the hierarchy. The second factor centers around the hurt and pain that many, if not most, of them endured as a result of their homosexual orientation. As they will say unanimously, they did not choose to be homosexual. When they admitted that truly this is their sexual orientation, they began to deal with bigotry and hatred, with exclusion from the mainstream of life, and from the church. They want this to be known.

The Ratzinger letter is identified as "The *Pastoral* Care of Homosexual Persons." Any approach that claims to be pastoral will necessarily have to be in touch with the people it wishes to serve. From all appearances, this document was not based on hearing the experiences of the people it wishes to serve in a pastoral way. William Shannon asks some very pertinent questions in *The Vatican and Homosexuality* concerning the lack of consultation by the Congregation for the Doctrine of the Faith. "Why was such consultation of the bishops omitted? . . . . Did they feel no need to learn about the pastoral practices already going on in many local churches? Did they believe that they possessed *a priori* all the truth necessary to address the topic of this letter? . . . . How much credibility can be given to a document that ignores the ongoing experience of the many local churches?" A part of that experience is described in these stories.

I believe that we can be faithful to the traditions of the Roman Catholic church and at the same time reassess the stance of church authorities on homosexuality as articulated in the Ratzinger letter. I know such reassessment is possible on the personal level from my own history. Like many of my generation, I have participated in the homophobia that permeates our society and church. I was able to surrender that homophobia only when I came to know homosexual people as persons and not as abstractions. The more I had to reflect on the experience of these women and men, the more I was forced to give up preconceived assumptions about them and form a new understanding. The claim of this book is that a true pastoral approach begins here with the stories of gay and lesbian Catholics. These stories must be heard before moving on to ethical considerations. They can help us see what is life-giving in our tradition and what is not. The purpose and plea of this book is "listen to the stories."

PROFESSIONAL VIEWS:
THEOLOGIANS AND PSYCHOLOGISTS

WILLIAM G. STOREY

Bill is professor emeritus of Liturgy and Church History at the University of Notre Dame where he taught for twenty-one years. He was married for twenty-six years and is the father of seven children (two deceased). He and his lover, Philip H. Schatz, are co-owners of Erasmus Books in South Bend, Indiana.

I'm a late bloomer. It has taken me most of my life to come to terms with my sexual self, to accept my homosexuality and to work toward a full gay identity. Family, church, society have all conspired to keep me firmly within the heterosexual camp while my deepest self has been crying out since childhood for a different identity, truer to my real feelings. A long and painful process of self-discovery has finally revealed that my true self is homosexually oriented and demands the love of another *man.*

I was born and raised a Canadian in a largely Anglo-Saxon and Protestant small town—a town with rather rigid, if fairly inarticulate, sets of morals and expectations. My parents were as guarded and prudish in matters of sex as the folks next door, and yet there were contradictions all about me. At our summer cottage I ran nude during much of my early childhood and nobody remarked on it; in town we boys swam naked off the docks in full sight of my grandparents' home; in high school compulsory nudity reigned in the school pool. At scout camp we learned the joys of masturbation. At church camp even more exciting surprises awaited us; although the rules, of course, forbade it, we learned to slip into each other's beds and experience further titillating facts of life. Were there any qualms of conscience? Not really! A maiden aunt gave me a pamphlet on one occasion that warned against the horrors of masturbation, but considering the source and my own experience, I immediately disregarded it as the product of virginal envy.

And yet, finally, I was caught up short. My French-Canadian maternal grandmother was a Catholic. Early on I was intrigued by her crucifix, her rosary, her prayerbooks; they breathed an atmosphere a bit more exotic than the dreary Protestantism that surrounded me, and appealed to my romantic nature. But there was more to her favorite prayer book than appealing pictures of the Mass and the imaginative and endearing phrases of the Litany of Loretto. It also included the dreaded "examination of conscience" before Confession, the strange and intriguing paragraphs on the sixth and ninth commandments, the fateful words on sexual impurity. It provoked my first taste of bad conscience. Could what I and my pals were doing be "sins against purity?" Who could I ask? What would I ask? I was, for the first time, experiencing a foretaste of decades of confusion, embarrassment, guilty silences, and stern repression.

For reasons too numerous to enumerate here, at eighteen I abandoned the Anglicanism of my youth, subscribed to the Creed of Pius IV and became a Roman Catholic. My priestly instructor and I rather easily agreed on the existence of God, the divinity of Jesus, the virginal motherhood of Mary, the visible and infallible church established by Christ and the other great verities of the Quebec Catechism. When we came to the Ten Commandments, however, he was more embarrassed by a discussion of the sixth and ninth commandments than I was! Both then, and later in the confessional, I learned two tough facts: one was that practically everything relating to sex was a mortal sin; the second was that nobody was going to give me a theology of sex, a viewpoint on sex; I would have to try to survive in the face of absolute prohibitions and embarrassed silences. A subsequent parish mission, given by experts in hell-fire and damnation theology, confirmed my suspicion that I was in deep and shameful trouble.

Daily Mass, visits to the Blessed Sacrament, and frequent confession, urged upon me by a spiritual director, became desperate attempts to ward off sexual temptations so that I might become as "pure" as possible. Somebody put in my hands *The Spiritual Combat* by Lorenzo Scupoli and that just about completed my course in nervous scrupulosity. The upshot of such nervous tension was that a year later I decided to enter a strict religious order to safeguard my hard-won chastity. Fear of the world, the flesh and the devil, allied with a tender devotion to St. Francis of Assisi, led me to join a rigid province of the Capuchin Franciscan Order. In the novitiate I expected to discover the "perfect joy" of St. Francis but instead was immersed in a place of repression, bad food, lack of sleep, bodily austerities, and major forms of psychic deprivation. I was particularly struck by the fact that our novice master meticulously analyzed for us the niceties of the vows of poverty and obedience but never deigned to give us a single conference on the vow of chastity or what it might entail. There were veiled warnings, hints, and rigid prohibitions, but no explanation whatsoever. Sex continued to be the unmentionable topic both before and after the first vows.

Nevertheless, after the probationary period, I took the three vows, advanced to the House of Studies and to an even more stifling situation. Now I was living in the midst of a large group of attractive young men of college age who prayed together, studied together, ate together, and "recreated" together twenty-four hours a day, seven days a week. The Rule of St. Francis and the Constitutions of the Capuchin Order were supplemented by a special set of detailed Rules of the House that would have to be seen to be believed. Looking back I think they were dictated by one overriding fear: that we might come to recognize the homosexual tensions that bubbled just below the surface of our monastic existence. The great central rule of the house was, No Particular Friendships! What exactly that might mean was, of course, never put into words. Ignorance, coupled with a raft of almost obscene hints, was supposed to frighten us off from the Unmentionable.

The result was that we all lived in an extremely close but friendless existence that brought with it unbearable loneliness. Thanks to the rules, the cultivated neuroses of our superiors and the spies in our midst, we were "pure" all right but were also nervous, distraught, ill-at-ease, uncomfortable with one another and, very often, physically ill. Insomnia, indigestion, and depression afflicted me from the first weeks in the house of studies and added immensely to the burden of five hours of daily choral prayer, a heavy scholastic schedule, and other duties and austerities. True to my original intention, however, I obeyed every rule and command to the letter until my mind and body collapsed; I was—like Martin Luther—a perfect monk in the eyes of my brothers and superiors while, all that time, I barely survived from day to day under terrible psychic duress. When my doctor warned me to leave the Order or suffer a total breakdown, I took his advice (despite the violent opposition of my superior) but returned home—overwhelmed by a sense of failure—to uncomprehending parents, a disappointed pastor, lost friendships, and a miserable factory job of boredom and isolation. My worst problem was that I felt I had failed to live up to a noble ideal for reasons I simply could not comprehend. I had lived by every rule, written and unwritten, of the Order; I had tried with sincerity and generosity to persevere in my vocation despite every form of discouragement and illness; and yet there I was, an ex-monk, adrift in a sea of troubles and fresh temptations.

In my new loneliness and confusion, my only friend was another ex-friar who had left the Order about the same time I had. He understood some of my problems, shared with me his discoveries in poetry and literature, and tried to cajole me into a more humane existence. Starved as I was for friendship, I found him appealing in every way—including sexually. Naturally, I hastened to confession to admit my aberration and was brutally confronted by a totally unsympathetic confessor who ordered me never to see my friend again. He was an "occasion of sin" and had to be sacrificed without any looking back. Piling confusion upon confusion, I was also gratuitously informed that such sexual attractions were signs of deep moral perversity; they were sick, sinful, disgusting, and should not be so much as mentioned among Christians. He also ordered me to recite five Hail Marys any time I so much as thought of such perversities; I added these to my daily Mass, daily Breviary, and other devotions but could not quite shake off all memories of my good friend and of the good times we had together.

In time, other confessors tried to be more helpful. Some suggested that my perverse tendencies were perhaps a cross sent by a loving God to try my purity and patience and that my salvation lay in a pious, uncomplaining, and life-long celibacy. Others hinted—almost obscenely—that since I hadn't tried women yet, I didn't know what real sex was all about. They suggested a quick courtship with a "good Catholic girl," thus allowing for the permitted joys of connubial bliss— plus all the children the Lord might send, of course!

The latter advice looked to me like an attractive as well as sanctioned "out." God had provided a remedy to my sinful condition; a good woman would cure me once and for all of my deviant ways. Spiritually resolute, I set about meeting and courting attractive Catholic women in the hope of the promised cure and a fresh, new, happy life.

It almost worked. By dint of effort I became friends with two remarkably fine young Catholic women, learned to enjoy their company, and thought seriously of spending my life with one of them. In the meantime there was, of course, no sex and, to my surprise, very little sexual attraction, but I put this down to a special grace and didn't let it worry me. If they wondered about my lack of ardor, I presume they attributed it to my obvious piety and strict adherence to all the church's laws—an attitude they themselves shared.

The only flaw during this happier period was that, thanks to new friendships made through school and church, I had three quasi-affairs with Catholic men that contributed to my self-doubt and self-loathing. Although not very long, very deep, or even very sensual, these friendships enraged my confessor and added to my confusion. Such actual encounters with real, rather than imaginary, men might have shaken me out of my mental stupor; they might have warned me off from marriage and set me on an entirely new track. They didn't, however, because mentally and emotionally I still inhabited the realm of the Catholic confessional and its peculiar sexual theology. Up to that point in my life, I had never even heard the word homosexual, much less the concept, and therefore had no intellectual tools—not even terms—for understanding my true situation.

The upshot was that I continued to embrace the Catholic ethic and the woman I loved, and tried for over twenty-five years to be a faithful husband and father. Until very late in our marriage, my wife didn't know of my peculiar temptation; I didn't think it was fair to burden such a lovely person with a loathsome secret and, later on, it seemed too late to share what had been concealed for so long. Besides, for some years, the temptation subsided in the face of the joys and responsibilities of young parenthood, the demands of graduate school, and spiritual direction. Nevertheless, temptations simmered just below the surface and, as I settled into the teaching profession, I discovered—to my dismay—that I was continuously attracted to my more interesting male students. I liked them, I loved them, I doted on them but, of course, I never touched them. That would have been a sin and I was still very much in control of my actions—if not of my imagination. More agonizing than my attraction was the fact that I soon discovered that at least some students, less scrupulous than I, were interested in seducing me! Still and all, I learned nothing new from these close encounters until a series of shocks obliged me to consider my condition from fresh angles.

The papal encyclical *Humanae vitae* was the first breaking point. The subject of birth control had agitated our Christian Family Movement group before 1968, but as obedient Catholics we had pretty resolutely closed our minds on that subject until the Second Vatican Council, the renewed discussion of sexuality, the appointment of the Birth Control Commission by Pope Paul VI and its final report, and then *Humanae vitae* itself. We read it, we discussed it among ourselves and with our distinguished pastor, and found that we disagreed with its arguments and its conclusions. It was particularly dismaying to discover that our beloved, highly spiritual, and deservedly famous pastor could not persuade us to the encyclical's truth. Both he and we were shocked at the realization that such faithful Catholics, with so many children, could reject papal teaching in good conscience.

In my dismay after the long session with our pastor, I telephoned our bishop—John J. Wright of Pittsburgh—and asked if he would come out to the house, meet with our CFM group, and discuss the encyclical. Although he had every reason to know how devout, sincere, friendly, and well-educated we were, his response was uncharacteristically abrupt: "Absolutely not! The Church has nothing to learn from lay people in these matters; the pope has spoken, obey him. Besides, I don't like discussions on sex; it's a nasty subject. Goodbye."

A few weeks later, however, I noted that Bishop Wright preached a stirring sermon on that very subject to teenagers attending the Student Mission Crusade at Notre Dame. He wanted to make sure that nobody misunderstood his absolute fidelity to *Humanae vitae*, and realized he would get no back-talk from thirteen- and fourteen-year-olds.

Humanae vitae and its aftermath were a great shock to us all. Authoritative attempts to impose its flimsy arguments, while bishops and theologians around the world demonstrated their inability to accept its teachings, was a breaking point for us. Once we grasped the point that the sexual rigidities of the past could be seriously questioned, the whole sexual teaching of the church was thrown into doubt. What became painfully obvious was the church's fallibility in such matters and its stubborn adherence to its all-too-fallible opinions.

Two practical results followed almost on the heels of *Humanae vitae*. The first was that my wife and I began to practice birth control with a good conscience. We had seven children already and were worried we might have eight or nine or ten. The second was that, for the first time, I began to suspect that the moral advice I had been given on the subject of homosexuality was perhaps not totally correct. I began to wonder if my feelings for men were as frightful as I had been repeatedly warned. That didn't resolve much yet but it did, at least, get me to stop confessing "temptation" to unsympathetic or hostile confessors. What a relief!

Two further events took place in 1967–68 that furthered my education and undermined my faith in Catholicism. The first was a brief romance with Pentecostalism. Its only connection with this story is that that little love affair was somehow based on the sneaking suspicion that only a miracle would cure me of my love for men. Pentecostalism promised miracles; and, for a short time, the emotional upheaval it delivered lessened my "temptation." Disillusionment soon set in, however, as I discovered that the charismatic phenomena did nothing to cure me and that the movement itself easily sponsored worse forms of repression and denial. As I drifted away from what came to be called the Catholic Charismatic Movement, I realized in my heart of hearts that miracles were no answer to my sexual dilemma.

The other event that changed my life was returning to Notre Dame to teach in a time of change, turmoil, and excitement. For me it was a land of promise that challenged me, as never before, to grow both intellectually and emotionally. Theology students literally forced me to think more deeply about subjects that had troubled me all my life—especially homosexuality. At first they puzzled me and frightened me by their openness. But little by little I came to the realization that my salvation lay in being available to them.

One decision that grew out of this acceptance was participation in a directed reading course in psychology from the noted priest-Jungian, Morton Kelsey. Reading and discussing Freud and Jung for a semester revolutionized my whole point of view and brought me to understand that repression was not the answer to the baffling questions that haunted me. These masters of the inner life taught me to accept my whole person—conscious and unconscious—and to live gracefully with the results. They taught me to accept the fact that I am drawn primarily to men and that I had better learn how to handle that basic fact of life before proceeding much further. But they didn't teach me *how* to do all this. Practical decisions about family and friends and job began to loom so large that I became paralyzed anew.

I temporized, I hesitated, I compromised and went through very trying times as I accepted more and more that I was indeed homosexual but was not living homosexually. Now that I knew my true nature it seemed futile and increasingly impossible not to act accordingly: *agere sequitur esse*, as the Scholastics say.

Without dragging in the names of beloved friends and comrades who assisted me—willy nilly—in the struggle, suffice it to say that their affectionate support enabled me to break free from my fears, real and imaginary, and to choose a new way of life. I "came out" to more friends and family, set up in my own apartment and tried to learn how to be not just homosexual but gay. Despite the pain and alienation I caused and experienced, I was shortly convinced that I had done the right thing for everybody.

In the meantime Philip had entered the picture. I had known him rather superficially for a decade while he was an undergraduate then a graduate student at Notre Dame but ours was never a close—much less a sexual—friendship. During the finale of the personal struggle outlined above, he reentered my life, we spoke with candor of our respective paths, and gradually fell in love.

After several delays, he moved to South Bend, we bought a house together and then a business. In the ten years we have been together, it would be impossible to imagine a relationship more loving or an attachment more fulfilling than ours. We enjoy a spousal relationship that is a true marriage of minds, hearts, and bodies in every way—except legally! Since we have lived together quite openly for ten years and since I have gotten involved in a certain amount of public controversy at and with the University of Notre Dame, we have experienced some external constraints that have not always been pleasant. Whatever price we have had to pay, however, we feel it has solidified our relationship and deepened our commitment. The only sadness I feel periodically is that I did not discover my sexual identity earlier in life and that I had to wound my wife and children in becoming who I am.

The result of our decision to be and act as a couple has been a growing process for many people, and especially for some of our "liberal" friends. A few have turned away from us but most have grown with us and accept us as we are.

We hope that our life together is a witness against the institutionalized lie that gay people are inevitably promiscuous, unfaithful to one another, and unable to maintain a lasting relationship. Had we still felt at home in the church, we feel that we would have much to contribute to its understanding of sexuality and of dedicated relationships. As it is, we have left its hostile and unyielding environment for a riskier and freer existence on our own.

As a church historian I may take the long view of things but I don't have time to wait for a Galileo-like rehabilitation—centuries later. Yes, *Humanae vitae* and all it symbolized was the great turning-point. In 1968 the papacy had an opportunity to admit that it had been wrong on the matter of contraception. It could have abandoned a false position and with greater humility and candor worked toward a more positive and accurate theology of sex and marriage. Instead, contrary to the advice of his own hand-picked commission, Paul VI obstinately clung to the "traditional" teaching and decided to bolster the authority of the magisterium against the voice of reason. His decision proved a calamitous one for the church in general and a final one as far as we were concerned. It was Bishop Wright writ large: the church has nothing to learn from the laity, gay or straight—especially on the subject of sex.

The Pope's successor seems to have learned nothing from the worldwide reaction to *Humanae vitae*. He and his curial enforcers seem determined to sacrifice gay people on the altar of expediency: gay people have been gratuitously insulted, as never before, in the recent papal pronouncements on sexuality, and most of us have gotten the message loud and clear. Even if Ratzinger and company could change their tune—*per impossible!*—a return to the church is quite out of the question. We have discerned the true face of the Roman church and find it to be the antithesis of the Gospel; it is a false and pernicious religious system and gives the lie to its claims to be the church of Jesus Christ.

MARY E. HUNT

Mary holds a doctorate in Philosophical and Systematic Theology from the Graduate Theological Union, Berkeley, California. She is co-founder of WATER (Women's Alliance for Theology, Ethics and Ritual). She lives in the Washington, D.C. area.

I grew up in Syracuse, New York. I did not go to Catholic school until junior high school. I went to public school because it was closer to home. My mother, who had been a teacher, felt strongly about having the kids home for a hot lunch. Going to a public school I think kept some of that early "Sister says" stuff out of my life.

I went to Marquette University as an undergraduate in 1969 and had a very good experience. Antiwar, civil rights, and inner city work made it exciting. I was "seduced" into theology by some good people who were there. I was studying psychology, and planning to go to law school but I got interested in theology.

Then I went to Harvard Divinity School in 1972. At Harvard I became interested in feminist issues. I was with people who were studying theology to become ministers although I had never thought much about ministry. It became clear to me that in college and graduate school I had always done something in addition to my academic work, whether campus ministry or resident advisor in a dorm. I realized at that time that there was a distinct separation between the academic route and the ministerial route in theology.

I came out as a lesbian in 1974. That's when I had my first love experiences with women. My experience as a child with my mother was this: I would say I love Suzie and my mother would say no, you like Suzie and you will love a man. My mother was correcting my grammar; I was using a verb in the wrong way. That's how I learned about gender-inflected language, and how there are verbs that you use about one sex that you don't use about the other. My mother thought she was correcting my grammar, but I knew she was really correcting my view of relationships. It took me up short because I knew she was wrong. My experience was that I did love this person, and this person was a woman. I think a lot of parents do that kind of teaching, ostensibly to correct any misconception their kids might have, and effectively expressing disapproval of same-sex love.

My parents were not thrilled when I came out. Like a lot of Catholic parents, they were upset and wondered where *they* had gone wrong. They did the usual kinds of things. My father was rather vehement, but my mother smoothed the waters as best she could. I know what the pain of rejection is, and it's no fun. But we need to forgive people and move on. My sister has been supportive from the beginning and continues to be. She is proof of the fact that you can come from a strict Irish Catholic family and be straight and be supportive.

I moved to Berkeley shortly after I came out. I lived six years there as an "out" lesbian in a very supportive environment. Then I went to Argentina to spend a couple of years teaching. That was a wonderful experience. That was a very repressive time in Argentina, 1980–1982. There was an underground lesbian network there. I have many friends in Argentina.

Then I came to Washington in 1982 and started WATER (Women's Alliance for Theology, Ethics and Ritual). I became more involved in the progressive Catholic lesbian community. I have always seen sexual preference as one of many justice issues around which I focused my work and my writing. The question I have now is whether heterosexism and homophobia are really a different kind of analysis than sexism or whether they are of a piece. I haven't figured that out yet. I do know that they go hand in hand. I'm writing a book on women's friendship called *Fierce Tenderness: Toward a Feminist Theology of Friendship*.

I'm thirty-six, so most of my Catholicism and my study has been post-Vatican II. I came out as a lesbian when I was twenty-two. That was the time when I reflected on my earlier life experiences in high school and college. I could look back and say, oh, I was a lesbian then too, but I didn't have a name for it. By the time I came out as a lesbian I had already been dealing with what it meant to be a Catholic who was a woman. I withdrew from the church in my twenties, as many people do. I distanced myself from the church as much as I could, being a student of theology. I had the interesting experience of going from Marquette where I was an undergraduate, to Harvard where I was a graduate student. At Harvard it was so overwhelmingly Protestant that I felt very Catholic. There was never a time when I didn't identify with being a Catholic, though there have been times when I'm not so sure about being a Christian.

I often talked about myself as being post-Catholic, as being post-institutional. I never went through a time when I thought I might be a Methodist, for example. I think Catholicism is a more ethnic experience than all that. From my early twenties, when I came out as a lesbian, I certainly understood that the church's position on homosexuality was clear. As I didn't agree with the church's position on birth control or women's issues, I certainly didn't agree with it on homosexuality. I have never felt myself outside of the church, though I have experienced from my family and from church officials and others the dissonance of being a lesbian who is Catholic. My study of theology helped in this.

Men and women have a different experience of church. As a woman I don't have the same problems as men. What are they going to do if I come out as a lesbian, not ordain me? They are not going to ordain me anyway. We have to remember that men can be church in a way that women can never be church, i.e., as priests. It never occurred to me to become a woman religious. We had very poor role models as nuns. That would have been one route to go to be "church," but it never crossed my mind. Besides there is a different relationship that women have with the institution in terms of what it means to be church. That's why I continue to use that expression, "to be church." Until you can be something you are always outside of it. That's the sinister genius of Roman Catholicism: to prevent lesbians and gay people from being church, so that we are always reacting to something that we are not a part of in an integral and intimate way. That's very powerful ideology to keep us separated.

If people want to be church, this seems to be the bottom line: if you are going to hang around these things for better or worse, then it's really a question of whether it's just going to be a critical effort at putting down the institutional church's position or whether there will be constructive work. My measure of peoples' good faith and integrity around this is when there is also constructive work. Otherwise, I think therapy is useful for venting emotions about things that have come down from the church. It's very difficult for me to get hired in a Catholic school, for example. My Catholic university teaching days are severely limited if not nonexistent. I can deal in a therapeutic situation with how angry that makes me, but I think the more important thing to do is what we try to do with WATER. We try to create a place where the kind of constructive work that needs to go on for the whole

I don't mean to be harsh about people who are angry. I think anger is a very important thing, and there is more than enough material for very righteous anger among lesbian and gay Catholics. But if that is all there is, then that's the ultimate victory for people who would have us be other than full human beings. At this time I'm not willing to concede the whole tradition of the Jesus movement to the institutional church.

In talking about the constructive phase of theology I would draw a parallel between what I know best, which is feminist theology and the experience of gay and lesbian Catholics. I talk about a *period of preparation* where the ideas or the insight is born and is given first expression. Then we enter into what I would call a *critical phase* where we look at the whole theological project critically from a new perspective. In other words, in feminist theology we rethought church history, we began to look at language, we looked at ethics, we looked at the systematic and philosophical foundations and discipline. This whole panorama of critical rethinking took place in the sixties and seventies for the women's issues. Then we moved into the eighties and we had a whole new moment, what I would call a *constructive moment*. Instead of being critical of what had been there, feminist scholars began to say, Aha! There's something new, constructive for the whole church to learn, not just for women but for the whole church.

That's the best parallel I can come up with to how the lesbian and gay experience is being integrated into the theological mainstream. The first work, at least that I know of, on the lesbian and gay issues in religion was written in the early seventies. It was a book by Sally Gearhart and Bill Johnson called *Loving Women, Loving Men*. Sally Gearhart is a professor of speech at San Francisco State University and she was brought up in a Protestant, more fundamentalist tradition. Bill Johnson was the first openly gay person from the United Church of Christ who was ordained.

A lot of people in mainstream Catholic theology who were reading Rahner and were caught up in the Second Vatican Council had no idea that this was going on. The fact is it was there. Some of Malcolm Boyd's early work, even some of the Metropolitan Community Church was there. We don't see it sitting on the shelves next to Schillebeeckx or Rahner, but it's very important in terms of raising these questions if we think ecumenically. I see that as a period of preparation.

I think the critical period had works like John Boswell's *Christianity, Social Tolerance, and Homosexuality* and some of the nascent work of others of us. Robert Nugent's collection *A Challenge to Love*, for example, is probably the best example of a good critical treatment. So I think in the theological world we are just beginning to get there.

What's interesting is the development of lesbian and gay groups in virtually every major Christian denomination, and that the lesbian and gay critique on the part of the people who have left the Church is as rich a contribution as what's been written by people who have stayed. One of the advantages that the lesbian and gay movement has had over certain other movements theologically is that we are doing our work at a time when many of the insights of Latin American liberation theology have been taken seriously, particularly the doing of theology from base communities. We live in base communities.

Thus you have a way in which lesbian and gay experience can be taken seriously without having to defend why lesbian and gay experience is different. We already had black theology, feminist theology, Native American theology, Latin American liberation theology. All of these have chipped away at the sort of normative theological structures and made clear, at least to progressives, that *experience* needs to be taken seriously. In a remarkably short time the particularity of experience has been taken seriously. This sets the tone for the acceptance of lesbian and gay insights on their own terms, which is not to say that we are going to have completely and utterly new things to say. But there is now a framework for saying that *particularity* is important. That means that our starting point is much further down the road than when the first article in feminist theology came out in 1960. That was the first time in the history of theology as I know it that it was suggested that a starting point as a woman or starting point as a man might influence the doing of theology. So a lesbian/gay perspective will obviously be different.

I think that homosexuality has been one of the untouchable topics for very "good" reasons in terms of the internal logic of the institutional church. Number one, anything sexual is suspect. Number two, since so much theology was done by clerics, the articulation of things sexual was coming from people who were publicly vowed to be celibate. So we have a kind of "Catch 22" when you come down to the experience question. Because if we are right that experience is formative in terms of how ideas are articulated, then that whole institutional tradition is limited. I think that as sexuality itself is something that we can talk about, as celibate experience becomes one of the many experiences out of which people theologize, and as women's experience is taken seriously, then we can have a much stronger starting point in our diversity.

I am personally persuaded that the lesbian and gay piece of the theological analysis in the Catholic Church will be a linchpin not only in changing our sexual ethics, but also in getting at questions of authority. Authority patterns have been tied up by both the confusion of the priesthood with decision-making and the exclusion of women and non-celibate people from the ministry. As those things begin to get sorted out I think we will move a long way toward a more participatory church.

I think that homosexuality is the linchpin because it is the hidden secret of a lot of persons in leadership who create a homosocial environment. I think once you begin to crack that, and people have to talk honestly about who they are and what they do and are held accountable for that, there will be a maturation in the church.

I think another thing that is crucial is AIDS. If you look at the trajectory of lesbian and gay issues in the Catholic Church what you see is a kind of peak probably around 1984. I think we had a certain plateau of acceptability then. I think that plateau has been eroded if not turned back by the actions of a lot of bishops against Dignity chapters, which in my judgment is, at a conscious level, responding to the so-called October letter, the Ratzinger letter. In that letter homosexuality moved from being morally neutral to being "intrinsically morally disordered." I think that is a watershed where the church began to backpedal in a significant way.

A lot of what is going on with the bishops around Dignity chapters is a response at an unconscious level to AIDS. Not to embrace those persons with a serious medical problem as people is sinful. As Kevin Gordon has said, and I think he said it better than anyone else, it's not that the churches will judge AIDS, but AIDS will judge the churches.

We are at a point now where gains that have been made are being eroded. That's a good sign for me in a perverse kind of way. I think what we have seen in other movements is that once you get to a point where there's been constructive work you always see a *backlash*. There's a period of preparation, then a critical period, then the beginning of a constructive period. The way you know that constructive period is making some inroads is that there is some backlash. I think the current backlash is proof that we made a very big dent in this thing.

I think there are two reasons for the backlash. One is because virtually every Catholic family is touched by homosexuality, literally every Catholic family. If the Kinsey reports and other statistics are correct that one out of ten people is lesbian or gay in our population, and I think those are low numbers, and you have in a Catholic family an average of six people, you are already going to have half your Catholic families affected. The fact is most of us have larger and more extended families than that. The other thing is that the institutional church has made such *faux pas* around birth control, abortion, self-insemination, and certain other of the sexual issues, they have so offended many good people that they really cashed in a lot of their chips.

The most obvious case is the church's position on so-called artificial insemination, particularly in the case of married couples who are having problems with fertility and for which a little extra help from modern technology will produce their family. I think the church's position on that has been so outrageous as to put the church in a totally untenable position on other sexual issues. It reminds me of what a famous feminist theologian once said when she talked jokingly about imprimaturs. Imprimaturs, she said, are useful because they help you whittle down the pile. If you see an imprimatur, put the book aside. There is a funny way in which the Spirit works in these things. The church has really played out its options on a lot of these issues. That's why groups like WATER are so important in the work that we do. The church has not solved the moral dilemma for folks, but people still deserve to be accompanied as they make moral decisions.

I would put the Ratzinger letter in the category that I call "theological pornography." I think it is an apt phrase in the sense that pornography has three components. First, it objectifies persons like myself. I live in a monogamous, committed lesbian relationship very happily. I have for many years and hope to for a long time. I consider myself a normal, usual kind of Catholic lesbian or gay person who lives what I consider a morally appropriate lifestyle. I don't consider myself virtuous or better than anyone else. I have my limits and failures, but I happen to live in a way that I consider morally appropriate. I think that to compare my lifestyle, my committed relationship, with behavior that is promiscuous, that uses persons sexually, that is irresponsible in terms of transmission of disease, is simply to objectify all of us. That's what pornography does.

The second thing that pornography does, including theological pornography, is to trivialize sexuality. It focuses on a kind of narrow understanding of sexuality, particularly genital sexual expression, which I consider to be highly appropriate between consenting adults in responsible situations. It trivialized that in the sense of talking about what it really doesn't understand. I have never heard from the Vatican any statement that reflected in an authentic and adequate way the experience of lesbian women. I consider sexuality to be part of the goodness of creation. When used and enjoyed and benefited from in a mutually responsible situation, I consider it to be a very important part of life. I do not consider it to be *the* pinnacle experience of human existence, but healthy sexual expression in the context of a responsible relationship is not to be trivialized. Pornography does that. The Ratzinger letter does that as well.

The third thing the Ratzinger letter does that makes it pornographic in my judgment is that it leads to violence. There is discussion about the relation between pornography and violence. I don't think it's necessary to split hairs over whether pornography causes violence or prevents violence, that's the porn debate. The issue at stake is that there is an integral relationship between pornography and violence. The Ratzinger letter has unleashed violence in the actions against Dignity chapters. I think it has almost sanctioned violence because of the statement that we should not be surprised if certain violent activities accrue because of persons who are homosexual.

I think for those three reasons—the objectification of persons, the trivialization of sexuality, and the close connection to violence—that the Ratzinger letter ought to be seen as theological pornography. I think it should be ignored and people should be counseled not to support the church economically until some correction is issued. Theresa Kane said at the Conference of Catholic Lesbians that we can't expect from the church what it is constitutionally unable to provide. By constitutionally she meant in terms of its own internal makeup. You set yourself up for frustration if you do that, she said. That was very sage, because what she was saying to the first gathering of Catholic lesbians was to be church. Don't expect that the church is going to be for you.

The primary Christian responsibility is not to change the church but to be church. It is hoped that a secondary result will be the transformation of the institution. Then we shift the power dynamic from *looking* to "the" church to *being* church. We literally change the way in which language is used, e.g., "I'm leaving the church." "I'm going to church." "I'm going to change the church." It's all "out there" language. But to *be* church, which I consider the primary mandate coming out of Vatican II and from the Gospel, is much clearer and much more exciting, much more fun and much more creative. I don't want to trivialize the changes. We have to make changes. But the primary agenda is clear and I think that is where the hope is, in being church faithfully.

JAMES ABDO

James is a psychologist with the student health center at a college in the southwest. He was married and has two children.

I don't think that my background is quite typical of many students who make it to Notre Dame, in that I was a product of public education. Notre Dame was the first Catholic school I went to. Yet I seem to have embraced a Catholic frame of reference of morality. That got highlighted for me when I arrived at Notre Dame and I saw that many of my peers were beginning to un-stuff themselves from a lot that had been put in during their parochial school years. I was more hungry than ever to explore some theological issues. I have always been grateful for the public school background, in that I didn't have the feeling that I had been stuffed in that way.

I was born in the midwest with an ethnic mix. My mother is German, which accounts for my looks. My father is Lebanese. It's not necessarily a mixture that I would recommend, with the fieriness of the mid-eastern blood and the order and constrictedness of the German blood. I don't know if they mix very well. My mother was of Protestant background and converted to Catholicism. Although my father belonged to the Marionite rite, since we lived in the suburbs we went to a Roman Catholic parish. My parents were associated with the church in terms of their routines and behaviors, but I don't think it ever integrated itself into a part of their reflection on the way that they ordered their life values.

I had the option to go to Catholic school or public school; I chose the public school, and that was okay with them. I remember regular attendance at religious education classes. I took very seriously what was presented to me in my Catechism lessons. As an adolescent I identified with how the church organized issues around sexuality and morality. In my adolescence I sort of cut myself off from a lot of my more rebellious, adventurous curiosity, the more typical developmental energy that an adolescent would be expected to go through. That was done out of a sense of righteousness that the church promoted. Growing up in the '50s and early '60s that righteousness was still very prevalent. It was not yet the age of diversity or debate or questioning. I probably identified more with being a Catholic than I did with my ethnicity. My father wasn't particularly identified with his ethnicity, nor my mother with hers. So if I was to distinguish myself from other people it was by being Catholic, particularly in the public school.

Being a professional who has paid a lot of attention to adolescent development gives me one way to depict what happened to me during my adolescence. It's not a particularly unique pattern, especially for those who are rigorous about their academics and attend institutions with a reputation for higher learning. During their adolescence there is a tendency to cut themselves off from the adolescent energy and become adults very quickly. In the Jungian terminology of archetypes, it is the polarity between the Senex and the Puer. The Senex being the old man, and the Puer being the archetype of youth. Some youths do an all-right job bearing the tension between those two and are able to integrate the two. Other youths overly identify with the Puer and may be delinquents or troublemakers. For a while they usually get a lot of attention because they are stirring up the system. Youths that don't get a lot of attention are those that overly identify with the Senex, cutting themselves off from the Puer energy because they are doing what everyone in authority would hope they would do. They study hard, their language is nice and clean, they volunteer. They get reinforced for their behavior. Where they suffer is with their peers. They lack spontaneity and earthiness because they identify with the structure and with order. Surely during my adolescence there was a major shift in my peer relationships, in that I had a lot of characteristics that should have kept me more included. I was an athlete, I was bright, I got good response to the way I looked, and yet there was a rigidity around morality and how one should behave that didn't allow me to be part of groups.

In my early adolescence, age thirteen to fifteen, I really began to see that there was this longing to have male bonding. There is no doubt in my mind that I went without that bonding. The rigidity that I carried, and identification with certain values, particularly as they are translated into Catholic terminology, just kept that bonding from happening. My longing to be with male peers took on more and more eroticism. By mid- to late adolescence, that translated itself into a lot of erotic desires that I was not open about and did not share with other people. It put me in a strange dilemma, in that I wanted to be open to sharing with someone. Had there been the right person that I was attracted to, I probably would have involved myself in some type of experience. On the other hand I had this whole Catholic morality that would have left me very guilt-ridden and made me very hard on myself. I suspect that I carried around this inconsistency much to my detriment. As it turned out, during my adolescence I did not have an experience. My intensity kept people off. As I approached my late teens, the need was more intensified. I dated women but there was not a lot of psychological energy around that. In terms of my sexual identity, I have learned as a therapist not to buy into any type of labels about peoples' sexual orientation. I don't have any objection to the terms gay and straight, or homosexual and heterosexual, being used about behaviors or lifestyles or about communities. I think it's important to talk about the gay community, and for people not to be afraid to associate with the gay subculture, because that fear of association only reinforces homophobia. On the other hand, I'm certain that when youths come to me and ask the specific question, am I or am I not gay, I'll tell them they are asking the wrong question. It's not that simple. People aren't pre-wired. I tell them, why don't we take a look at who you are sexually, and be a good observer of yourself before you use labels. I'm not making a pitch for bisexuality either. I'm pushing for an exploration of one's sexuality.

For me the eroticism took on the desire to be bonded with male adolescents. I'm not sure I knew what that meant without any experience. What I needed was permission to ask some very broad questions. But I didn't get that permission; I didn't run into the right type of people for that until I went off to college. This is where I have a love-hate relationship with Notre Dame, because that was the first setting I was in that had older adults around who made it clear that I could ask questions about my sexuality in an open manner and have it still be spiritually appropriate. Yet the whole atmosphere was pretty rigid and judgmental. It was this way across the whole country too, but Notre Dame lags behind in terms of opening up. There were not visible gay communities, no alternative lifestyles that were available. I went to Notre Dame having absolutely no sexual experience, and that includes masturbation. That emphasizes the degree to which I had cut myself off from my own physical needs and permission to explore. It wasn't that I had this great urge to masturbate, and out of Catholic morality I showed great discipline and courage not to do it. It was more tricky than that psychologically.

For me it was that I never allowed myself to put together all the ingredients of exactly what it was. So that even though I talked as if I knew what it was, had I the need to explain or spell out what it was I probably couldn't have done it. I did a lot of editing and censoring based on value judgments. Needless to say, I was a fairly uptight individual when it came to being comfortable with my body and my sexuality. That changed somewhat in college, due to meeting certain people who gave me permission to ask questions about my sexuality. The first person I disclosed these impulses to was one of the priests at Notre Dame. I was surprised that he didn't have more of a horrific reaction to it. I guess I had classified myself as much more the exception than I really was. I continued through my undergraduate years not having any experience of a homoerotic nature.

The other event that happened was that I met my wife-to-be at St. Mary's during my second year at Notre Dame. With her, I really couldn't sort out the nature of my sexual feelings, because my sexuality was very undifferentiated. Physical touch was pleasing. Though there was anxiety around it, there was surely responsiveness in my body because there hadn't been any before that. Yet my psychic energy was translated in my fantasy more toward men than toward women.

For two more years I kept this issue to myself, indicating to her that there were things we needed to discuss if we were to continue the relationship. Our sexual activity was limited. We got involved in some heavy petting when I finally experienced orgasm. After that experience I began to include masturbation in the way I took care of myself, which was a real needed shift for me. I finally became a sexual being. After that, we had an intense discussion, at which time I disclosed to her the homoerotic part of me, even though I had no full sexual experience with anyone. It was fairly upsetting to her. In retrospect, from her point of view she took the stance that because of my lack of experience this was just something that needed to be worked through. That an experience with a woman would sort of turn it around, which in retrospect was not the best assessment of the situation.

I really presented it to her in a way that made it clear to her that this was not a type of energy that I wanted to exclude from myself. Earlier I would have wanted to have this removed from me, but it became clear to me that this was a tremendous source of my creativity, and my ability to invest in work and relationships. I intuitively sensed that you don't just cut yourself off from this sort of energy, or try to artificially turn it around. I presented it to her as a part that was important to me, but not necessarily one that I assumed would be played out in any particular way.

Several weeks after this discussion I asked her to get married and she agreed. We were married after my senior year. I entered into a marriage still not having any direct sexual experience outside of petting. Throughout this time I picked up a degree in theology as well as one in the social sciences. I determined that I wanted to go into psychology in graduate school, even though I remained very interested in theology. It was pushing me to ask more relevant questions for myself. The department was designed to give people a broad and stimulating education without having to go on to graduate studies in theology. It had a lot of flexibility, and was helpful to me in my introspection. There's a lot of paradox that goes on here. One could say that the institutional church in externalizing morality was very detrimental to my adolescent development, and yet the spiritual rootedness of the church and its understanding of inward journeys was instrumental in getting me to explore myself and accepting my sexuality. It has played both the constructive and destructive role.

I truly sense that had it not been for my experience at Notre Dame I may not have been able to explore my sexuality, at least on a symbolic and introspective level. Even when I did explore it behaviorally a lot of it was done as a result of my prayer life. I did not face the crossroad that many people perceive they face, where you have to choose between being honest about your sexuality and giving up your religious identification, or keeping your spirituality and abandoning your sexuality. It didn't work that way with me.

Up until just a few years ago, my role in carrying my sexuality, especially my homosexuality, was done within the context of the church. I had seen myself as a person who would do my best to tolerate the church's stance on sexuality by trying to change things inside as opposed to outside. The insight came to me several years ago about early modeling in the church. What does one do when one's experiences begin to differ from one's tradition? The insight surrounded the origins of its founder. Jesus was born a Jew and died a Jew. He clearly had some spiritual experiences in the desert that so radically differ from what his tradition was saying between the relation of the individual and Yahweh, or more appropriately, Abba. He emerges from that experience and challenges people to think about that connectedness in a way different from what his tradition was saying. And yet, he dies a Jew. He never proclaimed himself anything but a Jew, even though his experiences were different from that tradition. His followers, who were originally Jews, somewhere came to the point where they said, our experience so differs from what it means to be Jews, that we are going to become something other than Jews.

Do you stay within your tradition even though your experiences are at odds with it? Or do you reach a point in time when you leave your tradition because the discrepancies between who you are and where your tradition is become too great? For most of my adult life I have assumed that I was following the former, that even though my experiences were different from my Catholic tradition I could stay within it. But I'm getting ahead of my story, and I'll come back to the point where that decision had to change.

I was in my mid-twenties and several years into my marriage when I had my first sexual experience with a man. It was clear to me that in this homoerotic area I was much more like an adolescent, seeking playfulness and adventure, than I was like an adult, seeking some deep erotic bonds. There was this missing adolescence in the homoerotic realm. During my twenties and into my thirties the challenge was how to let the adolescent live and give him experiences. From my mid-twenties on I was able to share with men in a homoerotic way that took on a lot of meaning for me. But they weren't incorporated into my ongoing lifestyle. It was clear that my marriage and my responsibility to that marriage came first. That was tremendously influenced by my Catholicism. One took a vow and kept within that vow and didn't have the prerogative to change that vow. The only thing that made me challenge that was the depression I was in and out of during those years. I fought a lot of battles with a lot of darkness. There is probably little that can come into my office as a therapist that really threatens me a lot, disturbance or darkness or destruction. I feel that I have been there inwardly.

I was in a marriage where my spouse didn't understand introspective work. She didn't need it. She was put together in a way that made her outgoing and aggressive as a professional in her field. She would look at her spouse, who was working with his dreams and keeping journals and having long conversations with mentors. This was bewildering to her; it caused resentment that she was not included. And of course there was the difficulty of me being connected with other people sexually. The challenge we had was a sense of competition which probably did as much as anything to hurt our relationship. She felt that if I was having the opportunity to have these experiences, she damn well was going to be able to also. Out of a sense of fair play I wasn't going to say no, you can't. She also had relations with other men, although not that frequently. We fought many battles, and I thought we had crossed enough terrains that we could continue the marriage. I was a bit naive in that. In our mid-thirties she decided that the marriage was no longer feasible, and threw in the towel. We got into an adversary relationship which ended in a way I would not have preferred. I certainly don't perceive that I could have denied my homosexuality and remained healthy, and particularly spiritually healthy. But it has cost me a lot.

Even several years after the time of my divorce, I was still a member of the church. The turning point for me was in October, 1986, when the Vatican came out under the signature of Cardinal Ratzinger with a letter. It was a significantly different document than the church had put out before. Formerly, statements were based on theology, and even though my theology was different from the theology the church was promoting, I would bear the tension. This letter was not about theology, it was about pastoral care and psychology, mental health. It was basically setting guidelines about how to treat homosexuals. It was so contrary to everything I know as a professional, as an ethical human being, as a person who has some concerns about what it means to carry one another's burdens. I felt the line had been drawn, when my particular growth and inner journey so differed from what the institution said was required. I chose to stop being a part of the church. I'm an individual who went to church for thirty-some years; I rarely missed and found the liturgy very important for me. One day to stop all this and not miss it at all is fascinating. I would have thought that there would have been a significant void in my life. That has not been the case at all, and I'm not sure how to explain that. I am very leery that most individuals can journey well by themselves, going without a community, or without a tribe. It takes a unique individual to do this. On the other hand, I haven't found another formal community yet.

My mixed feelings about the church were highlighted this past week when my new partner and I went to a play called the "History of Sexuality." It was outrageous. The dialogue between sexuality and the Catholic Church was extreme. From a psychological point of view it didn't rattle me, but on one hand there was an identification with the anger of the playwright and on the other hand there was a sadness because many of those symbols have been important to me in my journey. I find myself being the devil's advocate in that when I'm with psychologically aware people whom I feel are spiritually naive and have written off spirituality, I try to press them on where I feel they are shutting down. I'm amazed at colleagues who can do intakes with college students and not find out what their religious background is. On the other hand, I've had my fill of religiously-identified people who are fairly unsophisticated and dishonest psychologically, not wanting to call a spade a spade. They don't want to deal with the impulses in their own inner life, and don't integrate that, so they lay judgments on other people, and project all they don't tolerate inside themselves on institutions and on other people's lives.

I feel a sadness in my separation from the Catholic church, insofar as it takes stands on social issues, particularly in the third world and in Latin America. It's fighting some brave battles in regard to social justice and liberation theology. I am no longer part of that, mostly because of its stand on sexuality, and the very destructive burden it's laying on gay people. The whole issue of the feminine in church and the role of women is hardly dissociated from the homoerotic. The feminine is so restricted and demeaned and kept out of the dialogue in significant ways. There is no way the homoerotic can be integrated without the feminine. The church continues, as does the general community, to artificially polarize people as gay or straight. There is no psychological data that can be produced to show that people are polarized in that way. There is no real operational definition of what is gay and what is straight. People self-select, and nobody knows on what criteria.

What is the reason for the fluidity that women have about their sexuality that allows them not to polarize questions of sexual orientation? And why is it that men are constantly being presented with the frame of reference that they are or they aren't? If you ask the majority of Americans when did we come upon this notion of homosexuality historically, they would probably be surprised that it is a twentieth-century conceptualization. Before the twentieth century, people were either supported or condemned by what they did, not by their orientation. It would be naive to say that most peoples' lifestyles don't form a consistency over time that is basically oriented toward the same sex or the opposite sex. But when it comes to their individual identity inside, there is a lot of complexity involved. If we were in a more tolerant climate where people could be asking open-ended questions and be good observers, that diversity would blossom.

Another part that my Catholicism played was the emphasis on keeping sexuality in a relationship context. I did less shopping around and exposing myself to a lot that causes problems. I haven't been exposed to the same health problems some others have had. I don't feel righteous about it as much as lucky. But surely my Catholicism, with emphasis on relationship, played a part in slowing me down.

If the church is so convinced of the truth of its position as stated in the Ratzinger letter, then to be consistent it should ask about forty percent of the clergy to leave. As an institution, the church is benefiting from the love that people are sharing in a homoerotic way, and yet it doesn't even want to acknowledge its existence. This hypocrisy can, from my perspective, only lead to destructive results. If I have any major concern about the health of the institution it's that if you take a look at the New Testament, you see one trait that people are warned against over and over, and that is hypocrisy. Church people get split between their experience and what life has taught them, and what they preach and teach to other people. Surely there is hypocrisy between the role that homoeroticism has played in the Catholic church and the official stance the church takes in its condemnation of homosexuality. It would do well to tend to its own house first, to make no comments to people outside the church, and to begin to examine the role homosexuality has played with its own members. If it could gain some insights into this perhaps it could avoid the hypocrisy that can be fairly destructive. It's a shame that the radicalness of the New Testament in challenging structures and authority on that hypocrisy has been lost on the institutional church.

The name in this story has been changed to protect the privacy of the individual.

CHARLENE MATTINGLY

Charlene is a clinical psychologist. She has lived for the last three years in a committed relationship with her lover, Patty.

I was blessed with a good family. I was raised Catholic and although the schools I attended were very strict and rigid, my parents were very loving and did not take an authoritarian or fearful approach. From them I learned about a loving God, and about saints who loved little children. I didn't get the hellfire side of Christianity that some people got. I have a younger brother who is also gay. This, of course, we didn't know until we were in our twenties.

We are a close family, and the most difficult thing for me and my brother in dealing with our gay orientation was to disappoint our parents. Initially they were hurt and wondered what they had done wrong. But never once did they reject us. That is something for which I am grateful. They had to come to terms with their tradition in order to fully accept us. Even before they came to understand, they accepted us. That was incredible. My father was faced with a terminal illness and my mother gave her whole life to caring for him. He was able to recognize that this kind of caring is something no person should be denied, no matter what one's sexual orientation. That was when we were really able to talk about it. Now my mother accepts Patty as her daughter.

I have known gay people who have been as lucky as I have been with parents and others who have been disowned by their parents when they found out their children were gay. In fact, my own family has sheltered people who have been thrown out of their houses. The gay experience ranges from people telling their family everything to only part of the truth, where family members will indicate that it is okay but we are not going to talk about it. People seem to have varying levels of acceptance.

As for me, I don't know when I became aware that I was different. I knew that I never fit in all that well with the other girls. In childhood I was nearsighted and asthmatic, and definitely not sports-minded. I was an independent, quiet kid who read adventure stories and wanted to be Long John Silver. I was the kind of kid who alternated between ambitions of being a sailing captain and digging up dinosaurs in the back yard. I never saw myself as being a housewife like mommy. I think somewhere along the line I grew to realize that I didn't want to have a crush on Erroll Flynn like all the other girls. I wanted to be Erroll Flynn and get Olivia de Haviland in the process.

If I had known anything about what sexuality was or what it was about, I think I would have known what was going on by the time I was about eleven. I became extremely protective of this little girl friend of mine. I was going to take care of her. Looking back on it, that should have been the tip-off. I had a crush on the little girl who sat in front of me in class when everyone else was having a crush on Donny Osmond, or whoever the teenage idol was at the time. I didn't feel guilty about it because I didn't connect it with sex. I didn't find out the whole story about where babies came from until I was thirteen, and even then all I knew about sexuality was that it had something to do with boys and with being a dumb girl. I never thought of myself as being a dumb girl and I had no interest in boys; therefore, what I felt could not be sex. It was all very simple because it seemed so cut and dried. Later I started to realize what the feelings were and had the good sense to keep my mouth shut. It's amazing sometimes how the feelings we have do not connect with what we know about the world.

I was going through high school when the women's movement was just getting started. Expectations for girls were not as rigid as they had been. In my part of the country girls were expected to go to college. So my having academic ambitions was not unusual. What was usual was that most of the girls were busy trying to be prom queens. Being in an all-girls school it was easier to be the brain, the egghead. I was quite happy in this role. I was under no pressure to date, and that was fine with me, because most of the boys I knew were idiots anyway. In sophomore year I fell madly in love with a girl in my geometry class. We were the best of friends all through high school. We were as close as sisters and people tended to think of us as a unit. Oddly enough, neither we nor anyone else understood what the real situation was. I had an idea that there was more there than was being expressed, but I didn't know what it was I was feeling for her.

It was in my freshman year of college that I finally realized that I was gay, what that entailed and what decisions I would have to make, and how my relation with the church would be affected. I realized that I was going to have to think through a lot of things by myself. It was a difficult time, but being a female in the 1970s I was faced with having to think through a lot of things by myself, that was a given.

At that time we had a lot of double messages going on. One was that we should get an education but we should also be housewives and produce children. Right away that set up conflicts for me. I knew there were parts of the church that I was going to have to accept that were not right for me. I was going to have to keep my relationship with God separate from my relationship with the church. I went through a stage when I was extremely rebellious. I was opposed to the church and to organized religion. I was reading books with titles like *The Gospel of Irreligious Religion* and the work of Thoreau. Later I began to see that I could have a relationship with God within the context of the church in which I was raised even though I didn't agree with that church. I think that coincided with the maturation of the relationship with my parents. It was the process of being able to disagree with them but still like them, and be part of the family and yet not have to be exactly cloned from them. I think the two of them ran parallel. I left home and came back home. I did the same thing with the church.

I went to Catholic elementary school and a Catholic girls' high school. When it came time to go to college I was determined not to go to a Catholic college. I went to a very small private liberal arts college about fifty miles from home. I lived in the dorms with people of every possible persuasion. At that time I basically went to Mass on holidays. I remember going back and forth with a certain amount of guilt. In college we read a lot of the Church Fathers. It had a funny effect on me. In one way it intensified the guilty fits; then again it became obvious that the world of the Church Fathers and ours was so different that I saw the need to think things through for myself.

What helped me make the shift from the rebellious stage to an acceptance of my tradition as a Catholic was Dignity. My younger brother introduced me to Dignity when I came home during one period of my life. I wasn't much into the gay community at the time. Bars didn't appeal to me since I don't drink or smoke. I was kind of out of it on both levels. When I went to Dignity with my brother I felt like it was homecoming. Here were people in my community, the gay community, where I could be accepted. They were people who were doing some fascinating thinking in philosophical terms. At the same time they found a way to not be fenced in by the church but to work from within it. I continue to be involved in Dignity.

Many women have suffered so much under the patriarchal church that they simply want nothing that is associated with it. I have nothing against that. I read a lot of things associated with those traditions, but it just doesn't feel like home to me. This leaves me in a position that I belong to a tradition that is hostile to fifty-one percent of the human race. This applies as well to straight women, and in a way they are more affected. The only way that I have been able to resolve it is not to hold my God responsible for the sins of my church. I have had a lot of help with this, especially with some Sisters and friends involved in pastoral ministry. These women have such a tremendous knowledge of early church theology and feminist theology that it sheds a whole new light on the tradition. Listening to them reminds me that the original thrust of the early church was not patriarchal. That was not Jesus's intention. It came out of the Middle Ages. By approaching it from that perspective I feel comfortable within the tradition. I find myself getting very defensive when I hear some of the right-wing groups speaking with the authority of the Christian tradition and in the process diminishing women. I get angry at that but I have a place to go and people to talk to that help me realize that this is not the way it has to be. If wasn't for this support I would probably find myself praying privately or stepping out of the tradition.

What I hope for is that, as time goes on, those in positions of authority in the church will come to realize that women and gays and ethnic minorities are as much the church as the traditional European male patriarchy, and that these groups will be a force for social change. I would hope that church authorities will come to see the need for justice and mercy and equality and let go of judging. The fact that there have been so many wonderful clergy and sisters has been extremely hopeful. One of the things that dampens that hope is that the political climate is in a backswing toward the '50s. It seems that we are going back to the days of Joe McCarthy. So much of Christianity, especially fundamentalist Christianity, has defined morality as intolerance toward any minority.

This movement was in progress when the AIDS crisis hit. It certainly was not the cause of the backswing, but AIDS has certainly added fuel to the fire. We would have had to contend with this movement anyway, but because of the economic situation, politics and religious movements tend to get more conservative. On the good side what AIDS has done is to gather the gay community together and give it a new cohesion.

As tragic as it has been, it has had a positive effect on the gay community.

My study of psychology has shown me that psychology would like to grow up to be a science, but it is not there yet. The more I study, the more I know what I don't know. The best that psychology has to offer people is really a quasi-spiritual kind of awareness. The organized church has let people down when it has offered simple and patented answers. Psychology is on the way to making the same fatal error. What I find in psychology is a way to teach people to be less harmful to themselves. But because people also need an answer to some of the heavier questions about life and death, they aren't going to find this in psychology or in the printed material about self-help and growth. My studies have shown me what psychology can offer and what it cannot offer. But I won't look there for the ultimate answers.

If I had a chance to talk to the bishops of the Catholic church I would ask them to take another look at the spirit of the law. They have defined love, morality, and sexuality in purely physical, genital terms. In every aspect of what they call sexual morality in the church, from the role of women to the non-ordination of women, to the rules on birth control and homosexuality, what they look at is what people do with a certain portion of their anatomy, and they have totally missed the spirit of companionship, love, respect, and creativity. They have overlooked the fact that generativity and life-giving are more than biological. They missed the need of the community for diversity in the modern world. There is a place in society for people who are different from their so-called norms. The love of Christ has to be interpreted in that light. They also need to see the needs of people to love those that fit their own Godgiven temperament and biology. The pat, simple terms certainly don't seem to address these issues. They need to know how people really live, not how they think they should live. I'd like to invite them to come look at the reality of where and how people experience their lives.

The name in this story has been changed to protect the privacy of the individual.

TOBY JOHNSON

Toby is a forty-two year old psychotherapist who lives in San Antonio, Texas. He is the author of several books. An earlier novel, Plague, *is about the AIDS crisis. Other works include two spiritual autobiographies,* The Myth of the Great Secret: A Search for Spiritual Meaning in the Face of Emptiness *and* In Search of God in the Sexual Underworld. *He collaborated with the gay scholar Toby Morotta on the production of* The Politics of Homosexuality *and* Sons of Harvard. *His latest publication is a gay science fiction novel entitled* Secret Matter.

What seems to me the most important thing about my own Catholic upbringing and about Catholicism, is that ours is an intellectual religion. On a theological level it has been willing to discuss important issues. In the past it did this in a way that did not allow these theological discussions to get to the people. The theologians could discuss sensitive issues that didn't get into the parish. That no longer happens; today the discussion reaches the parish level. Some people then become more hardened in their belief because it is challenged, others throw everything out. It seems to me the appropriate middle road is to work toward a synthesis of what the mythology means. Unfortunately this is difficult to do inside the church. The institution seems opposed to letting that happen, although people are doing it anyway. Maybe this means that the institution will gradually be destroyed. I think that is what was supposed to happen. I don't think Christianity was ever supposed to have had a church. It seems clear that if Jesus was against anything, it was a church. The church put him to death. Then within a hundred years they founded another church and named it after him, and they put more people to death. Maybe we are at a point now where we are ready to hear the teaching of Jesus about the evils of religion. We need to recognize that religion is not owned by the churches. People can be religious without religion.

As Catholics we grew up valuing rational, intellectual discussion of religious truths, which is the beautiful thing that kept us from becoming literalist. The power of Catholicism is that it seems to adjust to reality in ways that biblical fundamentalists simply cannot.

I came out of a sort of mystical family background. My mother had several miscarriages before I was born and became very religious, which often happens in such situations. She was a convert to Catholicism and developed a great devotion to the Blessed Mother. I grew up with the understanding that my birth was successful in part because the doctor was willing to do a Cesarian section for the first time, but also because the Blessed Mother intervened. I had an understanding that there was something special about me, and that was because of the spiritual relationship my mother had with Mary.

I think I was like most young gay boys: I was very good and did everything right. That seems to be a hallmark of homosexual males. Growing up in the '50s, I had no idea of anything about sex. As I look back on it, I didn't understand the sexual teachings of the catechism class. The terms "purity" and "impurity" were meaningless words because nobody explained what they were all about. What I certainly knew in high school was that I did not understand other kids' interest in girls and dating, the things that would have been the beginning of normal heterosexual feelings.

I went to a Catholic high school taught by the Brothers of Mary. One brother was very important in my life. He taught me how to think and assisted in identifying me as a writer. By getting close to him, I began to have an attraction to the brothers' way of life. It seemed like an alternative to what looked like the sexual life of the other kids, which I saw as wrong and in which I had no interest. I was very mystical in high school. That has remained a theme all through my life.

Whitley Streiber, the author of the novel *Communion*, and I were close friends. He was influenced by the same Brother. There is a story in *Communion*, by the way, about how he and a friend set fire to the roof of his family's house playing with electromagnets. I was the friend. We interpreted that as proof that aliens were trying to stop us from finding out about their flying saucers. Although this was delusional thinking, it was appropriate for teenagers.

In fact I remember a time when I was little when I believed that I wasn't human at all but was from outer space. I think that was the way I sensed my being different—not being part of the human race—being homosexual. There is something about being gay that just doesn't fit. One of the very early crucial religious experiences I had was trying to decide whether I wanted to be religious in the conventional way or believe I was an alien from outer space. I couldn't claim both of them, so I eventually chose to be a religious, which means to me that my vocation flowed directly out of my homosexuality.

In junior year Whitley got me to read St. John of the Cross. One of my religion teachers told me I should not be reading that book, it was too advanced for me. He was right, I should not have read it. I'm not sure I have ever gotten over it. I still experience the feeling that the way God loves me is to foul up all my plans.

Anyway I joined the Brothers after high school. They were glad to have me because I was bright and had gotten a National Merit Scholarship. I went to Wisconsin for novitiate—one of the best years of my life. We had a wonderful novice master who abolished a lot of the crazy customs of the past. He imbued us with the idea that what was most important in life was personal responsibility. The next year in the scholasticate I got in trouble with this approach. I challenged those who tried to maintain the old styles of seminary life. I once accused the superior of being "old school" while we—the novices of my class—were "new school." I was thrown out of the Marianists at the end of that year. As I see it now, they got rid of me because somebody had to be taught a lesson. That was very traumatic at the time.

My best friend in high school had also gone off to religious life at the same time I did. He went to the Passionists. We corresponded over the years. During the turmoil of my novitiate I'd written him a long letter about all sorts of mystical stuff, all of which had an underlying sexual tone. The Master of Students read the letter, and that apparently cinched the fact that there was something odd about me.

Right at the end I had a conversation with one of the provincial officers who told me that the psychological tests showed I was gay, and they knew I was gay, and I would not be happy in their order. He never used the word gay, of course, and talked around it, but in retrospect I realized that is what he was talking about.

Another guy who left the same time I did, on whom I had a bit of a crush, was going to St. Louis University. I decided to go there too. In the mid-sixties St. Louis University was in the center of the liturgical movement. Early on in my stay there I met the Servites who were living in the graduate student dorms. I became fascinated with them. I hung around them, partly because I had a crush on the head of the choir. (He is now a gay psychologist in Los Angeles.) In my senior year I moved in with the Servites and sort of unofficially joined them. They were just starting the Catholic Theological Union in Chicago and after graduating I went on to Chicago.

By then I had begun to recognize my sexuality. I knew I was gay, though really didn't know what that meant. Nonetheless I became a sort of mentor for the seminarians. One of the things I was talking about in those days was the spirituality of sexual feelings, about how important it was to eroticize our daily experience—whatever that was supposed to mean. All this was an abstracted way of saying it's okay to be sexual. I was very popular because there were a lot of young gay men in the Servites. I developed a sexual relationship with one of the guys in my class. This was my first relationship. We would have sex and then get scared and guilty.

My teachings about the okayness of sex finally came to the attention of the Servite superiors. There were two priests—who were in irreverent gay jargon "fat old queens"—at one of the Servite houses who got in a huff and demanded an investigation. They started a rumor that there was a "hotbed of homosexuality" in the scholasticate and that I was the ringmaster. I acknowledged that I was gay, and that I was handling it according to what I understood my morals and virtues demanded. I was not disciplined but these two men who started the rumor were ordered under obedience to stop talking about it. The thing that impressed me with the Servites was that they recognized who their people were and they were honest about it. Because of all the turmoil in Chicago, I asked to do a year of novitiate.

Although I had acknowledged the previous year to the Provincial that I was homosexual, I don't think I quite acknowledged to myself what that meant. I had a great "coming out" experience the next summer while working in a psychiatric hospital as part of clinical pastoral education. I was able to admit to myself that I was gay and that was fine, in fact was a wonderful thing. This was 1969 and everyone was into acknowledging truth. I started novitiate with the Servites in the fall. My being openly gay created a lot of problems with a group of novices who were still in the closet. I realized that either I had to go back into the closet—at least not talk about things openly—or get out of the order. I couldn't stand living under all the pressure and I left after six months. The occasion for my departure was that a friend of mine was asked to leave, ostensibly for being gay.

By this time I had already begun to think of myself more as a Buddhist anyway. I had an important insight into what religion and mythology is all about: the significant thing is not the content of religious belief, but that these doctrines have the power to bring about mystical experience, at least in theory. The goal of religion is religious experience and not knowledge about a set of events that supposedly happened in the distant past. What saves us is that we get insight into what the doctrines mean. It seems that on many levels Christianity has stopped working precisely because it has failed to recognize that and has preferred doctrine to enlightenment and history to religious experience. To believe in the historical virginity of Mary, for instance, doesn't particularly help one become enlightened, though the image may be full of wonderful symbolism about nature and ecology.

I was born two days before the bomb was dropped on Hiroshima. I always understood that the bomb and I came into the world at the same time. I have a fascination for what the bomb means. I've never heard anybody mention, by the way, that the bomb was dropped on the feast of the Transfiguration, August 6. That's a very potent image: the day when Jesus turned into light. That doesn't mean anything literally, but it can be spiritually powerful.

After leaving the Servites I went to San Francisco. Thus I had an opportunity to be openly gay in a city where it was easy. Soon I started graduate school at the California Institute of Asian Studies, pursuing the Jungian, Buddhist thought that I had begun to get into with the Servites. While we were all semi-hippies at the school and very much into Eastern religion, I found myself often talking about Catholicism. In the classes I would show how there was a theme in Catholic tradition similar to this or that theme in Hinduism or Buddhism or Taoism. There are a lot of parallels, although most Catholics tend to deny this.

One of the things I'm fascinated with these days is the idea that a lot of gay men have had experiences similar to those I have had. They were in religious life as young idealistic students. In the church we saw so much promise: we were concerned about great social issues, and we were doing it within the church. The church was beginning to move, and the hierarchy was recognizing it. Then all of a sudden everything just stopped. The styles shifted a little without any change in the overall dogmatism and legalism. For many of us, this noble experiment was squelched. We were betrayed by the church. I didn't have any sense that the church was anti-homosexual—of course I didn't exactly know what these words meant. But I understood that to be one of the most beautiful parts of myself. My prayer life was involved with the people I was attracted to. Now, looking back, I see those years in the church as an important time in my life. I learned important lessons about living a peaceful, quiet life, living common life.

One of the things I learned about Buddhism is that all children go through monastic life for a while. Wouldn't it be nice for everybody to have religious formation of the kind that novitiate provides? Then go live life, and as you get older and retire, go back to the place of formation. We obviously have to do something about how we are handling aging and death.

AIDS has made our generation prematurely conscious of death and the transitoriness of life. I'm ready to go back to the monastery, but not in the church. It's time for us who have positive memories to begin our own experiment in putting together spiritual communities. At the end of my novel *Plague,* for instance, the main character goes off to what I called a "freelance monastery." And that's something I know I want to do in fact. I think there are a lot of other people in similar situations. Some of them do not have the monastic background, but for them AIDS has pushed an awareness of spirituality and a concern about preparing for death. I think especially for people who are diagnosed as HIV positive, an opportunity to move to the country at least during occasional retreats might be a way of reducing stress and thus offset the disease. I hope to spend the new few years founding such a freelance monastery with a guesthouse for retreatants and visitors. Monasticism is a wonderful alternative to the pressures of modern society, but, of course, not inside the institution of the church.

CURRENT RELIGIOUS

JOSEF SCHULTZ

Josef is a religious priest from Europe, studying for a doctorate at a major Catholic university in the United States. When he earns his degree he will return to his home in Europe.

I was born and raised in a simple, good, not very pious Catholic family in Germany. The region is totally Catholic. I had hardly ever seen a Protestant until I went to the university at age eighteen. That was the first exposure for me. Until then everything was Catholic. I went to a public high school but because everyone was Catholic, it was in fact a Catholic school. Religion is very much embedded in that society. Every year there was a big procession on the feast of Corpus Christi and on the feast of the city. The mayor and the representative of the government would walk behind the Blessed Sacrament, behind the clergy. It has always been that way, nobody questions it. I grew up in an atmosphere where Catholicism was not questioned about anything. Of course I was Catholic, of course I went to a Catholic grade school. If you went to a public high school everything was Catholic.

It's very difficult for me to go back to family life and analyze it in a fair way. As I look on it now, it seems more distorted than on first sight. You always think of your family as perfect when you grow up. When you look back on it you see problems. I was brought up with less Catholic guilt than some other nationalities. But the guilt trip that is all over people in my country is the guilt of the upwardly mobile middle class, which is that you have to work to arrive. So the pressure of study was always very high. I lost myself in developing to be a very cerebral, rational person. Work hard, do well in school, that's the aim in life. In that process I grew away at an early age from anything that was emotional. That's a big part of my story.

As I look back on it I cannot remember being sexually attracted by anyone other than men. But I never admitted to myself that I was

gay until I was twenty-nine. It took a very long time to come to grips
with that. I think that was due partially to the fact that sexuality in
my history was a non-issue. Sexual feelings were not looked at, were
not allowed to the conscious level. They were just not there. I grew
up to be a good little boy that never grows up, who always does his
duty. Little boys that don't grow up never become sexual.

Another factor was that I grew up consciously as a Catholic. After
age twelve or thirteen, after Vatican II, I grew up in the midst of
renewal of the liturgy and everything new in the church. I voluntarily
took part in that. I was part of a liturgical workshop in our parish that
prepared once a month a theme Mass for youth. I put a lot of time
and energy into that, and I enjoyed it. I worked with the chaplain in
the parish and I got to admire him very much. I still admire the man.
He is now a pastor in another parish. I started admiring him and it grew
into a feeling that I would like to be a priest like him. If you take these
two things—one, to be a good little boy that is non-sexual, and two,
the wish to be a priest who handed down the religion—when you
combine them you have the perfect match. Because priests by definition
are good little boys who are non-sexual. That's the way I perceived
priesthood for many years. I still struggle with that. The priest is a
perfect person who has no real engaging emotions and who is good
and nice and friendly, and hands down the tradition of religion that
he has gotten.

I was in high school when I first talked to my parents about my
desire to become a priest. I am grateful to them that they did not think
it was a good idea for me to go directly from high school into the
seminary. They encouraged me to study something else. First they made
me promise that I would finish the university before I would enter the
seminary. So I decided to study law. When I entered the religious
community there were two things that I regretted that I had to give
up, one was not to be able to teach in high school as I did during the
last year of my studies, and the other was not being able to practice
law.

During my university years, from eighteen to twenty-four, I was
still convinced that I was going to be a priest. Nobody questioned that
or challenged it. At that time I had not experimented in anything. During
my time at the university I met the priests of my future religious
community in church history. That was my first encounter with them.
I was attracted to their history and their ministry, so I decided to join
them. The decision to join was finally an emotional one. I felt very

comfortable around them and in their communities. Right after finishing at the university I entered the religious community.

I still see the novitiate as a very valuable time. Two important things happened to me at that time; one, I learned how to pray, second, I started learning to be honest about my feelings. I was very quiet and pious in the novitiate. It was a two-year vacation for me. The breakthrough in my life on an emotional level started at the end of the novitiate. We were sent to France for four months to live with the French novices. It was a very loose group, you did practically anything you wanted. I recall how I enjoyed that, going to the city and watching people. The next step for me was to go back home to study theology. The next part of my breakthrough occurred there when I touched upon feelings that I had always denied and put away. At that time there was another seminarian there who was a few years older than me. He was gay. He knew all along that I was gay, but he never confronted me. He was always reluctant to intrude into my space. But he was always there to talk, and would respond to whatever were my needs.

Where I lived, homosexuality was in the streets, it was not something that was hidden. Nor was it reserved to one part of the city; it was everywhere. So I was confronted with that. At first I was very much afraid of it. But I know now I was also fascinated by it. "Ben," I once said to my friend, "why don't we go to a gay bar?" We went, and I stood in awe before all those beautiful men. I still had that fascination in me for a long time and didn't know what to do with it. There was a still a block in me that kept me from admitting that if I saw a man that I was attracted to that I was gay. I didn't have a problem accepting that others were gay. I guess for me the rule was that if you are a priest you are not sexual to begin with, especially not gay. I wanted to become a priest, therefore I am not gay. That was the syllogism and it was working. My feelings were telling me that they didn't fit into the syllogism, so I just didn't do anything with them.

I finished my Bachelor's degree and went to licentiate studies in another city. I was there for three and a half years. After studying there for one year it was time to become a Deacon. At that time I still didn't have a very good idea of what was going on in myself. I started to work in a parish. By the middle of the year things began to change. One thing was that two or three of my good friends in my community left. I was thrown into a vacuum. Secondly, I started reading Genet, the French gay novelist. Again, I was fascinated by it and wanted to read more. Finally I came to the point where I admitted that I wanted to know whether I was gay or not. So I had my first sexual experience, and it was great. That for me was the break; I said, okay, I am gay. But that created a problem.

A lot of people have very negative experiences with the church in coming to grips with their sexuality. I didn't have the same kind of experience. My friend, who was by then ordained a priest, was there to talk to me. He directed me to another priest who was gay and somewhat older. He had a lot of experience in spiritual direction, and from that point on I considered him my spiritual director. They both applauded that I had come to grips with myself. They sort of dispensed me from everything. I still consider myself dispensed from anything that may be in the way of my growth. The fact that they were so supportive was very important to me. They gave me an image of what church can be for gay people, and, by analogy, for anyone who has come to grips with whatever in his or her life.

I think the first step that I had to take was to discover that I had a body, something that I had denied until then. I discovered that it is a good body, and that I can take care of it, and that it is good looking and that some people might find it attractive. As a footnote, I am amazed at how many gay people there are who are absolutely gorgeous and think that they are ugly. It is a common and widespread disease among gay people. It is probably a reflection of low self-esteem.

Then came the time for priestly ordination. The question was, should I be ordained a priest or not? Should my recent discovery be a reason for postponing? I came back very easily with the theological answer that the diaconate ordination is the real ordination, and priestly ordination is a follow-up that is automatic. I was ordained a priest and felt good about it.

My studies went well and they decided to send me to the United States to get a graduate degree. That's why I'm here. Ever since I was twelve years old I wanted to come to the States. That has always been my dream, and I am very happy. Another coincidence that worked out well was that Dignity is here. It gave me a place where I could be both priest and gay. Every aspect of my personality is accepted in Dignity. It was a wonderful experience. Before the bishop forbade us to have Mass, I was a regular celebrant. By being challenged to talk to people who are gay and struggling like I am, I wrestled with a lot of things on the spiritual, theological level. I was able to come to grips with these issues, and that is important for me. I also got a lot of good feedback from the Dignity members. They would value me as a person, and tell me that I was a good priest.

Back to my personal development, my first discovery had been that I had a body, and the second was to find out what relationship was all about. I think I'm still in that phase. For a long time I saw myself in a dichotomy. I saw two roads and I had to choose between one or the other. The one was to go on being a religious priest, but sooner or later fall back into a fairly classical way of living priestly religious life. Thinking "It's okay to fool around a little to get it out of your system but then go back into the ranks and lead a celibate life." The other way was: "Now that I have discovered my emotional-sexual side I cannot really live without relationship, and that will involve my leaving the community." At first I said, "Of course I want to remain a religious. This thing will go away. Eventually I will go back to my old pattern of a non-sexual lifestyle." The second step was to admit that there was a choice to be made, and that I was allowed to make a choice for either one of the two roads. I was with my provincial last summer and talked about all this. He knows that I am gay. He is very supportive and open. His approach is: "It's okay to be, not okay to do. We would like you not to be too open about it, because it makes people nervous." I told him what I was thinking about. He accepted the fact that I couldn't make a decision right now, so he said to go on the way I have been going. But sooner or later I will have to make a choice, according to him. The alternatives are to either leave the community and go with a relationship or to stay and be celibate. Now I think somewhat differently. I think that I have to stay because that's what God asked me to do, and that's what I will eventually be happy in. But my question right now is, what is the best way for *me* to give shape to the idea of being a religious and priest? Is it living in some kind of relationship, of whatever kind? Or will it be living in celibacy in the more classical sense of the word? This is the point where I am now. Perhaps I will leave the community eventually if I see that relationship is so important for me that it would take away the quality of my work as a priest. But it is more likely that I will stay, for that is what I feel called to. Perhaps I would like to go back to a celibate lifestyle, perhaps some kind of in-between.

In life you are never alone, there are always other people. I think that is a large part of the way Divine Providence will help me come to a decision: by showing what relationships mean to me in practice. It is very hard for me to be in the gray area. I have been there for several years now, and I will be there for another few years. That is a hard thing to do, but it is the only way to go right now. I think it would not be wise for me to jump to conclusions. I don't think it would be wise for my superiors to force me to jump to conclusions. That's why I find it difficult to be open with every superior about the fact that I do still have relationships which sometimes involve sexual contact. I strive to do this in a caring relationship of whatever duration, short or long. That's part of my life right now. I'm willing to talk with my superiors about that, but not every superior. It depends on whether they give me the feeling that they are free about the issue itself. A lot of our superiors are not. Many of them are gay themselves and have not come to grips with it. It shows in a lot of the anger that is evident in their language about the topic. I can open up and be free and try to discern with somebody who is open. I must admit however that I might project on certain superiors a lack of freedom which in fact is my own lack of freedom.

I came out to my family as gay after I was ordained. They accepted it. They will come to visit me this summer and I will take them to Dignity, and I think they will have a ball. For them it's easier to accept in the sense that they never expect to be confronted with me saying, "Mom, Dad, meet Jim, who is my lover." They can abstract from that.

This is my story, but I would also like to talk about how gay people could deal with the Ratzinger letter. The official church seems to be very anti-gay. My own personal experience with the church in terms of being gay has not been bad. My priest friends and my religious community has been accepting. That gives me an advantage over people who have had only bad experiences. Then I go to the next step and recognize how the official church writes about homosexuality, and I can get very upset. I think, however, we have to see it in the context of what the church teaches on sexuality in general. We look at how couples have been treated by not being allowed to make decisions about their own married life. That is probably more violent. At this point in time, I emphasize first of all the psychological aspect. The people who are the official church have personal difficulty with their sexuality and, therefore, you can't take too seriously what they say. Secondly, in the realm of sexual ethics there is no infallible teaching. So, as a good Catholic, I look at what the official church says about sex. I say, "This is an interesting proposal. They thought about it, but it doesn't make sense in the peoples' experience."

Certainly I do believe very strongly that the church is very much concerned about people. I don't think they sit in Rome trying to be nasty. There is some nastiness that might come through against their own will, but when you look at the letter of Ratzinger I think what he is trying to do is be compassionate, but he does it in a very clumsy way.

One of the most painful experiences for me is not that Cardinal Ratzinger writes a letter on homosexuality, but that he only says half of the truth. Even if it would be the teaching of the church revealed by Christ directly that homosexual acts are intrinsically evil, still it stands within the framework that nothing that is intrinsically evil is immediately sinful. It has to go through the conscience of the individual to make it sinful. By omitting that traditional teaching of the church, he misleads us. He is not being pastoral, he is not teaching the tradition of the church. The Pope and Ratzinger are not conservatives. Conservatives keep the traditions of the church, while Ratzinger wipes away whatever traditions he wants to. And that is what heresy is.

I strongly believe in the last authority of our own conscience. If in my conscience I come to the conclusion that certain things *are* good for me, they are good for me and cannot be a sin. Trying to fit into molds and to keep to directives that we have always been encouraged to keep is not always the best way to go. This is how I try to help others who come to me: helping them to come to their *own* decisions of conscience. The ultimate thing is to figure out what gives *you* peace. Where faith, hope, and love grow is where God works.

In the Dignity group I belong to there is the sense that *we* are the church, even though we have been banned. They can't kick us out and we keep trying to maintain relationships with the official church. Some people have been estranged from the church and they come to Dignity and find community, find a parish. Others come once or twice and realize that the Catholic church is not their cup of tea anymore. Another group come for a little while. This can be three weeks or three years, and subsequently they start going to a regular parish. I wish the bishops would really be open to the discernment of spirits and would go a few times to Dignity and see people who were estranged from the church come back celebrating and come closer to God. I can't see how this could be the work of the Evil One.

I have a book which helped me a lot. It is by a Protestant minister who is gay. He talks about how people ask him for justification of why he is gay and practices homosexuality. He says, "Of course it is intrinsically evil, because there is no intrinsic justification for anything a human being does, gay or straight. We are all and always sinful. If you want justification for anything you will not find it, except in the cross and resurrection of Jesus Christ. Justification is not an intrinsic part of any given action. It comes from the outside by divine grace." That opened my eyes. The whole point is not to try to justify ourselves, but to accept ourselves and to accept the grace that justifies us. And that grace is already there—in abundance.

The name in this story has been changed to protect the privacy of the individual.

SISTER ANN LEE, D.MIN.

Sister Ann is a member of the Sisters of Christian Community. She has dedicated her life to the poor in the field of education. The author of a book and several articles, Dr. Lee is currently writing a book about secular spirituality.

There were eight of us in my family, including my parents. I am the oldest, with two brothers and three sisters. My father was Catholic and my mother was Methodist-Episcopal. Today I can appreciate how this diversity of religion contributed to the ecumenical perspective I have today. Perhaps it also gave me a broader outlook on life in general, so that, later on in life, I would not reject out of hand my own lesbian identity.

My first memories of church are fond ones. They begin when I started Catholic school in fourth grade. I studied my catechism faithfully and made my first Communion with great fervor. My brother and sister and I used to play "Mass" with Necco Wafers until my dad told us we shouldn't do it. All in all, I was an introspective and sensitive child, deeply interested in things spiritual. In high school, I was already meditating, attending daily Mass, and doing spiritual reading. After graduating from Catholic high school with honors I worked for a year, recited the short breviary daily, socialized, and volunteered my services at a nursing home.

During grammar school, I deeply admired a few of the sisters. I remember counting candy money for Sister Augustine one day when I was in seventh grade. Suddenly, she asked me why I was staring at her. I turned dark red and felt like disappearing. It was during that same year that I also had a crush on a girl who was a year older than I. In my junior year in high school, I fell in love with my high school math teacher, who was a vibrant, strong, self-assured woman. She was kind to me and counseled me, never knowing that I was a budding lesbian. Despite my overwhelming adolescent admiration, she always kept a proper distance from me.

Interestingly, my sexuality was awakened by a beautiful and affectionate relationship with a young man in high school. We dated for three years as I struggled with my long-standing desire to be a sister. Again, just before entering the convent, I met another man whom I knew I could have married. Much as I wanted to be intimately close with someone, I also wanted to do something different with my life. So, after a year in the work force, at age nineteen, I finally found a small religious community I wanted to join.

With all the idealism of youth I wanted to give my life to God and others; but now I know that I saw opportunity in the convent as well. Not only could I get away from my family, which was as dysfunctional as it was functional, but I could also pursue higher education and have the opportunity to try out a great variety of occupations. More importantly, I had the opportunity to be near a sister I loved. I didn't know it at the time, but here my lesbian identity was blossoming forth. The sister I loved was lesbian, though to this day, she has no awareness of her homosexual orientation.

I didn't really know I was a lesbian until I was about twenty-five, and even then I never called it by name. I just knew I was sexually attracted to certain women. Between ages twenty-five and forty-four, I did a great deal of learning. My experience in structured religious life was good for me. I had no trouble with the Rule because my father ran our family like a strict superior. In community I found that my obedience, sacrifice, and hard work made me rigid and proud. After several years in religious life, my superiors wanted to send me to law school. I declined. I knew I was already too legalistic. I needed the balance of love in my life; that balance was the integration of my sexual identity with the rest of my personality. After nine years of canonical religious life,, I was ready to move into a less structured environment. Eventually, I joined a non-canonical religious community which allows me the freedom I need to live my own life and to serve the church I love. The past twenty-five years of religious life have been good for me.

Just this past year, I told my mother that I am lesbian. She asked me if I was telling her that to punish her. I explained to her that, for me, being lesbian is a positive experience in my life, another step toward growth. She didn't really understand, but she loves me anyway. She asked me what made me this way (somehow I felt she was asking me instead how I contracted this "disease"). I told her that I think many factors have contributed to make me who I am—as in all instances of being human. Perhaps it was induced by hormonal changes brought on by stress when I was in my mother's womb—she was married just before I was born. Perhaps it is environmental—my father molested me for many years as a child. Perhaps it is a political choice on my part—I have always detested the way women have been treated as inferior persons. In the end, what does it matter what combination of events gave me my lesbian identity? What is important is that I accept who I am and do my best work on this earth. Today, my being lesbian and being sister mean that I am on the cutting edge of change—and I am proud of that. Being timid by nature, I need to live a life that demands courage at all times.

About ten years ago I went for therapy in order to resolve the pain and hurt of being molested as a child. In order to live normally, I shut that pain out of my life for too long. Now I can see some of the positive elements of that experience: at an early age, I learned that authority is fallible; I also learned that I am responsible for me. This learning has carried over to my view of authority in the church in the sense that I don't look to the church for what it cannot give me. Despite its proclamations to the contrary, the church is no more godly and no less human than my father who wanted the best for me, despite his personal flaws.

As I love and accept my parents, so I love the church, but I do not expect it to understand me. I do, however, believe that the church will come to understand homosexuality in another hundred years or so. Unlike our parents, the church has the eons it takes for humanity to become enlightened in yet another area. Back in the early days of Christianity, no one would have thought that the church would abandon its tolerant approval of slavery. Back in the Middle Ages, who could have imagined the church abandoning its rigid, literal, biblical interpretation of the universe in the light of scientific observations by men like Galileo? In Darwin's time, no one could imagine the church expanding its literal understanding of the creation story to include evolution. So, too, the church will learn to expand its understanding of homosexuality; but I don't think any of us living today will see that happen. So my philosophy remains as I learned it from my experience with my father—I am responsible for me and I'd better make the most of it.

The name in this story has been changed to protect the privacy of the individual.

FORMER RELIGIOUS

JOE IZZO

Joe is a former Xaverian Brother who was dismissed from the Order because of his activities in the gay community. He now works for the Whitman-Walker Clinic in Washington, D.C.

I grew up in a very Catholic family, in the 1950s in Brooklyn, N.Y. I was the oldest and the only boy with two younger sisters. I went to a Catholic elementary school, and then to an all boys Catholic high school. My parents never talked much about what we should do when we grew up. They gave the impression that to be a priest or religious was good, but I never felt any pressure to do that. When I got into high school I had the Xaverian brothers as teachers.

I had no real awareness until I was about fifteen that I was homosexual. My first emotional-sexual awakening to another guy, which made me very upset, happened when the family went on a retreat during the summer in Massachusetts. There were a lot of families, perhaps sixty, at this retreat center. When we were there all the children were divided into age groups. I just happened to have turned thirteen that summer, so I was in with the teenagers. One day when I was in the locker room I was alone with this other guy who was about sixteen. I remember seeing him get undressed and being absolutely mesmerized. It was the first indication that there was something going on. I didn't even know that what I was feeling was sexual.

By this time I had been masturbating for years, feeling very guilty, and going to confession every time it happened. I had a very good priest friend at the high school, and during a retreat in my junior year I talked out the whole sexuality thing. For the first time I felt that it was not a bar for me to consider religious life.

By this time I had made up my mind that I wanted to be a teacher. After that retreat I decided that I could be a priest or brother. I went on a trip to the Juniorate of the brothers in Leonardtown, Maryland, in February, 1965. After that trip I made my decision to spend my senior year in the Xaverian Juniorate. That was basically a good experience. It was nice to be on my own. At the end of my senior year, one month before graduation, I had my first sexual encounter. It was with my roommate. We just wound up in bed together one night, and the sheer closeness caused us to have an orgasm without doing anything. I was terribly guilt ridden. I was trying to be holy, and according to my upbringing that meant avoiding sex at all costs. After graduation I made up my mind that I was going on to the novitiate. From that time on, with the exception of a few "trysts" with two or three other young brothers prior to age twenty-one, I was celibate until I was twenty-nine.

After I graduated from college I taught high school for six years. I basically sublimated my sexuality very effectively by becoming an absolute workaholic. Beside teaching a full load of classes, I worked with clubs and retreats and all sorts of activities. I was even assistant swim coach for three years. Don't think that wasn't a painful experience. But I was so well repressed that I could look at the guys without any problems being created. As I was finishing my teaching experience I got a phone call in the spring of 1978 from a priest at the University of Maryland about taking a position on the staff of campus ministry.

Prior to that I decided to spend the summer of 1978 doing a basic training in clinical pastoral education at Catholic University. It was during that summer that I realized what I had been doing with my sexual energy and drive. I had sublimated them by becoming an almost out-of-control workaholic. At the end of that summer I made a decision, even though my supervisor gave me a clean bill of health, to go into therapy. I knew that there was still something unresolved with me. I knew it was around the area of sexuality. At that point in my own mind, without sharing this with anyone, I decided I was bisexual.

I had, during my graduate studies at LaSalle University, gotten a Master's degree in religious studies with a concentration in biblical theology. It was during the summers of 1973 to 1977 that I completed that degree. It coincided with the years that all the liberation theology from South America was coming into the United States. It was liberation theology that made me view the teachings of the church in a different light. Part of my own liberation came from the study of Scriptures. By the time the summer of 1978 arrived I knew I had to do something for me. I started therapy, and spent all that year while I was in campus ministry in therapy. By the end of the year, my therapist got me to the point where I could admit I was gay.

During the first weekend of May I got involved in a conference sponsored by the Quixote Center called a "Strategy Conference on Homophobia in the Churches." I was asked to be a small group facilitator for the conference. I didn't even know what the word homophobia meant. I still hadn't fully come to terms with my own sexuality. That weekend did it for me. I realized that what I suffered from was not homosexuality, but the negative conditioning that I got from church and society, and that condition was called homophobia. I had internalized a lot of those myths about what gay people were like. The conference ended on Sunday afternoon. During the conference I had met a guy from Dignity and we hit it off very well. He took me to my first Dignity Mass that night, and I have been going to Dignity on and off ever since.

That summer of 1979, I must have read at least eight different books on homosexuality. The two that affected me most were Don Clark's *Loving Someone Gay* and a book by Glenn Bucher, a Lutheran theologian, called *Straight/White/Male*. To this day I think it is the best book on the issue. My next job was at Catholic University, and by that time I was mentally prepared to get involved in gay issues.

In the spring and summer of 1982, Bob Nugent of New Ways Ministry was getting ready to go to Yale Divinity School for a year's study. He and Jeannine Gramick wanted someone to replace him for at least that year at New Ways Ministry. This was after I left Catholic University and went to work at the Quixote Center. I decided I would like to do that, but to take the job I had to consult with the superiors in my order. A new Provincial had been elected that summer. I became the first test case of his authority. In September of 1982 he handed me an "ultimatum" letter. It basically told me that I had to cease and desist all my activities with any gay organization. He and his counselors had decided that I could not take the job at New Ways Ministry, because it was too controversial and I was too confrontational in my approach. I would be a source of conflict and embarrassment to the brothers.

I rarely took anything like that without a fight, and so we "locked horns" over it. After a few meetings, he hand-delivered a letter to me on the 15th of September and told me I had to get out of all the gay organizations I was in. At that time these included Dignity, New Ways Ministry, the Gay Activist Alliance, the Gay Men's Counseling Collective, and the Association of Gay and Lesbian Older Washingtonians. The previous Provincial and I got along very well. He understood what I was going through. When I realized that I was gay, I wanted to experience my sexuality, and I told him that. He took a very pastoral approach, accepting me where I was at the time. At some point he expected that I would have to make a decision to continue living in celibacy or to leave the order. He didn't set any deadlines for that, and we kept open communication going. In the summer of 1982 his term as Provincial ended.

I assumed that I could share with the new Provincial the way I did with the previous one, which was not the case. Everything that I shared with him that I thought was in confidence was used against me in a public forum. This is the text of the ultimatum letter he gave me on September 15, 1982:

Dear Joe:

This letter is to follow up in writing our conversation of this morning.

By our vow of celibacy we Xaverian Brothers commit ourselves not to freely engage in any sexual genital activity, with ourselves or with others, male or female, homosexual or heterosexual. By this vow we commit ourselves to this abnegation for the sake of the kingdom of God. By your vow as a Xaverian Brother you have undertaken this commitment and publicly profess it to your Brothers, and to the world.

If you do not believe this, if you do not hold this commitment, you should withdraw from this congregation.

If you do accept this commitment, then you must make a reasonable decision whether or not you can live it. Given your past behavior in this regard, and given all the help we can offer you (fraternal support, professional psychotherapy and counselling, and spiritual direction), and that of divine grace, can you live a celibate life within the congregation?

These are the two questions I want you to address during the next two weeks. When we meet September 30, I would like a decision regarding them:

a. either you hold that this is what your vow commits you to, or you ask for a dispensation from your vows and withdraw from the congregation.

b. either you judge that you can actually live this commitment, or you ask for a dispensation from your vows and withdraw from the congregation.

If you decide that you want to live a celibate life in the congregation and that you can do so, I shall do all that I can to help you make that decision a reality.

Besides asking you to decide these questions, I impose upon you two other things:

1. First, that you withdraw from the gay community

2. Secondly, that you cease to counsel anyone—male or female, homosexual or heterosexual, formally or informally, with remuneration or without.

I see these two things as necessary for you at the present time. If you decide to remain in the congregation, therefore, I want you to close off your relationships with the gay community and to bring to an end all your counseling services.

We are both aware that these are serious and difficult decisions. I encourage you to give them very careful and prayerful consideration. I suggest that you seek the advice of a wise and prudent person, one both knowledgeable and experienced in religious life.

I shall hold you in my prayers that you may truly listen to and follow the voice of the Holy Spirit in your regard. Please do the same for me.

Our appointment then is for 9:30 a.m. September 30 here at Kensington.

Sincerely and fraternally yours in Christ,

Provincial

That was a tall order. I thought about a number of people I wanted to consult. I consulted with a canon lawyer who informed me that the letter sounded like the standard cease and desist letter that begins the canonical process of dismissal. I knew I wanted some counseling and consultation. A person whom I respected at the time was Theresa Kane. She read the letter and said, "Joe, it seems to me that this is not the working of the Holy Spirit." She also felt that the Provincial was not working independently, but that there was pressure on him coming from Rome because of my reputation as a "gay activist." It was she who recommended that I talk to him about other brothers who knowingly violate the vow of poverty and have separate bank accounts. Why is he so rigid on this? After that talk and mulling it over myself for the next two weeks, I wrote him a letter in which I explained that I was willing to attempt to live a celibate lifestyle. At that point in life I valued the ministry far more than any sexual needs. I questioned the two conditions he imposed concerning my involvement in the gay community, and my continued counseling. I challenged why he was stripping me of my ministry and support system. I further requested a meeting of the entire Provincial Council to discuss these issues.

He received that letter from me on the 30th of September. He read it, looked at me, and said, "What's the meaning of this?" I said, "It seems perfectly clear to me." He said, "It sounds like you don't accept my conditions." I said, "That is why I am requesting a meeting with the entire Provincial Council to mediate this difference between us." He said that they would be coming in eight days but they wouldn't have the time to set my case as a special agenda item. I had already sent each of the Counselors a copy of my letter. They knew my request and knew the issue. When the Provincial heard this he went through the ceiling. He said, "You have tied my hands." I knew there was a power play going on between us and I was ready to fight for my rights.

The Council decided not to meet with me, but several of the brothers responded to me by mail saying that they were willing to consider this and were happy to mediate. They decided at the meeting on the 8th that they would convene a special session the following weekend. On the 17th of October, 1982, I met with the entire Provincial Council. I was well prepared. I was willing to share anything that they wanted to know. The Provincial asked me to come in prior to that meeting and to sign a release statement allowing him to share anything that was in my personnel file with the Council. I agreed, stupidly. He and the province attorney drew up this agreement. He then went to my personnel file and extracted all my letters to former provincials and highlighted certain sentences, all in a way to justify his case that I was an unfit member of the congregation. He tried to show that I never conformed to the Xaverian Brothers' lifestyle, that I was always asking questions and causing trouble.

I was given a chance to speak first that morning. I presented my whole case within an hour. They asked me questions, I answered their questions. We took a break for lunch, and after lunch the Provincial started. He spent the next five hours, point by point, detail by detail, running me into the ground as the most unfit brother that had ever come through the order. I was actually horrified, and without being melodramatic, I felt I was being crucified by the man. From my point of view, it was a distorted perspective as to who I was as a person, and what my commitment as a vowed brother had been. They asked if I had any response. I told them that I saw no reason to answer point by point things that I had written, or conversations I had that were ten or twelve years old. I told them it was a senseless exercise and I could not understand why the Provincial needed to do this.

At that point one of the brothers spoke up and managed to put me together again. He was held in high esteem. He said that he had lived with me, that he knew me all the years I was a brother, and that he could not agree with what the Provincial had said about me. He knew a different Joe Izzo. I was stunned. By this time I was so emotionally wrung out I didn't know which end was up.

No decision was made. They asked for a cooling-off period. During that time I was to seek counsel, and perhaps move out of the area for a while and get a new ministry. I thought about it for some weeks.

The weekend the Council had met for the first time was the Columbus Day weekend. I had taken Monday off and went with two friends to the mountains. We wound up being in the general area of Emmitsburg. We were near Mother Seton's foundation home. I said to my two friends that I would like to go in and spend a little quiet time there. I went into the chapel where Mother Seton is buried and knelt in front of the altar, and prayed for guidance that I would know what to do. I guess I was there about a half hour in absolute silence. I was not hallucinating but a message came to my mind that was as clear as if you were speaking to me. The message was, "If you are to serve the gospel of Christ in any capacity, be prepared to suffer." As soon as that hit me, I looked at Mother Seton in the sarcophagus and said, "Thanks, but that's not what I wanted to hear." Yet I knew that was the true answer. It made no difference whether I stayed in traditional religious life or left and took up lay life again. To live the gospel could be done anywhere and under any circumstances. That experience gave me strength to go through the following weekend and feel okay about the consequences.

My decision was that I no longer wanted to fight to stay in. It was going to be an uphill battle and I could no longer see any value to it. That's when I decided to leave and began to put all the mechanisms in place. I moved out of the community house the week after Christmas in 1982. I continued to attend Dignity, still thought of myself as a Catholic, but somewhere along the line I realized that everything about the Catholic church made me angry. Its attitudes toward women I think are at best antiquated if not thoroughly Neanderthal. It was not really the gay issue so much. I was still willing to struggle against the authorities on human sexuality issues. But I saw no hope for the change of attitudes about women by the hierarchy in my lifetime. It was basically on that issue that I finally decided I was so far afield from what Roman Catholicism believed that I no longer wanted to be a part of it.

I had found a very welcome home among the Society of Friends, the Quakers, as early as 1982 when I started going to their meetings for worship. I found it a wonderful experience to sit there at least one hour a week in contemplative silence and to share the faith experience of those present. That was very nurturing for me. When I decided to leave the Catholic church a lot of the spiritual energy that had been channeled into anger at the institutional church was now available for prayer and growth. My experience since leaving the Catholic church and becoming a full member of the Quakers is that I feel that I am in a religious community again. The type of work I do, AIDS prevention, alcohol and substance abuse counseling, and the populations I deal with—female and male prostitutes, intravenous drug abusers, people who are incarcerated—is basically trying to communicate the message that we can change our behavior. I believe very strongly that this is a ministry. I'm continuing to serve God by helping people to love as best they can to their fullest potential as human beings.

I am supported in that ministry by the other members of the Religious Society of Friends. I have been recently appointed to the Marriage and Family Relations Committee as the only openly gay person, with them knowing full well that my lover and I intend to be married under the care of the Meeting. I have been asked this coming summer to give one of the major addresses at the Friends General Conference. The theme of this year's gathering is "Nurturing the Tree of Life: Cultivating Justice, Healing and Peace." I've been asked to give the address on AIDS and Healing—how AIDS has been an instrument in healing for people; how this whole crisis has brought about tremendous healing and spiritual growth.

At this point, I see the hand of God working all of this. It is sad that there are still obstructionists in the Catholic church who continue to want the institution to operate according to the ways of a few human beings and block the working of the Holy Spirit. I see a lot of Catholics in terms of the AIDS issue beginning to respond in a very spirit-filled way. I think it even had a ripple effect on the bishops, in that they came out with a pastoral letter that was at least compassionate.

My Catholic roots are strong. During Lent in the mornings I still read the daily readings from the Lectionary and try to spend a little time meditating on them. As a practicing Quaker I don't have to follow liturgical seasons, but they still mean a lot to me. It helps me shake myself out of the lethargy of the day-to-day activities and realize that Lent, for instance, is a good time to take stock of myself. The nice thing about being a Quaker is that they have completely adopted the spirituality of monastic Catholicism. They talk constantly about people like Francis of Assisi, Thomas Merton, Meister Eckart, and Matthew Fox. You can't be with Quakers without someone talking about the latest book they have read, and invariably it is something that comes from the contemplative tradition of Catholicism. I feel that the best part of Catholic spirituality is still a part of me. The only thing that I left were some of the external trappings that really had no meaning for me anyway.

I think the future of the Roman Catholic Church is so much different from the past. I think the church will change, probably not to the degree that I would like to see in my lifetime. Therefore I choose to be outside of it. I think through the living example of Catholic women who are dedicated to Christian life, the powers in the church are going to be changed. It will probably take a long time and I'm too impatient to wait around. I think once the current generation of hierarchy has met their Maker there will be some changes. One of the things that is pushing the church in that direction is the state of the world. The fact that the Pope could come out in his encyclical and talk about the possibility of the church selling some of its massive holdings for the poor makes me think maybe the Spirit is still working in the institutional structure.

There are some compelling reasons for the Catholic Church to change, because the existence of humanity hangs in the balance right now. The American Catholic bishops are beginning to deal with the global injustices, economics, the threat to survival from the nuclear arms race. I think the church needs to lead the way to a humanity that is unified. One issue obviously that they have to deal with is sexuality. Our understanding of sexuality at this time is considerably different than it was at the turn of the century. We know a lot more scientifically, sociologically, and psychologically about sexuality. We know that sexual orientation is not something that people choose.

KATHY SHORTER

Kathy owns and manages a store in Washington, D.C., which features both local and international crafts. She lives in a committed monogamous relationship with her lover. She was formerly a nun.

I grew up in a pillar-of-the-church Catholic family. I am also an adult child of an alcoholic. I graduated from high school in 1968, which was an exciting time. I was encouraged by the nuns in high school to be very involved in many of the current issues such as the peace movement, civil rights, etc. I came of age with a concern for social justice in the forefront. I think that because of the alcoholic situation at home, my mother in her own good way fostered my involvement in these things, partly because she thought it was right and also because it was a way for me to be away from home and my father's drinking.

I went to Notre Dame College in New York City for one year. For some time it had been clear to me that I wanted to join a religious community. After my freshman year of college I entered religious life. As I look back on it now, I can see how it was a desire for an inclusive support group of which I could be a part in order to work among the poor, as well as a way to finally be a member of a functional family. I stayed only a short time, leaving confused and questioning how I was going to live out the life I had planned.

All the while I was with the community I never had any inclination about my sexuality. I dated in high school and college, always knowing that I didn't want to get married. However, if something came up where I could be with my women friends, I would always break a date. But I didn't see any kind of golden thread at the time. I knew I was different, but my sexuality was not an active issue. I returned to New York City to finish college after leaving the community. After graduation, I returned to Washington, D.C. to accept a position on a Congressional staff, and ultimately became staff director of the House subcommittee responsible for most health and environmental issues. I remained there for ten years, and for reasons both personal and political, I decided to leave Capitol Hill. I had purchased a home but hardly knew what it looked like because of the hours I worked. I left having no particular plans, and purposely took about six months off and found myself gardening, cutting firewood, painting the house, etc.

Soon I opened the store and both women and men ventured in who challenged my very limited feminist views, as well as reminding me of my previous interest and involvement in church matters. All of a sudden I was given permission to grow and become involved in several grassroots issues. I found myself listening to stories that sounded so much like my own. Neighborhood folks were telling me that my store was a comfortable place to be. I think it was in part this that moved me to begin a Master's degree in counseling, which I finished last year. I am currently co-leading an AIDS bereavement group.

Most of my life I have been involved in "changing the church," and have found myself around people who work for "social justice." Homosexual issues just never seemed to be included in those agendas. I've since found that it is a very selective brand of justice where one can simply say, "Justice stops here" when certain issues become too close or uncomfortable. I think it was the counseling training that clearly gave me permission to finally discover who I was. You can't get through that kind of program in an honest way without doing good therapy yourself and coming to terms with personal issues.

The church issues that deal with my sexuality and being a woman have been difficult, but it never crossed my mind to turn my back and walk out on my church. On the other hand, I do not belong to a parish or attend Mass. It has become too difficult for me. It was almost without my knowing that I was weaning myself away. For years I searched for an inclusive community, inspiring liturgies, and a group responsive to social issues. I thought I found one in a community at Catholic University, where a lot of good people gather who are also struggling. Something was still wrong. Only men could preside, and this was no longer acceptable to me. Probably not a day goes by that I don't wish I could go to church, but I think I've come to terms with the fact that now I cannot do so. The Dignity community is basically male oriented and still buys into the patriarchal structure. I really don't think most of the men in Dignity feel what we women experience. I realize that there are a lot of gay men and lesbians who still need to attend Mass. The question for myself became, "At what cost?"

I have never before felt the energy I have experienced by being part of "Women-Church." I think that for now, women have to be together, to share both pain and strength, and to celebrate what we have been for each other all along. The thing I am most comfortable with now, that I never, ever thought I would be, is that I've come to own the struggle. I know that this is where I belong, and I've found some peace with it.

It broke my heart when I left the religious community. There are many goals that I share with those who are still working within the structure. I have been with religious women who say, "I can't leave my community, although I would like to." We know that there are many lesbian nuns who are struggling with these issues. They have a difficult time talking about sexuality. We all do. Many can't do what some of us did and cross over that line. It is just too scary, especially if you don't have supportive people around you. It is overwhelmingly sad when you conclude that the built-in support that you thought was guaranteed is not necessarily there.

My father died fifteen years ago, and my mother has Alzheimer's disease, so in some ways I'm without a traditional family. I had surgery recently and the support of friends was so encouraging. My doctor jokes about how he had to report to about six people in the waiting room. Mary Hunt signed in at the hospital as my priest. When I woke up from surgery there were ten people in my room. I finally realized that what we were experiencing was community at its very best. It was there all along! Community was not just a word, or something to hope for—it was happening because we were a group of friends who loved one another and were willing to share struggles, console one another, worship with one another, and have fun.

Four years ago, while studying for my Master's degree, I became involved with a woman who was a nun. I didn't have a label for what it was. She had been involved several times with other nuns and she did not have a label either. She would not use the word lesbian. Neither would I. We talked about being "good friends," and used a lot of other euphemisms. Finally a friend said to me, do you realize what's going on? It was the gentleness of my partner and other good friends that allowed me to face the issue and name it.

Within the year she decided to leave her community. At this point she is glad she made the decision. There are so many women who are unaware of this dimension of themselves and do not have supportive people around them, as we did. There is a joke around that my partner and I run a shelter of sorts at our house, because we have so many -

people who feel at home with us and comfortable with the way we live. The really healing thing is to be able to talk about it. We try to offer that opportunity. It makes a crucial difference to have healthy lesbians who live "normal" lives surrounding us.

I do not think we made a conscious choice to "come out." It just happened and I think it was because we're in a safe place that our friends provided for us. My partner and I have been together three years and we plan to grow old together. My aunt and uncle are my only family now, but my partner is always included in all family functions and is treated as the one who matters most in my life. There are no questions asked. As far as other family members are concerned, I have always been considered "different" because of my political involvement. Both sides of the family are old southern Maryland farming families. My liberal views were never accepted there. I was the kid who wanted to stay in the city, and that was unheard of. My mother always said, "Who cares what they think, do what you need to do." I hear how others talk about coming out to parents; especially how lesbians talk about their relationships with their mothers. I don't think my mother would be extremely comfortable with knowing I'm gay, but she would accept me. Unfortunately it's not an issue because of the Alzheimer's disease. She no longer knows who I am.

There are a lot of men from the religious houses who come to the store and talk very openly and freely about their sexuality. AIDS has certainly had a hand in changing attitudes. I don't know if that would have happened several years ago. However, I'm not hopeful about what will happen in the church. I think what we need to do is create alternatives. There is so much good, positive energy being spent on living on hope, rather than living as hopeful, creative people. I will stand out on the street and hold a protest sign saying "change the church," anytime. I think that is an important political act, and I will do that, but in my own faith life I'm not very hopeful it will help. I'm much more comfortable with the idea of insisting that we *are* church, that we won't be pushed out.

I thank the nuns in my life, because they made it possible for me to love women. Despite their intentions, they started me off in that direction. I'm sure some of them would hate to hear that. They were the ones who gave me the "credit card" to love myself. Certainly they were the first strong women, beside my mother, in my life. They were the ones who were getting things done. They were the avant garde in making changes in the church and social structures, and I liked what I saw.

When I first opened the store, many people would come in and say, "What a ministry." I would turn red and deny it, but I guess my view of ministry has expanded since then. It does matter what we sell or buy. I have helped to educate customers and I have surely been educated by them. For instance, seven years ago I wasn't concerned about sexist language. I certainly have changed. My customers have held me accountable and this kind of honesty and give and take has really paid off. My accountant often suggests that I have a good business operation and would make more money if I changed the location. But no one would bring me chicken soup when I am sick as they do in this neighborhood. It has become a place where people can check in and ask when the next SAS (Sisters Against Sexism) liturgy will be held. A lot of folks from out of town stop by to chat and to find out what's happening. I never cease to be amazed at what we can accomplish because we know one another. We can get the troops out in an hour. For some, I am seen as someone who didn't make it in religious life, and has fallen away from the church. That is not true. I am a lesbian who is proudly taking part in healing my church, being strengthened by my partner and other good women and men. In the truest Christian tradition, we are empowering one another to live the way we believe to be right. The hopeful part is that we are already doing this—we are on our way!

TOM CUNNINGHAM

Tom was a priest in the Dominican Order for four years. He is a vice-president at a bank in New York City. He is former treasurer for Dignity/USA.

I was born in 1942, in Boston, Massachusetts. I'm the only child by my father's second wife. He had three daughters by his first wife, who died. He was more of a grandfather to me than a father. There was quite a gap between our ages. He was around fifty-six when I was born. It was a lonely childhood being an only child and having old parents. I didn't have that active participation of my parents in a lot of the things I did. In fact I never even knew my father that well until my mother died, which was the summer of my seventh grade. He was the kind of person who was out in the morning at five-thirty and home at four o'clock at night, when he put a newspaper in front of him, and went to bed at eight-thirty in order to get up again at four-thirty the next morning. I think one thing that is part of me now that was very much part of him is being in that workaholic mode. Earn more money, build a better life, etc.

From the first grade I went to a Catholic school taught by the Notre Dame Sisters in Boston. I was very much into the good boy scene, being an altar boy from the first moment I could be. I was in the choir. In many ways I was looked upon as being Sister's pet. I was considered a goody-two-shoes compared to a lot of the other kids. I tended not to experiment a lot with things. If someone told me something was wrong, I pretty much accepted it, and there I stayed. That entered into my own sense of justice and I didn't violate that.

I think perhaps the most significant issue that blasted me out of my own complacency was my mother's death. That event was an absolute tragedy. When I think of what was foisted on me as a boy of thirteen, I wouldn't wish it on my worst enemy. There was so little communication between my father and mother that she never told him how serious the operation was that she was going to undergo. From my checking back in the medical records, it looks like a botched-up surgery. She died from internal hemorraghing the night after the operation. The feeling of abandonment was enormous. When I came home the night my mother died, all the family was gathered in the back parlor. My father came over to me, simply said, "Your mother died," turned and walked back to the undertaker who was setting up the funeral arrangements. I was left standing alone with fifteen sets of eyes on me, leaving me to decide what to do next, and I cried.

Then I went to high school and the nuns were a predominant force in my life. I had the Dominican Sisters and again became a workaholic in school. I never considered myself a very good student but I was very good to have around. I would erase the board and paint the walls. In fact, I am still friends with one of the Sisters I had in that school. She was someone I could share my feelings with. She was very responsive to that. She was both my teacher and my confidante. She probably knew more about me than anybody else. With her help I started to develop a relationship with my father, but it was more like grandfather to grandson. It stayed that way until his death when I was thirty-one and he eighty-six.

Again the church stood out to me as a place to go for refuge. I went from being an altar boy to being supervisor of altar boys, to being in the choir, to being involved with the nuns and with CYO. We had a retreat in my junior year of high school at the Dominican House in Dover, Massachusetts. It was my first time to meet a religious community of men who to me lived the life that I saw the sisters live, as opposed to the life the diocesan priests lived. Whatever impression was made on that weekend trip lasted.

Looking back on elements of my life other than the religious, I think I was a late bloomer sexually. I had a lot of difficulty trying to understand that. I went to one of the parish priests and was told not to bother to understand it, to get it out of my mind. Being the obedient boy, I put it out of my mind. In hindsight, I know that I was not attracted to women in any way. I tended to be the one who would work at the refreshment counter or sell tickets at the high school dances. That was a comfortable way of getting out of dancing with a girl. I was too busy doing all those other things. At the prom I chose a girl nobody else would choose, and just put up with it.

At the same time I was feeling a physical attraction to boys, but in no way knowing how to interpret that or even how to talk about it or get counseling. The most I could feel was wanting to catch a certain bus that would get me to a certain bus stop at a time that this other guy in my class would get to that bus stop so I could walk the three blocks to school with him and maybe become his friend. That is the most I could interpret as an attraction. We never had physical education in school. It was a small parish high school.

When I got into the senior year of high school, I thought about going into the Dominicans. I was working part-time at the drug store and thought also that I'd like to be a pharmacist. I entered the Massachusetts College of Pharmacy after high school. Halfway through the year I realized that was not my scene at all. I realized that I really wanted to go into the priesthood, and it would be a great tribute to my mother. So in I went; I was ordained in 1970 and was in the active ministry for the next four years.

I was very naive. All the statements in the seminary about not having particular friendships I interpreted as not getting too close to somebody emotionally, because if he leaves it will affect me. I was naive about what was going on in the seminary. There were gay relationships developing there. All of a sudden two people would leave at the same time; overnight they were gone. It dawned on me that, well, that was their particular friendship and that was more important than studies. I went through all the years of training and got very involved in the religious education scene at the Dominican House of Studies in Washington, D.C.

I received my theology degree from the Dominicans. Then I was the first Catholic student to enroll at Wesley Theological, a Methodist seminary, and received my Master's degree in religious education. I remember the Dominican director of studies said to me, "You will never be one of our scholars, but you are good to have around." That's a statement that has stuck with me these years. I am good to have around. I washed the cars, I kept things well managed.

I was always involved with youth in carrying out my religious education and pastoral duties. There was a certain emotional involvement with a few of the guys I dealt with, but I guess I always translated it as, they are looking to me as counselor and confidant. I guess I saw it as being similar to what the nun back in high school did for me. What wasn't given to me, I went out of my way to give to these teenagers. I recall how I enjoyed seeing these young men's bodies when we would go swimming. At the time I never gave much thought to that in terms of trying to analyze it, or realize it as a sexual attraction.

In 1974, I made a decision to take a year's leave of absence which led to a permanent leaving of the active ministry. It started like this: I was suddenly transferred from the suburban New York parish in which I was working for two years to be a chaplain at a boys' high school in Charleston, South Carolina. The transfer resulted from a conflict between me and an older priest in the house. The Provincial's decision, which was a lack of decision, was to transfer both of us to opposite ends of the country and that would solve the problem. That was probably the last instance as far as I can remember that I observed the role of the good Catholic obedient boy. I was very involved in what I was doing and everything was about to suddenly end. There was no way to redress the issue, or mend the rift with the other priest in some way. The Provincial's point about the transfer was that this is how it has to be in obedience.

I went down to Charleston and visited the high school. In many ways the assignment was attractive, yet my guts were being ripped out in the whole affair. I'm not being transferred there as a normal transfer, but because of an unresolved issue back in New York. Getting back to New York, I went for an evening walk, and in the course of that walk I said, hell no, that's the end of the good Catholic boy who always does what he is told. I came back and called the Provincial on the phone, woke him up, and said I had to meet with him the next day. He was too busy the next day, so that even rubbed it in more. So it was the following day. I went in and said, "I'm sorry, I'm not in a position to pull up stakes and start a new life in Charleston as if nothing happened in New York." His response was, "You have to go." I said, "No, I don't have to go. I need a break. I'm telling you that. I have psychological reasons for this, and I need to be in charge." I said, "You have ripped the guts out of my soul and I need time to recoup." He refused to discuss it any further. He called me back in the next day. He was adamant and angry. I said, "I'm not going to go, and I want a year's leave of absence."

I don't know where I got the guts to do it, but I told him he was handling the whole thing very badly and he ought to be ashamed of himself. I said, "If you don't want to talk with me about this then get whomever you want to talk with me." After that, everything was with his secretary, who was very much of an administrative-type person. He took my health insurance card and cut it in half, asked for the rectory key, and gave me two hundred dollars in ten dollar bills, saying "Goodbye."

I went out and bought my forty-dollar suit. Then I got to that point where I wondered if I were doing the right thing. The parish was in an uproar. They sent a delegation to Cardinal Cooke to see if something could be done. He wouldn't deal with an internal Dominican Order matter. It was a closed issue, but there was a lot of hurt going on in the parish. Fortunately for me, one of the men in the parish, the head of my former high school religious education program, who was a former priest, offered to get me set up for interviews with companies.

One of the four interviews was with the bank where I still work, fourteen years later. It was perfect timing, walking into that particular job. They were interested in employing me because of my educational training. They felt it was a skill translatable to personnel-related work. I worked up the ladder from being a $200.00 a week personnel department clerk to a vice-president in banking operations.

That was a break from the church. The baby went out with the bathwater. I left everything behind me. I took off the Dominican habit, put on the forty-dollar suit, and that was it. I literally walked out the door with $200.00 to my name. Since then, the church scene for me has been one of great distance. At first I would have nothing to do with it, then that disposition softened over time.

I thought, here I am, thirty-one years of age. I guess I'm going to have to get married and do it soon. I made efforts to meet women at bars and realized it was all out of my ballpark. I was doing it more out of a feeling that I have to do it than wanting to do it. I think of the women that I would plan to meet at the information booth at Grand Central terminal, take out to a perfectly lousy dinner, and be glad that the evening was over. She would get on her train to go home and I would get on my train to go home. Once I started to get serious, and I guess that was my panic stage. Eliane invited me to her family for Christmas. That's when I realized she was bringing me into the family. They loved me; she loved me. I really started to get uptight.

That's when I started exploring what was going on in me. Why don't I like this? I started reflecting all the way back to high school; why was I behind the refreshment counter instead of out on the dance floor? Up to this point in the seminary and priesthood, I was able to dismiss the issue of women. I now found myself addressing that seriously. One night at Grand Central, I bought the *Advocate*, a gay magazine. As I read through it I found myself excited and at ease. This magazine is saying something to me like nothing else has. I started to go to some gay bars in New York City. Eliane, the woman I was dating, was getting more serious and I was getting more close-mouthed. She was looking for me to get more serious and I was looking to step back. We had a heart-to-heart talk, which was the last time I saw Eliane.

I really got into the gay scene back in the mid-'70s. It was certainly a different type of scene from the straight bars. I didn't even want to walk in the doors of the straight bars; the whole thing was totally alien to me. I did it but hated it all. I found the gay bar scene something I liked, but found it difficult in terms of trying to establish any kind of rapport with the scene. In the beginning I was so uptight that I would find a place in the corner to stand and look, afraid to talk to anyone.

In reading more periodicals and magazines I learned about Dignity. I made a phone call to the number listed. At that time in New York City chapter meetings were in people's homes; Mass was celebrated by a gay priest. It was a small group and was very attractive to me. It was a chance for me to put the pieces back together in terms of my own religious background and the issue of being gay. One of the people I met from the beginning is still one of my best friends today. I met a heck of a lot of nice people there. From that I got involved in the Gay Men's Health Crisis, a voluntary clinic in New York City for gay men. I met many new friends there, and realized that the volunteer mode is a more productive way of meeting people than the bars.

My volunteering led to a relationship of about seven months with one guy. We still remain friends. Through the local Dignity chapter I volunteered for the National Convention Committee when the convention was here in New York. Because I work for a bank, I went to a regional meeting and was asked to run for national treasurer of Dignity, which I did in 1985. I was reelected in 1987. This was another opportunity to meet a lot of fine, sincere people who have become damn good friends. I realized, however, that a lot of my friends had different zip codes, and geographical distance doesn't help day-to-day socializing. The impact of AIDS in the city, and the fast life, pulled a lot of my local friends away. One of my closest friends was diagnosed in 1985 as having AIDS; he's still alive but suffering and withering away.

One thing I realized last year is, I'm forty-four years of age, I haven't really been in a serious relationship of any duration. I have a damn good job, but I find I'm getting fed up with the city. I bought a condominium on the shore of the Hudson River seventy-five miles north of the city. There is a very active local gay and lesbian social group and I joined it. Three months later with the help of new friends I started a joint Dignity/Integrity chapter, known as the Mid-Hudson Chapter for Catholics, Episcopalians, and Friends.

I find myself now celebrating the fact that I've come a long way. I've reached a stage where I'm not going to be so closeted about my gayness. I'm not necessarily looking to be an activist or out in the open all that much, because my private life is my private life. Now I realize that my years in the active ministry were a significant portion of my life. I don't regret it. I guess what I'm finding is that I'm being called to a ministry within the gay and lesbian community. I'm finding that I'm respected because of my background and I'm proud of it. I went through hell because of what happened in 1974. The experience led me to being much more comfortable with myself.

I am very angry at the church as an institution. I find individual priests very understanding. I'm impressed with the advertisements on the local TV stations about "Come back to the church for Easter." They did the same thing for Christmas, with a scene of mother, dad, and kids. I've felt they should have a disclaimer statement at the bottom saying this invitation is not extended to self-affirming gays and lesbians. I am not one of those invited back to the church. If I were dying of AIDS, or if I felt badly about my orientation, I would be welcomed. The Cardinal here in New York has made that evident. If I say my gayness is a gift from God, he would look upon me as perverted.

In looking back at my own life, there is no way I can say my being gay is not a gift from God. I know that it is not something of my own making. I know what I've gone through to explore it, and the hurt involved. I remember a sister in high school once making the comment about me being a very sensitive person, that I would be subject to a lot of hurts. I believe this is an integral part of my gayness and emotional disposition.

When I look back on my priesthood I thank God for what happened back in 1974. I don't know if I would have explored my own gayness if I were in the priesthood. Or if I did explore it, would I have done so in a way that would have been real sleazy? I've seen that with classmates I've known in the seminary. Having to drive a long distance to make sure they are far out of the parish, and then looking for a bar or picking up some kid on the road. I get incensed by people identifying the sleaze as the predominant way gays and lesbians are. That's not my scene. I feel affronted by having such a stereotype imposed on me. My own personal morality is as high as it ever was. Again I find myself angry with the institutional church for not supporting me and not helping me define the ethical issues. No longer will I take a simple yes or no.

In the Dignity organization we have a task force devoted specifically to sexual ethics. Trying to define what you do with this body of moral theology in terms of being gay or lesbian. I need as much direction as the next person does, but I need it in a way that allows me to be true to my own gayness. My gayness is a given and I have to know how to deal with it. In many ways when I came out in my mid-thirties I was acting like a teenager. I'm glad I went through that relatively unscathed. I was neither physically nor emotionally harmed.

Back to the church, there was something political behind the Ratzinger letter. The way it was presented so insensitively. Why was it issued in English? The easy answer is that it comes from a surfacing of the strong homophobic attitude. Why, on Halloween of 1986, did that happen to be an issue? There was no lead-up to it, like a conference or a challenge. This is the reversal of a hands-off attitude by church leaders. The previous realization was that there are a lot of homosexuals; they didn't like it but they realized we are people to be dealt with. The Ratzinger letter switched all that. It said, this is an orientation that in no way has any good to it. It is a disorder.

Through statements like this, as well as others, the church is losing its credibility. If God appeared and made the statement, that's one thing. But it is a Cardinal in Rome making a statement based on a crass observation of natural law. There is absolutely no validity to that. Like many others, I now take the position, I don't care what he or any church leader says. That's their problem. It presents a problem for me to the extent that I want to read the statements from Rome with a certain validity. That's the good Catholic boy in me that reacts that way. But as a mature Catholic man who realizes his gay orientation, I can't give any validity to these statements about disordered orientation and my being intrinsically evil.

What bothers me is that there are those who believe that God made this statement. I see the institutional church again taking the role of being the leader of the poor unwashed immigrant. That was fine for my father and his parents. I find myself saying, wait a minute, I need to give this some thought. I'm not at the point where I think all morality is up for grabs. But I have to listen to my own heart, and the Ratzinger letter in no way reflects my experience. I'm angered by the power of the church in confirming a homophobic stance and the resultant violence that follows from it.

The New York Roman Catholic Cardinal is so vocal about so many things. He is a politician without credentials. Recently I met the New York Episcopal bishop. The experience was delightful; he is so down-to-earth and so spiritual. That's what I look to if I'm looking for a church leader. It amuses me that the Episcopal bishop is not in the papers. He is doing his work as a bishop, not a politician. I don't question the Cardinal's spirituality, but I don't experience him as a spiritual leader. I'd like to meet him for ten minutes and just have him listen to my observations, but that's not possible. It's abominable that he is on the President's Commission on AIDS.

I am presently a facilitator of a discussion group composed of persons with AIDS. It is a very sobering experience and one from which I come away after each meeting with a renewed realization of my mission in life. I am still a priest, not formally recognized nor garbed, but a person with a mission and a gift. I used to look on my mission when in the active ministry as one of ministering to others; now I look on my mission as ministering in the midst of and with others. You see, my gift of gayness is not something to be hidden under the bushel basket, but a gift to shine. I have a challenge also. My gayness is a gift from God; I have to return that gift to God in better shape than when it was received. That's my life mission; that's my purpose.

DOROTHY FISHER

Dorothy lives in Washington, D.C. She was a nun for several years.
She is now the manager of her own business.

I am the oldest of five children. I spent seven years in a Catholic school, then finished in public high schools. Early in life, I did not have a name for what my feelings were, but I can remember in grade school having crushes on all my women teachers. When I got to high school it continued, but all my other friends were having crushes on the male teachers. I knew enough not to say anything, but it didn't stop. I dated men when I was in school and after I got out. I realized that I was more attracted to women than men, and I knew I wasn't the only person in the world but I didn't know how to make contact with other gay people. When I was about nineteen somebody took me downtown to one of the bars. The women I saw there were not women I identified with or wanted to be identified with. I enjoy being a woman and I enjoy being feminine; that's not what I saw there.

At age twenty-five I went into the convent and stayed for three years, knowing about my sexuality. But it was no problem, because the vow of chastity means not to act sexually. It didn't matter whether I was heterosexual or homosexual. I left, not because of poverty and chastity, but because obedience just did me in.

The summer I left the convent I had my first relationship with a woman. She had also just recently left a religious congregation. I think I wasn't ready for the kind of relationship she wanted. She was ready to settle down and get married; she had had other relationships and knew what this was all about. I was totally intimidated.

Down the hall of the apartment building where I lived was a very nice man. I had not been there long when he knocked on my door one evening and asked if I was okay, because he noticed my car hadn't been moved for several days. From that time on we were on a passing

relationship. One night, when I was returning from the movies, he was
sitting out on the stairway nursing a gin and tonic and crying. I asked
what was wrong and he told me he was gay and had been with someone
for eighteen years, and that his partner had just died. We started talking
and he said he had never told anybody. I looked at him and said, I
am too. I think it was really a gift of grace. For him to choose me
to tell when I was struggling with so many of these things just fit
perfectly.

He was the person who told me about Dignity. He offered to take
me to one of their gatherings. One Sunday we went together and as
we walked across the Georgetown campus I ran into one of the kids
I taught in high school. She saw me and said, "Sister, Miss Fisher, what
are you doing here?" I told her we were just walking around the campus,
and we turned around and left. I didn't have the nerve after that to
just walk into this gay Mass. I wasn't willing to risk it. We went back
another Sunday.

The Washington Dignity community is just fabulous. I was elected
as a delegate to the convention in Miami last summer, and that gave
me the opportunity to talk to a lot of people. Women are under-
represented as a whole, but the guys here are so incredibly supportive.
Any of the things the women want to do, they are right out there with
us. They are concerned about inclusive language. We have a lot of
feminist gay men in our community. I got quite involved in Dignity,
and over the next four years I struggled over whether or not I had made
the right decision to leave the convent. I was very secretive about my
sexuality, and about going to Dignity for Mass. I had a lot of questions
about my decision to leave the convent, so after three years I went
back. I stayed one year and left with a clean conscience. This is a
wonderful life and great for some people, but it is not where I need
to be.

I left in 1986, and then got involved in a relationship. I didn't leave
because of that, nor was I involved when I was in the convent. We
are still together, although now we are separated and trying to put
things back together. By working with the people in Dignity my self
esteem has improved. I don't feel a need to be so secret about my
sexuality, nor am I ashamed. I went through a period of life thinking
that if I'm not like the rest of the world there must be something wrong
with me. I'm not self-conscious about those things any more. I want
this relationship with Loren to work out; I'm just crazy about her. I
am concerned that we in the gay community don't seem to support
relationships. Often when there are signs of trouble, people kind of

hover, waiting to see what will happen, then move in. Maybe it's just because we don't take our relationships seriously that they don't last.

I'm out to my dad. My parents are divorced. They separated when I was fourteen and tried off and on to get back together. They were divorced when I was thirty. My father is in the middle of three boys, and both of his brothers are gay. The youngest brother has been out since he was eighteen. Everyone suspected that the older brother was also gay, but he was very closeted. One summer when he was here my father sat him down and asked if he was gay. He said yes and started to cry. My dad went over and hugged him and said, "I just needed to know that." They have been so much closer since then. It's a terrible secret. I know that for me it's not the biggest part of who I am, but I feel that when I'm not open about that, there are a lot of other things I can't be open about. It's nice to tell people who you are and trust that they will be okay with that.

When I told my father, I called him and said, "I need to talk to you. Can you come over?" He came over and we drank coffee and ate cookies and listened to music. It got to be about eleven o'clock and he said, "It's Monday night and getting late, you said you needed to talk." I said, "Well it's hard." He looked at me in complete seriousness and said, "Do you want to sit on my lap?" I said no and proceeded to tell him my secret. He had wondered about me before. When his wife, his second wife, got back from a trip she called me. She invited me to join my dad and her for dinner and wondered if Loren could also join us. Then she said she had been told my news, and that she was just fine with that. They have been so incredibly supportive. They like Loren and include her in all the family gatherings. They even go to Dignity Mass with me at times.

I'm not out to my mom. For her things are right or wrong, black or white. I remember when I was younger how she would talk about my gay uncle in not very nice terms. I've been kind of afraid to tell her, not knowing how she would react. In some ways I'd like to wait to tell her when things are going better with Loren and me. Loren is an officer in the military and I certainly wouldn't want my mother to make any well-placed phone calls. Loren only has a few more months before she retires. Maybe then I will tell mom. I think that if my mom doesn't know, she suspects. I'm out to three of my four younger brothers and sisters.

There is a woman who has been my "other" mother since I was about eighteen, a person I worked with. I told her right after Loren and I got together. She didn't take it badly, but I think that she was uncomfortable with it. I think what happened is that over time she came to see that I really loved Loren. She finally got the idea that it was the quality of the relationship that made so much more difference than the sex partner. In the meanwhile we would talk about things, and that's been a good experience.

I have another friend who was just floored that it took me four years to tell her I was gay. She said, "I love you. Why do you think that would make a difference?" She is my age, and has been very happily married for about eleven years. She is so tolerant. I think that as she has gotten to know me she understands some of the prejudices gay people are up against. She gets angry on my behalf in a way that I can't. Once there was a garden party to which about eighty lesbians were invited. Since Loren was out of town, I invited this friend of mine to go with me. I asked if she would like to be dyke for a day. She went and was so comfortable. It made me so happy.

In my first job I was a top administrative person. I was so paranoid that someone would find out about me. I think I was afraid that I would lose professional credibility if people knew I was a lesbian. I didn't want people to think less of me. That was before I really came out to myself with total acceptance. Then I went into business for myself and I didn't have to rationalize or justify who I was. Now I work at a large non-profit organization in Washington. First of all there are laws in the District protecting homosexual people from discrimination in employment. My boss is gay, one of my colleagues is gay, the assistant to the president is gay, and several other people are gay. It's a good place to be. I feel safe there. I'm not flaunting my sexuality, but I don't feel the need to hide.

I think that there are subtle ways in which the gay community discriminates against its own. I was going to be on the planning committee of Women's Alternative, a group that plans alternative events to the bars. I was going to a meeting held at the Washington Ethical Society for the planning committee. That same night there was a church meeting of the Ethical Society. I had gone from work, so I still had on my suit and my grown-up-lady high heels and my briefcase. I walked into the room and they took one look at me and said, "Your meeting is down the hall." I looked at these women in blue jeans and flannel shirts and said, "No, it's not. This is my meeting. I'm here to plan the dance." I know I tend to steer clear and sometimes make judgments before I get to know people, just as they made a split-second judgment about who I was and where I was to be. This seems to happen more with women than men. Women also tend to be more closeted in their jobs. Maybe it's because it's easier for gay men to climb the corporate ladder than women. I know a lesbian woman who is very high in her company, but is terrified that she would be found out.

The position of the church, as described in the Ratzinger letter, makes me very sad. This is not a club I belong to, this is what I believe. They can't take that away from me. I will still go to Mass, I will still seek out the sacraments. I like the opportunity to go to a Mass that is specifically for gays and lesbians. The homilies are usually prepared with us in mind, making application to our lives. We have problems and face discrimination in ways that other people don't experience. It's nice to have our religion help us meet some of those needs. I know a lot of people who have left the church because of the way they were treated. But the energy they use in being negative could be better put to use to work for change. We will not do anything to effect change from the outside. We might not do anything to effect change from within either, but I'm not leaving. I spent a period of time looking around at other churches. I tried on other religions, but I ended up back in the Catholic Church. That's home.

I think that in Dignity our job should be to put ourselves out of business. We should do all we can to support ourselves and one another, emotionally and spiritually, but also work for change in the church. Not only the official church, but the local parishes. I dream that we could go to parishes and say, here we are. We look just like you, we believe the same things, we want a lot of the same things out of life. We are not really different. We could say who we are and be accepted. The church and the local congregations aren't there yet. I hope someday that will happen. Since we don't have children, we have a lot more disposable income that we could contribute. We have more time we could offer in volunteer work. There are many needs in parishes that we could plug into and be supportive of. I'm not willing to do that until I can be "out" about who I am. Now a lot of us are denied the access to the kind of community that being in a parish would allow. Parishes are being denied the talent and time we have to offer.

The name in this story has been changed to protect the privacy of the individual.

JOSEPHINE BRUNI

Josephine lives in a committed monogamous relationship with her lover in New York. She works for a parochial school in the area.

I'm the middle child of three from a very Catholic Italian family. It's a very warm family that is extremely supportive of all members. I went to Catholic school from kindergarten to fourth grade in a very conservative parish in east New York. When I was fifteen we moved to Queens and because the schools were overcrowded I could not get into a Catholic school. I was in public schools the rest of the time. At a very young age I was interested in religion. I was fascinated by the nuns. When I was in ninth grade I decided to enter the convent, which I did when I was twenty-one. I stayed in the community for four years. I have now been out of that for four years.

As I look back now I see things that pointed to my being a lesbian. I don't think that when I was in the community I ever knew who I was. I came out as a lesbian two years ago. I came out full force. Before that I was having the feelings but never knew the word. I did not know how to identify it. All through my life growing up I always knew I was different. I was not attracted to boys like my friends were. I think that's what led me to enter the convent. I interpreted not being attracted to men as being attracted to celibacy. That really wasn't the case at all.

It was while I was in the convent that I met another nun who knew she was a lesbian, and I got involved in a relationship with her. That was instrumental in my leaving the convent. That was the great realization that I'm not meant to be celibate. We stayed involved for two years while she was still in the convent and she felt that she could not leave, so we decided to put an end to the relationship. We remained friends. I spent the next year and a half just wandering around, not yet being able to put the title lesbian on it. I didn't really know what the whole gay community was. I thought that I had just had this unique experience.

A year and a half later I met Sylvia, who is my present lover. I knew she was a lesbian. I was working at a shelter for the homeless at the time and she was coming to the shelter as a member of Dignity. A lot of the Dignity members were volunteering at the shelter. That was my first introduction to the gay community. I was meeting homosexuals for the first time and was getting very comfortable with them. At the same time a gay fellow who had AIDS was sent to live at the shelter with us. I was part of the live-in staff. He was just released from the hospital and had no place to go. He came to the door and said, "Hi, I'm Craig. I'm gay and I have AIDS." That was my introduction to the whole scene at one time. It was Craig and his honesty, and Sylvia being very open about who she was, that got me thinking about who I was.

I talked a lot with Craig. I found myself being more and more attracted to Sylvia. I guess it took me a year to make that first step to approach her about a relationship. At that same time there was a Dignity convention in New York. Sylvia invited me to go to the convention. We spent a week in New York, which I call my coming-out party. I was with three hundred gay men partying for over a week. It was a lot of fun. I've been living as a lesbian ever since and am very, very happy.

As far as the church is concerned, it has been a constant struggle, especially coming from the religious background that I had. I always felt very close to God. Because of what is going on in the church right now, I have had to draw a line between the church and God. I've had to reevaluate who is God, what is the church, and separate God from the church. I still go to Mass on Sunday. I'm active in Dignity. We try to plan a lot of alternative liturgies. I'd say I'm still as close to God as I ever was, but I'm not as close to the church. I'm fighting not to leave the church, because it has been a big part of my life.

I've been living on Long Island for about two years, and attending the local parishes has been just awful. We went shopping for a parish. We found one about twenty minutes away that is a good compromise. They seem to be welcoming to all types of people. There are very poor, very rich, and everything in between. They don't seem to be uptight. Belonging to a parish and attending regularly is important to me and to Sylvia. We also participate in Dignity. I am also a member of the Conference of Catholic Lesbians.

I have recently come out to my family. It's an ongoing struggle. I felt as though I could not go on hiding who I was any longer. I know that they worry, being the concerned Italians that they are. My father would not stop worrying until I was married and settled down. So I felt that I had to tell them that I was settled. I felt so alienated that telling them could only make things better, they could not be any worse. I was hiding a whole section of my life. They are trying very hard to understand. My mother is doing better than my father. He has made it clear that he doesn't like the situation. He wishes it could be different, but he will always be there for me. I guess that is all I can really ask for. I'm twenty-nine, I have a sister who is twenty-two, and a brother who is thirty-three. My parents asked that I not tell them. I suspect that my brother knows. I will give them time before I tell them. There is no real need to tell them now.

I am vice-president of the local Dignity chapter. I served one year as vice-president then became president. Presently we have seventy-eight members in Nassau. Twenty-three are women and the rest are men. Our chapter works hard to make women welcome. The men are very welcoming. Recently we had a Love-a-Lesbian night, where each of the men was asked to bring a lesbian. We had a woman speaker who was very inclusive in her talk. I also support the Cathedral Project. I plan to go every month. It's kind of scary because of my job. The first time I went with sunglasses and straw hat.

There is some competition between the Conference of Catholic Lesbians and Dignity, because there is a local CCL group that meets in the area. Dignity can't offer what CCL offers. A lot of the women who go to CCL don't go to Dignity because they don't want to be part of that male patriarchal church. I can't blame them because I feel the same way sometimes. I feel that I need to be empowered by the women. Even with Dignity there are times when the men give the impression that they don't understand women's spirituality. They don't understand why women are offended by not using inclusive language. They don't see it because they don't feel it. So I can understand why a lot of women don't want to come to Dignity. I probably stay because the men in our group are so wonderful. They really do make me feel welcome. Dignity is made up of people who want to stay active in the church, whereas CCL is not. It consists of women with a Catholic background that are looking for more women-centered liturgies. They are two different styles.

I try to dismiss the Ratzinger letter as coming from people who really don't understand. I look at myself and all the people I know, and hear the term "intrinsically evil" and I think, are they nuts? I have never met a group of more loving, giving people than the members of my communities. When the letter first came out I was angry. I have now put it aside and try to consider the source. They will learn. The church has always been so far behind what is really going on. I keep reminding myself of all the people in the past who were held to be wrong and finally vindicated. The reason I stay is that there is hope that things will change. I have two different experiences, the priests and nuns I deal with in everyday life, and the Ratzinger letter. The people I deal with that affect my everyday living also see the Ratzinger letter and other things going on in the church as something that is not in their reality. These people know who I am and they accept me. They don't see me as "disordered."

The people I worked with at the shelter eventually knew I was a lesbian. There are two nuns and one brother there. I shared with them who I was and they were totally accepting. Those are the kind of people in my everyday life who are important to me as being the church. Church is not Rome but the people I meet every day.

One of the hardest things I had to face when I came out was what to do with my straight friends. They were all waiting for me to bring a man home. When I was not doing that but was bringing this woman with me it made a difference. Some are still waiting for me to marry a man. I'm now beginning to say I'm not going to get married. I'm still in touch with my straight friends. One of them had a difficult time accepting, but she eventually came around. I've been making my choice one by one in telling them. I don't want to live with a mask on anymore. I don't like living a double life.

Where I work I have to be more careful. I avoid certain things, and there are major parts of my life that I don't share. So I find myself pulling back a lot. I don't want to get myself caught in a lie. What I ended up doing was saying that I share a household with another woman friend. If I slip and say "we" I don't get caught, because they know I live with someone. I find it difficult. Everybody talks about their husbands and boyfriends. I feel like the odd one out because I'm not sharing. For Valentine's Day Sylvia sent me roses. It was like "Twenty Questions"—where did the roses come from? Who are they from? I had to be very vague. I loved the roses, but I wanted to kill her for sending them.

One of the things that disappointed me about the church was when we were forced to leave the church where Dignity met. It was a painful experience. We are now relocated in an Episcopal church. That is painful.

That's when I had to admit that they are wrong. They have been wrong before. I can't believe what they are saying. I will not internalize it. I think I'm the best person to know who I am and what I am doing. I have a good sense of when I am sinning, and I know that my lifestyle is fine. I have been in a committed monogamous relationship for two and a half years. I am not the type of person who has ever been promiscuous. I made a commitment and entered a relationship that I consider a marriage, and I am living like that. I dare anyone to challenge me face to face. There is no way anyone can convince me that I am doing anything wrong. My marriage is the same as my parents' marriage.

The name in this story has been changed to protect the privacy of the individual.

MALCOLM MACDONALD

Malcolm lives in a committed monogamous relationship in Austin, Texas. He is an Adult Probation Administrator.

I was born in Chicago, in a very Catholic neighborhood. I have two sisters and a brother. I am the youngest in the family. My father was an alcoholic. He is deceased now. My mother is very religious. She is a pillar of the church, and a confidante of the pastor. I grew up in the old-time Catholic Chicago ghetto where Father Ryan the pastor ruled the neighborhood. He would patrol the street at night, and send the kids home if he thought they were out too late.

One of my jobs as the youngest child was to wake up my sisters and brothers to make sure they got to Mass on Sunday. The religious experience wasn't a family experience where we would all go together. In its orientation it was more obligation than anything else. My dad stopped going to church, but it had less to do with religion than the fact that his life was just lousy.

I went to Catholic schools for sixteen years, grade school and high school. After high school I joined the Holy Cross Brothers. I was with them for four years, two at their junior college, then two years at Notre Dame. I graduated from Notre Dame. I didn't attend a public school until I went to graduate school. One of the events I remember about a religious education was when I was a sophomore in high school and learned what was mortal and venial sin, with all the details. I often think how unfortunate it was they didn't have computers in those days to keep accurate track of all the nuances of sin.

By the senior year of high school we were more influenced by Vatican II and were taught to have an informed conscience and live by that conscience. I have accepted more of what I was taught in my senior year than in my sophomore year. I never felt the need to reject Catholicism, nor even the organized church. As I get older I see how similar are all organizations. They consist of people who are initiating their own agendas. The church might have hypocrisy in it, but so does government and every other organization. I have always felt comfortable with my own belief system and no need to reject what is my tradition.

As far as the gay issue is concerned, I see a difference between the official position and the real daily pastoral practice which is often done with love and care for individuals. I don't feel that I'm supporting an organization that is going to kill me or destroy me in any way. I think it is inevitable that the official opinion will change. They just move at a different rate. I know in my work with government some people move at a more rapid rate than I do in some areas. So I'm the conservative in that regard. And again, I move faster than others.

As far as sexuality went, I was never taught anything either in grade school or high school. If it happened I don't recall it. Sexuality was totally unknown to me. I had feelings toward other men, but because of my strong inhibitions and being a child in an alcoholic family with all the denial that was going on, my main agenda was just survival. Sexuality was almost a non-issue through high school. Even into college it was a non-issue. I was aware of feelings but did nothing about it. In my senior year at Notre Dame I encountered one or two people sexually. I felt uncomfortable about this, but had nobody to talk with about it.

I joined the Holy Cross Brothers in 1966. I was with them one year in novitiate and three years in college. I left in the summer of 1970. This period allowed me to get into a quiet time and establish a certain stability. My brother has said he can notice this as making me different from other family members. They never had that opportunity. They had to move from one crisis to another. I am more relaxed and don't approach life as intensely as they do. I don't have this strong sense of right-wrong that my siblings have. My experience with the Brothers was good. I experienced some good teachers and a lot of other good people.

I had several excellent teachers at Notre Dame, especially Father John Dunne. He was responsible for forming much of my thinking. I was there from 1969 to 1971. I also had some very good religious experiences at Notre Dame, including knowing Father John Griffin, who was a very lovable human being.

In 1976, ten years after graduating from high school, I started going to the bars regularly and started dating men and having lovers. This was a very mysterious thing for me at that age, experimenting in a very private and closeted way. My experience in coming to grips with my homosexuality was more of an evolution than any particular occasion. When I was at graduate school, a group of us went home for Thanksgiving. One of the girls in the group was lesbian, and she was telling us how much fun the gay bars were. She took us all to a gay bar. I and another girl hung on to one another because we were uncomfortable. It ended up that she was lesbian and I was gay and neither of us knew about it. At school I went to a counselor and talked about the gay issue. He encouraged me to flow with it and not be too uptight. That eased me some. Then I started to get to know people and formed social relationships. I have been with my current partner now for eight years. He is director of a research institute.

I was a conscientious objector to the Vietnam war. As an alternative service to the military I negotiated with the board to teach in inner-city schools. This is what I was trained for in college. But because of some aberration in the law the draft law ended for four months and I was able to get a 4H deferment. I continued to teach in the inner city for two years in Cleveland, Ohio. That was a very frustrating experience and I got burned out. Then I went to a private Catholic girls' high school in Chicago. I discovered that I wasn't meant for teaching. I went to graduate school in New York focusing on criminal justice. Then I transferred to the University of Texas in Austin and got a degree in public affairs, concentrating on criminal justice. I worked for the Welfare Department for a couple of years, and then moved into my present work which is in adult probation.

I was elected president of the association I belong to, the American Probation and Parole Association. So I play a leadership role in my profession nationally and internationally. I have spoken around the country and in Japan and Australia to promote the profession. A lot of people say that I was one of the key persons who challenged our association to reach its potential. I happened to come on the scene at the right time, although I do work hard at this job. A month ago I spoke to the President's Commission on AIDS, and I serve on an advisory board of the National Institute of Justice's Probation and Parole Issues and AIDS Project. Being gay, and with my professional competence and the respect that I have, I could go in to speak to the commission with an assurance that my terminology was sensitive to the full understanding of the issue. I published my statement to all the membership, and now I'm one of the people in the association that people call when they want information on the topic.

If homosexuality is a disorder, as was stated in the Ratzinger letter, so are greed, revenge, distrust, and many other things. As I read more on families of alcoholics and other dysfunctional families, I realize how rare the truly functional ideal family really is. In working with people I see a lot of disorders which are so much more dysfunctional than what people do at bedtime. There are so many other problems; it seems that all the discussion of sex must take place because it's just fun to talk about sex. I figure that this is a group of people with an opinion that I just don't agree with. I wouldn't mind sitting down with them and talking about it, but I do have a lot of other things to do. It doesn't affect my life. I suppose if my life weren't filled with a lot of other things I might pay more attention to what they are saying and be annoyed. I just discount what they say, but not disrespectfully, because I think the Pope promotes some very positive values. I accept what I see as good and discount the rest.

CONFERENCE OF
CATHOLIC LESBIANS

KAREN DOHERTY

Karen is a business executive for the American Management Association in New York City. She was married, and now lives with her lover.

I come from a very mixed ethnic background. My earliest American ancestors came over in 1629; they were English. I also have French, German, Irish, Norwegian, and Dutch in my background, both Catholic and non-Catholic. I was exposed to both Catholic and Protestant beliefs. I ended up with the name Karen because the Norwegian side of the family was so infuriated when my mother married an Irish Catholic. She was disinherited. The name Karen was a balance to Doherty, to reflect the other side of the family. My mother was taken back into the family after I was born. As the family began to marry into other backgrounds there was less religious tension.

I went through public elementary and secondary schools, but attended a Catholic college, Trinity in Washington. As a child I had to attend religious instruction classes, but I also attended Methodist Bible school. I remember enjoying the Methodist instruction a lot more than the Catholic instruction. As a little girl I loved to hear the stories. By the age of seven I held in awe the mystery of Catholicism. That made an impression on me that stayed with me the rest of my life.

One of the things I enjoyed about Catholicism was the sense of humor, of how people could look back and trade experiences of how we played pranks and mischievously got around the system. This all held me in good stead when I grew up and became a business executive. How to have a sense of humor in a dire system, how to beat the system, and how to be friends.

I think because of my mixed background I was not imbued with as many Catholic superstitions as were people who had a totally Catholic educational background. The first prayer I was ever taught was from a non-Catholic aunt. I am appreciative that I don't have all the negative

103

focus of pain, suffering, guilt, and shame. My early focus was on thanking God for the beautiful things. The first God I knew was positive and the giver of happiness. As I grew up I began to associate the Catholic Church with negative things. But I was always very firm about my Catholic identity. I was taught the Protestant version of the Our Father and was rebellious. I had to take a stand for my religion, so I would say the Catholic version.

My great-grandmother grew up in the court of Queen Victoria, so there was a certain amount of aristocracy in the family. There was also a certain amount of grinding poverty because many of the folks lost all their money in the crash of '29. This had something to do with my character formation. It brought with it feelings of responsibility and shame.

I first became aware of my sexual orientation at about age twelve. It was very frightening because of the stereotypes. Lesbians were those swampy, devious, horrible creatures. I didn't want to be that. But I was aware that I was more attracted to girls and wanted to spend more time with girls than boys. Like any youngster, especially a Catholic youngster, I was indoctrinated in the belief that you will get married and have children. When I would talk about being a nun with my family it was discouraged. They felt that nuns lived a barren life. I considered religious life for a little while. When I asked a priest if nuns could go swimming and he said no, I decided that I didn't want to become a nun. That was my first and last attempt to choose a religious vocation.

At age twelve I was accepted into a private Catholic girls' school. Papers were signed, uniforms bought, and I was ready to go. At the last minute I pulled out. My reason was that if I was in an all-girls school, it might come out that I had these tendencies, so I would be better off in a public school. I decided this by myself without consulting anyone. That was my first real acknowledgment that this was something I wanted to stay away from. I remember all through high school haunting the "L" section in the public library. Of course, any book that was there contained the words "deviant" or "pervert" and reinforced my fears. I played basketball for CYO and I remember when I was seventeen having a vivid sexual dream about one of the girls who played on the team with me. It frightened me half to death that I would even have such a dream.

I redoubled my efforts to be accepted, to have boyfriends. I really learned how to play the game well. I dated, I became very homophobic about any other kid who was "queer." I avoided it, and yet was fascinated by anybody who I thought might be gay. I remember having a big crush on my freshman English teacher. I would wait until the class was out, then walk by her and say hello. I didn't get over my crush for her until I graduated from college.

When I was a senior in high school I looked around at colleges. I think my reason for choosing Trinity was that I wanted a Catholic school. I went to visit and recalled it as being a very warm and friendly place. My experience there was very good, and I would recommend the place. They give the appearance of being very conservative, but they are not conservative in teaching. We had a free rein to question and challenge and to use our imagination. I wish they would take a stronger stand on the women's issue. I experienced the nuns as human people, which is missed by a lot of other folks.

I was learning to play the heterosexual game. I had a date every Saturday night. I didn't see my life as having a choice other than being married. My mother and father were open to talking about sex, other than homosexuality, which was talked about in a derogatory way if the subject came up. We were free to talk about sex, but free to talk and free to do are two different things. I was repressed sexually, like many Catholic girls, but also I was very curious. I couldn't stand it any longer and decided I had to go to bed with somebody to find out what it was like. I "fell in love" with a Georgetown law student. We got engaged and married. He was the first man I ever went to bed with. It was great. I really enjoyed it. This was at age nineteen, and my budding sexuality was still a stress and strain.

Looking back at high school and trying to tie these things together, I didn't realize it at the time but my sponsor for confirmation was a lesbian. She brought her "friend" with her. This woman gave me a prayer. I kept that paper and came upon it recently. I wondered what possessed me to keep it all these years. I wish I could go back to my sponsor now and say that was really courageous of you to have your friend give me that gift. I keep it in my prayerbook. She was my gym teacher; I took her name at confirmation.

My first experience of falling in love with a woman was with my best friend in college. We met in the infirmary. I was resting after exhaustion from parties and running around. She was in there with flu, and we just hit it off. We have been best friends since that day. I fell madly in love with her and have loved her ever since I was eighteen. I have never told her that I have been in love with her. We told each other that we loved one another, and you would have to be blind not to see that it was something more to me. Unfortunately she is straight.

I happened to get married because my friend decided she didn't like Trinity and was going back to Missouri. I was so mad at her, I thought what is the thing that is going to annoy her the most? That would be for me to get engaged. In the beginning of my sophomore year I found myself a nice law student. The very first person I called to tell about my engagement was my friend. I know that she was distraught, which made me feel wonderful. She came back to Trinity when I was a junior, and by that time I was married and was living in an apartment with my husband. But the next two years I was a third "roommate" with her and her assigned roommate. I woke her up in the morning and got her off to class, being the best friend who was always there.

At this point I wanted to go to bed with her. One night when I was a senior, I called my husband and said my car had a flat and I was going to stay at school. I knew her roommate was out and sensed that something was ready to happen. The one night in three years of college that she didn't come home was that night. I waited until three in the morning for her to come home. She never did. I fell asleep and got up for class. I never cranked my nerve up after that time. I folded right back up into the closet after that.

I was repressing all this by saying, I'm popular in school, I am married, I've had plenty of guys dating me. I wore long hair; I would never have short hair. After I came out, I had short hair for a long time, until this summer on retreat. I had a vision that I should grow my hair long to start to incorporate more of my own femininity. Now I am comfortable enough with my lesbianism that I don't feel I have to have short hair and wear jeans. I can be me by wearing skirts and having long hair. At Women Church Convergence all the straight women had short hair and wore jeans and looked like lumberjacks and all the dykes had heels and dresses. I think lesbians are becoming comfortable not doing the "butch" things.

I married the law student. We both graduated the same year. He grew up in California and I in the East. Neither of us liked where the other lived, so we compromised on Alaska. I lived there from 1974 to 1978. During that time I was adopted by the Tlingit Indians. This has been a major influence on my spiritual life. I was never into cult or psychic things, but this opened me up to seeing spirits and the spirituality of another world in a way I have never contemplated. Through their dancing and other ceremonies, I experienced an incredible new way of feeling about myself. It was a remarkable experience.

My husband and I ended up being unhappily married. We were very much involved in the environmental movement in Alaska. He was an attorney in charge of environmental affairs. We were there during the controversy over the trans-Alaska pipeline and the offshore oil development. I will always praise him for getting me involved in the environmental issues. It is one of the positive things that has survived our marriage. The other thing he pointed out to me was that I had absolutely no business being married.

I had two experiences with Catholicism when I was married and when I was divorced. I had a real problem with breaking my marriage vows. My husband at the time was an alcoholic. I had a drinking problem that I knew I had to get out of. I went to see a priest to talk about it. He said, "There is nothing I can do to help you out of the marriage." I said, "I pulled a shotgun from his hands two days ago when he was about to blow a cat away from the window. I don't know if when I walk in the door tonight he will be there with a gun." He said, "I'm sorry. There is nothing I can do for you." The one time when I really reached out to the church for help I couldn't be helped. What came from this experience was the realization that I will have to rely on myself and not expect the church to help me. This was the beginning of my independence from the church. What I also remember about that priest is that he was in agony giving me that information. I could see that he was torn between what he felt and the advice he was forced to give.

In Alaska you can be divorced within thirty days, which is what I did. I know I disappointed my husband by not being the kind of wife he expected, but as long as I was being my own person and not fitting a lot of the stereotypes, things just didn't work out. When the issue of children came up, I said I would be glad to be a mother and stay with them when they were infants, but once they reached a certain age I wanted to go back to work. Would he stay with the children at that point? He refused to do that, so I decided not to have children. I have from time to time missed having children. I can feel my biological clock running. I thought of possibly having a child with a gay man, but with the kind of life I have chosen I want to devote my life more in the future to being prayer-centered rather than having a child.

My second experience with the church was with the man who finally counseled me into facing up to the fact that my marriage was not good. He was an ex-priest. I really trusted him. I recognized the goodness in him. He was more of a priest to me than the man who was still official. He looked into my heart and he challenged me. He didn't give any textbook answers, but made me answer by looking at who I was and why I was continuing the marriage. He made me face the fact that the marriage was over. I remember thinking how unfair it was that this man was an ex-priest. So I had both positive and negative experiences with church. The marriage ended in November of 1978.

After that marriage I almost remarried. I met a man in Connecticut and was engaged. My girl friend from college asked me to come to St. Louis to visit. I took that invitation gladly and when I got back I broke the engagement. It was obvious to me that I chose my girl friend over my fiance. It was at that point that I said I have to sit down and begin to think about this and see what needs to be faced. It was around February of 1980 that I called Dignity for the first time. I didn't do anything about it until May when I called again, found out where they met, and went to my first meeting. I "came out" in May of 1980. It was at Dignity that I met Christine Nusse. We were lovers and friends, and now are friends and companions of the heart. We were together for over seven years. We just broke off this past October.

When I went to Dignity I felt that the worst part of coming out as a lesbian was going to be facing the Catholic church and my Catholic background. I've gone through a lot of my life saying that my Catholicism hasn't been important to me, but it always sneaks up on me. Even though at times I say I don't care, I really do. I worked for a while with Dignity New York and ran into a lot of heavy weather with the Dignity men, especially when I was a rabid feminist. A lot of it was centered around inclusive language. There was a liberal wing in Dignity, and we were trying to get the church to accept us as we are. A split occurred in 1982. The pivotal issue was over having our unions blessed. The people at St. Francis Xavier refused this, and we felt it was morally disagreeable to worship in a place that would not recognize the blessedness of our unions as couples. We wanted to leave St. Francis Xavier. They agreed that four times a year we would meet elsewhere to have these unions blessed.

The bulk of the people in Dignity do not want to make waves, and want to be accepted by the church. They are not interested in women's issues or ordination. I have not been involved with Dignity since 1982. We left with other Dignity members and for about a year and a half we had a base community called Lesbian and Gay Catholics. That petered out. Christine and I started the Conference of Catholic Lesbians. We have been active with CCL now for five years. There are members all over the country, and a few from overseas.

Many women who say they don't care, really do care about being Catholic. They feel a spiritual void in their lives. They still love the ritual, mystery, and ceremony of Catholicism. But they also have negative feeling about the church, more as women than as lesbians. Personally, I do two things. When I'm out in business I often go to five o'clock Mass. I'm there with a cross-section of people who also want to go to church. I feel a tremendous sense of community with those other strangers. I still light candles. I think the feminine defensiveness has burnt off, so that when I hear sexist language I understand where they are coming from. It's not that important to me anymore. I think what helps is that I also have CCL liturgies in which I am with other women, and where my identity is being expressed as a lesbian and a woman. I need both at this point.

I know who I am. I can call myself a lesbian. I can call myself Catholic. I'm comfortable with this. I don't need a bishop to tell me who I am or what I can do. I don't need that anymore than I need a lesbian activist who says you can only be a lesbian if you wear short hair, etc. I'm not trying to reconcile all the oughts and shoulds and stereotypes in identifying myself.

I was the person who went to the Chancery to pick up the Ratzinger letter, so I'm probably the first person in New York who read it. I was dismayed. Since I was not looking to the church for approval, I was not hurt by it. I was surprised and not surprised that they identified homosexuality as an intrinsic moral evil. I think the potential for violence is going to show up. That was the worst part. I think it helped a lot of comfortable gay and lesbian Catholics to get off their fannies and start to see how things are. The church would be wise to make it just comfortable enough to stay in the closet, so that we could get by with some crumb of dignity while staying there. The more radical the church is in opposing us, the more people will come out.

I think Cardinal O'Connor made a mistake in closing St. Francis. They had their Mass and could pretend to be good Catholics. By closing it he riled up the gay community. I think the major shift is that it is forcing people to go from being a child Catholic to being an adult Catholic. People are beginning to say, this is who I am, and I don't need the church to tell me who I am. The weight that was once given to Catholic authorities is not given any more.

I continue to care about the position the institutional church takes because it affects my life and the lives of many others. I also feel that it is important to challenge this church. We lesbians and gays don't need to be told whether we are Catholic or not. Those of us in Dignity and CCL claim our own tradition, our Catholic tradition, and we will not be kicked out. I hope that we will never again hear the statement by some lesbians and gays, "I know I'm not wanted, I feel they have kicked me out."

I am out to people in my office. Once they got to know me as a person, then found out, it helped crush their stereotypes. It's a risk but it is worth it. Some of my classmates at Trinity were more accepting than others. I told them that I was the exact same person they once knew. What prompted me to come out at work was that my company was going to do a briefing book on AIDS. I realized who was going to read this book, major personnel people, and if we did it wrong and encouraged homophobia, the whole cause would really be set back. So I wrote a note to my boss, who also graduated from Trinity, to say that I knew someone who was an expert on gay men's health issues. A couple of days later we had lunch, at which time I told her. I made sure the book was not homophobically slanted. I wasn't coming out in order to come out, but because the issue forced it.

My mother and father found some Dignity literature that I had left around. The roof of the house blew off. They made comments about my long hair. How could I be a lesbian and have long hair. My mother said, "If I had kept you home cooking and not let you go out to play basketball this would not have happened." They discussed which side of the family it came from, and every other possible chestnut you could imagine. Christine was from France and at that time was not an American citizen. My mother threatened to go to immigration and report her for turning me into a lesbian. I said, "If you do that I will never, ever walk in your door again." I think that threat registered with my mother and father. After a period of time things improved. When Christine and I broke up, they were concerned that they would lose their relationship with her. They continue to stay in touch.

I was one of the delegation to meet with Cardinal O'Connor in 1985 to consider his opposition to the civil rights bill. My impression of O'Connor is that he believes strongly in what he believes and has a lot of integrity. I think he had some feeling in saying no, I can't accommodate you. I'm here to enforce the laws of the church. I wish I could help you, but I must do what I have to do. It took guts to meet with this very hostile group and be very straightforward and say what he believed in. We were treated like human beings. He made a point to shake everyone's hand.

Probably the hardest judgment call I ever had to make as a lesbian activist was when I was asked to be interviewed for the *New Yorker* about O'Connor. What should I say, I have an audience. I could say he is miserable and insensitive. But I couldn't do it, because I can't believe in my heart that he is a bad person. He is a person I would fight to the death, but I don't believe he is evil. I couldn't use that medium to get my point across, although the temptation was there. I could not use him as a symbol of our discontent.

BARBARA MULRINE

Barbara lives in New York City's borough of Queens. She is a bookkeeper at Christine Nusse's business. Until recently, she was a member of the Collective (Board of Directors) for the Conference of Catholic Lesbians (CCL). She is still active on national committees and in the two local CCL groups.

On my mother's side of the family there are two Dominicans: an aunt, who is a nun, and an uncle, a priest. My grandmother was a member of the Third Order of St. Dominic. I don't know if that factored into the aunt and uncle's decisions to become Dominicans. My grandmother was a daily communicant, of course, and once my grandfather retired he joined her. I remember how my grandmother would have to drag and bully him into getting up and dressed for the eight o'clock Mass. I think his reluctance to budge from bed had more to do with not being able to deal with the long hours of aimlessness that stretched before him during his days of retirement than going to Mass in the morning.

On my father's side, the only person I ever got to know to any degree was Granda. He was born in Scotland. As a young boy Granda left the small town where he was born and went to a junior seminary in Aberdeen in the Highlands. When he was seventeen or eighteen, he went to a college and seminary in Vallodalid, Spain, where he received his Ph.D. in theology. Three weeks before his ordination, according to family lore, he left on the pretext of testing his vocation, never to return. My father, when he was home, had to be persuaded to go to Mass. He studied in a Franciscan seminary for a brief time after college, but I believe that was on Granda's wish list and was not something my father wanted or felt he was called to.

My mother, for all her devotion to the church and the Mass, resisted any organized or pressured kind of activity that was not prescribed by church law. We were an Irish-American family, and as such, I think we were affected by Jansenism to some degree. There was a vast chasm between our bodies and our souls. For all the family's religiousness, it was the nuns who taught me in Catholic grammar school, and the parish priests who formed me as a Catholic. I probably would have been a scrupulous kid in any event, but they gave me the permission and blessing to be so.

Very early on I was aware of my sexual orientation as a lesbian. I remember the pull toward girls and women when I was a small child, but I lived in a predominately female household, and I never recognized my sexual feelings for what they really were. I kept trying to turn the thoughts off because the Church would label them "impure," and society wouldn't approve of them either. I grew to believe they were mortal sins, and I went through torment for many years.

When I was about thirteen, I realized I was zigging while everyone else was zagging. It was my last day of school in the eighth grade when I realized the depths of my confusion. I was in love with Noreen, who was in love with Richie. I figured something had gone wrong. I think that's the first time I recognized it in myself, and that was the beginning of repressing my homosexuality. I spent a lot of time in the confessional reporting my impure thoughts.

After high school, and until I was in my late twenties, I dated men with a vengeance in hopes that this lesbian "phase" would pass; it didn't. I fell in love with a man, and thought that would be the cure, but it wasn't. When I stopped dating men, I gave up the struggle between men and me, and the struggle within me began in earnest.

I worked in an advertising agency for sixteen years, and I couldn't be out as a lesbian. The only ones who could safely be out were the gay men in the creative department. As long as they produced, they could be as openly gay as they wanted, but people like me, who were in the accounting department or the media, didn't have the same freedom. It was probably because we weren't seen as being vital to the workings of the business.

All those years I was very closeted, and there is a great deal of stress in being closeted. I feel very lucky to have the job I now have. It would be difficult going back into the closet after this. The issue of honesty is at the heart of being out, and I'm an honest person. To live in the closet requires you to be someone you are not, to play a role, and I find it difficult to be someone else. Lack of honesty in one part of my life could lead to a creeping dishonesty in other parts of my life. Where would it end? Who would I become?

It's easier to be out in a city like New York where there is a large gay and lesbian community. That's not true in so many other parts of this country. I know a woman officer in the Army, who wasn't far from retirement, who had to stay buried in the closet if she didn't want to lose retirement benefits. She tried to attend one of the CCL national conferences but backed out at the last minute because of fear of being caught. She attended a subsequent conference but was terrified that someone would spot her. I had to admire her courage for being there, and I felt badly that she was forced to be so closeted.

I feel very lucky to be where I am when I see what others go through. There are times when I ask myself why I'm spending so much time with CCL work. The answer is, because I care. There are many women out there in small towns who are struggling to be who they really are and be comfortable with it. Knowing that I may be of some small help to one or two of those women makes all the hours of work worthwhile.

When I was a child, I knew I was different from boys, but I thought the difference was basically biological. I never felt inferior as a little kid. I suppose that was because there were few males in my family. I remember memorizing all the responses in Latin that the altar boys would say so that I could get on the altar. It never occurred to me that I wasn't allowed. My mother asked me why I was memorizing the responses. When I told her why, she explained that I couldn't get on the altar because I was a girl. I was crushed at first, and then I became angry.

I went through the same experience when I was a little older. I lived in southern California at the time. I played baseball with the boys in the neighborhood. I wasn't a natural, but I worked hard and held my own. I was as good or better than some of the boys who played on Little League teams. Then, I discovered Little League was another thing closed to me because I was a girl. You can build up a lot of anger growing up knowing you're being discriminated against. If there's a positive side to the sexism I've experienced, it is that it's made me more sensitive to other forms of discrimination that society practices.

Women have always been told to be Mary-like. I have never been able to identify with the church's Mary because she wasn't real, she wasn't like anybody I knew or could hope to be. She was a figment of the male imagination, and an extension of a pagan myth.

I listened attentively to sermons on Sundays that had nothing to do with my life, and probably had nothing to do with the lives of a lot of the people in the pews, especially women. My most vivid recollections of sermons were around Paul's epistles which concerned women and the family. The message to women was clear: be pure, be obedient, be submissive, and don't open your mouth. Women seemed to be called to be half a person, a servant without a soul. I wasn't always angry about it, at least not as a child, but I always wondered why. Why was I given a brain and a voice if God didn't want me to use them? Why were men afraid of us?

I was in my mid-twenties when I realized how alienated I was from the Church as a woman. I often hear gay men talk about how they feel ostracized by the church because they are homosexual. These guys know what is it like to be an insider, part of the club, but they are angry because they're not welcomed as members of the club because of their sexual orientation. Women were never part of the club; we've always been outsiders. I realized one day that there was no place for women in the church, especially single women, let alone lesbians.

Today a woman is discriminated against in the church more than ever. Women can be lectors and eucharistic ministers, but one wonders how much longer that will be tolerated. The current Pope and those in power around him, like Ratzinger, are dangerous to women and gays—and any others who question their policies.

Consider, for example, the pastoral letter on homosexuality or the bishops' letter on women. The message is clear: keep them in their place, let them know what conditions they must meet to be accepted by God and the church. Ratzinger's Halloween pastoral letter was a dreadful thing. It really gave "fag bashers" a blessing. I know cardinals and bishops don't like to be told they are wrong-headed or sinful, but Ratzinger's letter was uncharitable at best and certainly sinful in that it could incite people to harm other people who happened to be gay.

I stop in church occasionally to make visits, but I rarely go to Mass any more; yet, I admit I miss the church (the building) and the sacraments. Women are voting with their feet and leaving the church in droves, but I don't think the hierarchy notices. They didn't notice them while they were there so why should they miss them when they are gone?

When I go to visit my sister in Florida, I go to church with her. This is a strange turn of events. She is a case of a pagan who has gone back to Christianity. She never believed in the church, despite her baptism and training. She was always fighting it. She knew she was a second-class citizen from day one, and she was having no part of it.

After her divorce and annulment, she remarried a man who is a practicing Catholic, and she's getting more and more conservative. Last Christmas I reluctantly went to church with my sister and brother-in-law, and I got so angry over the exclusive language and the idiotic sermon that I began to mumble. My relatives were elbowing me and warning me to be quiet. I was so angry at the end of Mass that I had to ask myself what sense it made to go to Mass. I get totally distracted from my purpose for being there.

In CCL we create our own liturgies. It took me some time to get used to them, but they hold more meaning for me and facilitate prayer and worship for me. We have readings from various sources, public prayers and psalms. Occasionally we have a Eucharistic celebration, but we have other rituals as well. What I miss most, I think, is the Eucharist, and I think that's true for many of us. The music we use comes from many sources. We sing songs from the St. Louis Jesuits and Weston Priory as well as from women composers, such as Carolyn McDade, Coleen Fullmer, and even Chris Williamsen.

What I would like to say to church authorities would be mostly about women's issues. I'm not personally interested in women's ordination, although I would support women who are campaigning for ordination, but I think church authorities have to understand that they have to give women more participation. Not just in parishes but on the institutional level also. We should be allowed to live our faith to the fullest as men are. For instance, I see no logical or scriptural basis for the exclusion of women from the deaconate, and I can't understand why women aren't being used in this role. Jesus treated women as equals; that is evident in the gospels. Why should the church do less?

I was at a wedding of a cousin recently. Someone who was close to the bride was the main celebrant and the pastor, who was a friend, concelebrated. There were two nuns on the altar beside the priests and altar boys. Both the nuns were relatives of the bride and groom. At the point of the homily, the main celebrant began a homily on the readings and then he turned to another subject. He talked about how women could do many things in the church today, but one thing they couldn't do was preach. He told those assembled that one of the nuns would be giving "reflections" on this occasion and on the readings. He repeated that she would not be preaching because women weren't allowed to preach. She gave a great fifteen minute "reflection," and I had to marvel at how dumb our church Fathers are. She has a Master's degree in theology and works on retreat teams but can't preach in a Catholic church. Our best and brightest women—some of whom may be more gifted than many a priest—cannot preach in our churches; they have to go to Protestant seminaries and pulpits to preach. It's a great waste of talent.

I would also like to remind the bishops that, although they claim that the basis of Christianity is love, they show a shocking lack of Christian charity when it comes to homosexuals. Gay people are often catechists, teachers, and other ministers and workers within their parishes and schools, and yet they would deny them the right to live openly as gay people, and call them "disordered." It would be nice if a few more bishops had the guts to do what is right as a Christian rather than what is politically correct and expedient. Archbishop Hunthausen had guts and did what he believed was right, whether the issue was nuclear disarmament or welcoming homosexuals into the Christian family, but he paid for it.

In this climate within the church it seems unrealistic to expect that other bishops will be willing to listen, let alone act in the light of their own consciences. We can't stop talking to them though; we're going to have to force them to hear us, to feel our presence, if we dare hope for a better future. I find myself hoping for an American schism. I hope—though it may be a fantasy—that there may be a chance for a reconciliation with an American church and disaffected Catholics, including gays and lesbians.

LORI RICE

Lori has a doctorate in social psychology. She was married and has a five-year-old son.

I am the oldest of five children. I come from a very traditional Catholic background. My father is Italian and my mother is Canadian French. We lived in western Massachusetts. I went to a parochial school through high school. To show how provincial and Catholic we were, we talked about the French Catholic church and the Irish Catholic church and the Portuguese Catholic church. I don't think I knew a Protestant until I was in high school. I have two aunts who are nuns, causing a lot of interest in church matters. I also remember saying the family rosary together every night.

A great moment of truth came when it was time to go to college. The nuns wanted me to got to a Catholic college. My dad was very supportive, saying I should try to get in wherever I could. I received a scholarship to Smith, which was the only way I could go to college. One of the nuns said after she found out I was going to Smith, "You won't last a week." I was bound and determined to make it. Smith was a wonderful experience for me. I really blossomed there. It was a happy and exciting time in my life. At Smith they believed that women should really be all that they can be. It also gave me a chance to see Catholicism from a different perspective. I was taking courses in religion that were not "Catholic" courses.

I then came to New York to get a graduate degree from Columbia. This was a big step for a little girl from western Massachusetts. Through all this time I adopted a kind of Catholicism that enabled me to look at issues like birth control and go my own way and make my peace with God. At this point I was still not aware of my lesbianism, but I was finding myself increasingly uncomfortable with the way the local parish did not speak to me as a woman. While I was at Columbia I married a Jewish man. We were married in the presence of a Rabbi and a priest. When we had a son I had him baptized and we also had a bris. This seems a little unorthodox but we were trying to make our own way.

My marriage became more and more troubled for reasons that had nothing to do with my subsequent discovery of who I am. I left my husband when the baby was thirteen months old; protracted negotiations and a divorce followed. It was after I left him that I became attracted to a woman and began an affair. That was my first lesbian experience and first conscious awakening. Looking back, I can see that I had many crushes on teachers throughout the years. I never identified this as lesbianism. I always attributed the fact that I was uncomfortable in the traditional role of the woman to my interest in higher education. I believed in equality for women, that women should work at whatever they chose. I thought that my confusion and discomfort was a result of my coming from a very traditional family. As I became aware of my sexual orientation, my marriage couldn't have lasted. As it was, it ended before I had to deal with my orientation.

Here I was, newly divorced with a little baby and a dawning awareness that I was a lesbian. What a dilemma I faced. How does one keep one's child when there is a father, and lesbianism is socially unacceptable? I am happy to know who I am, it is a great weight off my shoulders. I feel very authentic now. It was during the time that I was coming to terms with my sexuality that I heard of the Conference of Catholic Lesbians (CCL). At that time I had stopped going to church. After all I had gone through I was disenchanted with the church. As soon as I heard of CCL and saw the combination of Catholic and lesbian, I knew that this was the place for me. I could now explore who I was with like-minded women. It took me a year to find the courage to go to a group meeting because I am a person of action and I knew that once I joined I would become involved.

I was sitting on the fence because I knew who I was but for all intents and purposes it was not evident. I was a divorcee with a small child. Temporarily that was a safe place for coming to terms with who I was. I had a great fear of losing custody of my son. It was a very difficult time because on the one hand I knew who I was and was happy about being able to proclaim that, and on the other hand it was a very real risk. After sitting on the fence for awhile, I realized that I couldn't be a good mother if I were a tortured person. I then decided to go to the group meetings. I met a lot of wonderful women and I felt very much at home. It was a place where I could explore my spirituality, which had been dormant for awhile.

Since then, I am happier and happier by being involved with CCL. I am very thankful for having found this organization. My spirituality now takes a more personal form of work with a spiritual advisor, doing volunteer work for CCL, and participating in women-developed liturgies. I am involved in a lot of things, including being a mother and managing an office and having a lover, but I find my involvement with CCL a very nurturing part of my life. I met my lover through CCL. We do not live together now, largely but not exclusively because I want to keep custody of my child. My son knows of our relationship. After a lot of soul-searching I also told my son's father that I am lesbian. I did this because I was living under tremendous pressure fearing that he would use my lesbianism against me if he found out. I couldn't stand the ambiguity or the fear. So I decided to tell him. It was a risk but the courts can't take away my child simply because I'm lesbian. They could take him away if they proved he lived in an unhealthy environment.

My life now is an attempt to balance a lot of things. My relationship with my lover is very important to me. I know that I couldn't give up my child; on the other hand, I know that I couldn't live without this great love in my life. So we choose not to live together in order to prevent the court from taking my child from me. There are other reasons also, but that is the major one. It's a difficult thing. I don't walk around every day terrified that I will lose my child, but I realize that I would be very resentful if my life was held hostage to what my ex-husband might do. He has threatened a custody fight. He is also very erratic and may never initiate a court case. He is getting married again and this may affect my situation.

I am out to my family. It is difficult for them, although they think my lover is a wonderful woman. They are embarrassed by my lesbianism and can't understand it, but they continue to love me. It was important for me to tell them. I have told each of my three brothers and my sister. They reacted with varying degrees of confusion. Some of them still haven't accepted it very well. I have to give them credit for trying to meet me where I am. My mother has asked me not to share my orientation with other relatives. I don't broadcast the fact, but I also will not hide it. My lover and I went to the wedding of one of my brothers. I introduced her as my friend. If they were to ask more I would have told them. I think people only ask what they want to know.

We wear rings as a sign of our commitment to one another. We told my son that the rings meant we were married. The next thing we knew he was insisting that I must be a man. We finally discovered that he was confused because his father told him that two women couldn't be married. In my son's mind, if two women couldn't be married then one of us must be a man. We decided that the time had come to talk to him. We told him that we were lesbians and that meant that Karen and I love each other and that we are family. We also told him that some people think that two women can't love each other, can't be married, but we do. It wasn't really heavy duty, but I wanted him to hear the word from us when it wasn't being used in a negative connotation. I don't know what it will be like when he grows older and understands more. I'm sure there will be some difficult times.

In terms of my spirituality and religious life, I am now in a place where nobody can push me out. Cardinal O'Connor may say I'm not a Catholic, but that doesn't bother me. What CCL is to me is a place to find spirituality and outreach to other Catholic lesbians and to worship together. We also are working for exposure in the church. I don't pretend to believe that Cardinal O'Connor or the Catholic Church will radically change their position on homosexuality, but that doesn't mean that I have to walk around being ashamed of who I am and letting other people pretend that I don't exist. I exist and I'm quite happy about who I am. They have to deal with me; I don't have to accommodate to them.

The church is the people of God and I'm part of the people. It's not for the bishops to say to me that you don't count in this church, or what you do is sinful. I am loving and my sexual orientation is a facet of my personality, it is part of who I am. It doesn't totally define who I am. I am a woman, a psychologist, a mother, and I am also lesbian. I integrate all those facets of my personality and I have a lot to offer. I don't accept the idea that the church can shut me out because I am a deviant. If I were to go to any parish church, most people there would consider homosexuality wrong and against God's law. Whereas, I can go to CCL and be accepted as I am. It is the patriarchal church that tries to define and set limits on me rather than allow me to be who I am. I feel very comfortable as a woman of Catholic heritage and a lesbian. But I need some kind of spiritual life and I find it where I can.

I feel that I have nothing to be ashamed of. I want to proclaim who I am. When I came out to my sister-in-law, she said, "I'm so sad for you, you are on the fringe of society." I'm not on the fringe of society; you might want to put me there or society might want to put me there. I'm in the mainstream of society. I have a responsible job. I look like and act like a woman and I am a lesbian. It is extremely difficult for me to use a pseudonym in this book. Rather than not tell my story here, I chose to use a pseudonym. I want to make that point because I think that it is very important for people to have their stereotypes of lesbians shaken up. That is one reason why I came out to my family and at my office. For me it is important to proclaim who I am in as many places as I can in order to shake up the stereotypes. It is difficult for people to hold onto those stereotypes when they see actual flesh and blood people doing everyday things.

I am the manager of a large office and I supervise a lot of people. My secretary is a young woman who is extremely friendly to my lover on the telephone and who, I believe, has a lot of respect for me. She noticed my ring and asked about it. I told her that it was a sign of my commitment to Karen. She was shocked when we discussed it further and she realized what that meant. I had to give her a great deal of credit. Although she was shocked, she said, "I just have to think about this." She came back the next day and has been able to cope beautifully. Her prior relationship allowed her to continue to be comfortable with me and with Karen. It's that kind of thing that I think is the hope for the future, in society as well as in the Church. For many people homosexuality is a very fearful thing, and so it helps if they are able to find out that people they respect and care for admit their homosexuality.

I had no awareness of my lesbianism while I was married to my son's father. At a difficult time in my life I had to face my lesbianism. My intention when getting married was to be in that relationship for life. That's why we had the rabbi and a priest perform the ceremony. Having gone through all that, I intended to be together for the duration. To have that crumble was devastating. And also to have a young child to care for by myself was extremely difficult. While all lives are complicated lives, at that time it seemed to be a very complicated balancing act. I am now much happier than I have ever been. There is no more curtain between me and the inner me. It takes a lot of balancing and making choices to achieve that state.

This past year was the first time I marched in the Gay Pride Day parade. I was too fearful to do that before because my son's father might have me followed as he had in the past. I simply decided that I could cope with that possibility. I am a good mother. I have taken great pains with my life to balance what's best with my son with what's best for me. I do not live with my lover but I marched in the parade when my son was with his father. I did that for me. I was fearful before he was two years old that he would not remember me if he was taken away. To let go of that fear and be able to march in the parade was a sense of liberation. I would never claim that I am not a lesbian. I would always claim that I am living my life for the good of all of us involved.

The name in this story has been changed to protect the privacy of the individual.

DIGNITY

JIM BUSSEN

Jim is the former national president of Dignity, an organization of Catholic gays and lesbians. Under his leadership Dignity became more vocal and active in regard to the theological stance of the hierarchy concerning homosexuality. Jim lives and works in Chicago.

I grew up in a small town in southern Illinois, a town of about 5,000 people. The main industry there is farming. My dad was connected for a number of years with International Harvester. Our family was dependent on the farmer. Our family was very strictly Catholic, German Catholic. You followed all the rules right down the line. If it was a holy day you went to church. On Christmas if there were three Masses, we went to three Masses. Whenever there was forty hours devotion, you went. Part of the thing was that Mom played the organ for the church. She was going anyway, so the family went to anything that happened at church. The other influence on my life was my mom who was involved in many causes. My dad also encouraged this. Mom was chairperson of the county blood drive one year, she was chairperson of the Christmas bazaar for the local hospital one year. She continues to help out on a number of other projects. I was taught by my parents that you did for others all the time. They also placed a high value on education.

I usually hesitate to tell this part of the story, and I rarely do to any reporter because I don't want it to be played out of proportion. Simply because if the hierarchy or others see that someone with my involvement in Dignity is an ex-seminarian, they would say, Aha, he has an axe to grind. I really don't. I say it's relevant in the sense that I was very naive, growing up in a small town. Going to the seminary was good for me, simply because it opened up all kinds of doors in terms of growing up, in terms of exposure to people from all over the country. I was in a seminary in Belleville, for the order of Oblates of

Mary Immaculate. Although I was exposed to a lot of learning, I think anybody who went to the seminary in those pre-Vatican II days did not escape without some scars.

There was discussion in the seminary about homosexuality, although I didn't know what they were talking about. I was scared to death of it. The other talk at the seminary was about either cars or girls. I didn't know anything about cars, and I wasn't interested in girls. Then there was the constant discussion about particular friendships. Any time you made friends with anyone it was frowned upon. I think that is where the scars were made. You were afraid to make friends. You held people at arm's length, because you didn't want to get too close, because you were afraid this person might not be around tomorrow. That's why many left. If you were ever seen more than three days in a row talking to the same guy, you would be called in and told that you were forming a particular friendship. Because of that I can say I don't have any close friends from high school. I think that was the sad part of that segment of my education. The system didn't help young men come to grips with their sexuality, with intimacy, with friendship, and their emotions. I don't regret the intellectual end of it and the challenge of discipline.

When it was time for college they sent us to Lewis College. I now rely on the philosophy degree I have and the theology courses I had to be able to put in perspective some of the pronouncements that come from Rome. They seem to have conveniently forgotten their own church history, their own philosophy and theology. Historically the church has changed positions, i.e., slavery, collection of interest, etc. For me this seminary education has offered a solid background from which to work. I had four years of minor seminary, four years of college and a year of novitiate. It's part of my life that will never go away.

In terms of personal history this part of my life is important, but I don't like to bring it up with reporters because they tend to go after that as sensational. I don't think it's relevant for the battle between Dignity and the Church, or the struggle of lesbian and gay Catholics for recognition by the hierarchy.

I took temporary vows before my last two years of college. It was then that I really started questioning the whole idea. It's the time when you have to decide about whether or not you want to go ahead with ordination, and with staying in the religious order. By that time my naivete was beginning to leave and I was confronting my own sexuality. That was only one part of why I left. My major part had to do with obedience, since I'm pretty independent. More of it had to do with poverty, simply because I felt that if we were going to witness to poverty as an order and as individuals, I objected to a lot of what the order tolerated. I was often appalled by the comforts of some of the order members.

In terms of coming out it helped that one of the priests at the seminary was coming out about the same time I was. He recognized it in me before I was willing to admit it to myself. He and I would go to breakfast together quite often, and pal around a lot. One day we were walking around the campus and one of the glorious hunks passed by and he turned to me and said, "Did you like that?" I played dumb and said, "What do you mean?" He finally confronted me and said, "I think you're gay." Between the two of us we spent the next several months doing research together, in the *Summa Theologica* of St. Thomas and other places, trying to find any reference to homosexuality we could find. This was the early '70s and at that time there was very little gay literature available. We read everything we could get our hands on. With his help I came to a very good reconciliation between being gay and being Catholic. I was able to maintain my Christian Catholic identity and still be sexually active.

I had a very smooth coming out. I had a guy take me under his wing and bring me up in terms of gay life. He was a very street-wise man. I was twenty-one and he was in his late thirties. Now that I'm thirty-eight I have to be careful when I say older man. He was very kind but street-wise. As a young kid he had run away from home and was a hustler, but by this time he had a job and had put his life together. He took a liking to me and took me under his wing. Literally we went through all the sexual possibilities there are. He told me about all the kinds of venereal diseases. He showed me the so-called milk run in Omaha, which every city has. It was a two-square-block area near the gay bar where the hustlers or the guys going to the bar just stand around. By the end of the summer I was able to identify who was selling and who wasn't. To this day it has served me quite well in the sense that it saves me from some possibly embarrassing situations, or from some dangerous situations. As a former street hustler he had a lot of wisdom to share with me.

I am grateful that my coming out was relatively smooth. When I lived in Omaha I decided to come out to my parents. This was between 1969 and 1972 when gay organizations were springing up around the country. Another close friend and I started to host rap sessions in his apartment. We invited our friends over for coffee and dessert and talked. There was nothing organized, we would just sit and talk. From that we set up a dinner at a downtown hotel in Omaha. It was a first for

Omaha. We had a sit-down dinner for gay and lesbian people and we brought in a speaker, Louie Crew. There was a huge turnout. From that we had more people attend the rap sessions. We decided that Omaha needed a gay organization. Because Omaha was conservative, we decided that it ought to be a religiously-based group. While there is a large Catholic population we decided to be broader-based, so we wrote to MCC and invited them to send out a representative to start an MCC church. In many ways I have to take some credit for helping to start MCC in Omaha. The very first Sunday that they had a service was my last Sunday in Omaha. I had been accepted for a federal job in Chicago.

Once I was in Chicago I went to a Dignity service here and started to get involved. I got involved with the liturgy committee first, then got on the Board of Directors. Then I started to represent Dignity to the Gay Pride Committee and other gay organizations in Chicago. In 1976 I was elected chairman of the Gay and Lesbian Pride festivities. In 1977 I was elected the first regional director for the upper midwest area for Dignity. I was in that capacity until 1980. Between 1980 and 1985 I took a somewhat low profile. I needed some time for myself.

I was elected national president of Dignity in 1985. The president at that time decided that he did not want to run again. By that time I was chafing to get involved in something. I was getting bored with my job and felt the need to get involved. I got a phone call and the group said they had put together a slate. They had the vice-president and secretary and treasurer for the slate. Since it was so well thought out and put together I felt that it was meant to be, so I said yes. To be honest I had thought about running as vice-president with a woman running as president. In fact before that I had called a few women and asked if they would be willing to run for president of Dignity. In many ways I assumed I would be a caretaker president. After some turmoil in the organization things were put back together before I came. But we had no staff in the national office. I knew that living in Chicago would help to get the business end of it settled.

Our first order of business was to hire a staff person to prove that Dignity could manage this. Then all of a sudden there was dumped in my lap the Ratzinger letter, which forever changed the course of gay and lesbian involvement in the church. The Ratzinger letter was such a hateful document. Given my activist bent I was labeled in Dignity as a radical, whereas in other places I was considered conservative. I ended up being this very liberal leader of a conservative organization. I felt that the only way to respond was in kind. Once we were slapped in the face with that kind of harmful and unchristian document, we could not keep silent. If someone says why didn't you turn the other cheek, I respond that gays and lesbians have throughout history turned the other cheek. In good conscience we owed it not only to ourselves to call ourselves by name and be affirmed who we were, but we owed it to that vast group of gays and lesbians out there who didn't belong to Dignity and had nowhere to turn, and were now told that they were disordered. We had to speak to them. We had to reach them. We had to let them know that there are people who do not believe that they are disordered. It led to some of our chapters being kicked out. It led to an almost combative state between Dignity and the hierarchical church. It was not of our making. Following this came the full-page ad in *Newsweek*.

I don't know what drove the bishops to do that. There was no indication that Dignity was willing to change its pace, its tenor, or its tone. Dignity has gone along for eighteen years being semi-quiet, not really ruffling feathers or being overtly confrontative. As long as we had our Mass and had a priest for our liturgy, people were satisfied. I don't know what possessed the bishops to think that was going to change. Then all of a sudden they upped the ante by allowing the Ratzinger letter to be issued. It was issued in English, which is unusual for a statement out of Rome. It was obviously aimed at the United States, and at Dignity. If the bishops had any guts they would have gone to Rome and said this is harmful. Once it was issued it was merely a guideline, it was not a papal dictum. The bishops did not have to kick Dignity off church property. Some of our strongest supporters as bishops followed suit. Whatever possessed them to be traitorous? What kind of a hold does Rome have over them? There must be something in these people's closets. There must be some dirt someplace. I hold these bishops liable. I think it is past time for Dignity to stop mollycoddling the bishops and saying Yes, Father. There is no reason for them to have done this, especially for those who have some clout. I guess if they cave in for a fellow bishop like they did for Hunthausen, I shouldn't be surprised if they cave in over gay and lesbian people. They are now using the divide and conquer tactics with Dignity. The religious right in America has an uncommon ear at the Vatican. They still have their cohorts in Rome and I don't think we have heard the last of them. I think there will be more chapters booted out.

We have nineteen chapters who have been kicked out as of today. I just hope our chapters don't do what Dayton did. They buckled under and signed a statement that they accept what the church teaches about homosexuality. When you say you accept the church's teaching on this, you say you accept the Ratzinger letter, that you accept being called disordered. If you think you are disordered, what the hell are you coming to Dignity for? You need further help than we can provide. You need help from a psychiatrist.

The question is why do we remain in the Catholic church? Why do we still call ourselves Catholic? On a personal level, being Catholic is my spiritual home. It's where I find my prayer life, my worship community, my support system. Until the church doesn't provide that, or my anger gets so deep, I'm going to stay. Once my anger interferes with my spiritual life, or the support is gone, then I will have to look for another spiritual home.

Interestingly, in 1986, when Cardinal Bernardin opposed the gay rights bill, I became a public figure on TV. He and I were trading pot shots on the ten o'clock news. It is liberating to be totally honest and out. Even at work I did not get any anti-gay remarks. In fact all I got were supportive remarks. What I did get were anti-church and anti-Catholic remarks from both Catholics and non-Catholics. I have had any number of people come to me and say, Why do you stay in the church? Why are you fighting? Why don't you be like us, we just go to our parish and don't pay any attention to what the priest says or what the bishop says? Why don't you do the same thing and shut up? Or, some of the non-Catholics say, Why don't you come to my church? You can pray with me, Jim. Here I was being beaten down by the guy who is supposed to be reaching out to me, then at work I get this non-reinforcement from Catholics who don't care about the structured church, both those who have stayed and those who have left. And those who have left are very bitter, very angry. I think this has escaped the bishops' understanding. I don't think they fathom the chasm that exists between them and the people in the pews.

I stay because I think being Catholic is almost like being Jewish, or being of some ethnic background, especially for those of us who grew up in the old church. I'm not sure that kinds of identity exists with the young people today. All of the symbols and rituals gave us a real identity, especially where I grew up in a southern Illinois Protestant town. The Catholic church and the Negro church were down by the railroad tracks. All the Protestant churches were uptown near the town square. The Protestant cemeteries were all on the nice rolling hills just outside of town. The Catholic cemetery was a little plot of land right next to the city dump. I didn't understand those subtle discriminations until I left Greenville. When I look back on it I realize the subtle message that gives about what it means to be Catholic. I think this has given me the ability to understand the subtle discriminations against being gay.

I think there is a whole identity to being Catholic. When Protestants don't like their church, or they feel it isn't fulfilling their spiritual needs, they look around. They probably join another church. Whereas Catholics just stop going to church. They don't become something else. I think that tells us more about the identity of being Catholic than about the spiritual needs that are being met. On the other hand, I think, why should we turn the church over to the bastards? It's like voting. You can't complain about the mayor if you don't vote. You know you have another chance in two or four years. Although the church is not a democracy, there is still hope for a change. If you wipe your hands of it and walk away, who is going to help make the change? How does the Spirit speak to those people? Someone had to stay and fight. There is a certain level of satisfaction from staying in and being a thorn in their side. At this point I'm not about to turn it over to them. That's not a very spiritual motive, but I think there are various reasons why one stays in.

As far as Dignity goes, the recent actions have changed the face of Dignity. The chapters that have been booted out and have decided to fight and not go away and lick their wounds and say, oh, poor me, have grown by leaps and bounds. The ones that have withdrawn and licked their wounds are dying. The Washington, D.C. chapter is now the largest chapter in the country since being booted out. They have over three hundred people. Our Hartford chapter started out with around forty people; it is now one hundred and forty. Chapters that are self-affirming, and won't go quietly into the night, are growing. We are getting more activist people. They are people who want to be church. They have no argument with bureaucracy and they think there should be guidance and guidelines in moral matters. We are not fighting church dogma. We are only questioning one aspect of church teaching, which of course is very important to us. Young married couples are questioning one aspect of church teaching. Women are questioning another aspect.

All these areas have a common thread, because of the sexual misogyny of the church, the sexual myopia of the church. Dignity has upped the ante just like the gay and lesbian movement has upped the ante. We used to say that although in our lifetime we may see no change, we are fighting for future generations. Well, because of AIDS our lifetime has been shortened, we want to see some changes now. We have seen arrests at St. Patrick's Cathedral. The prophets went before the kings of old and said you are wrong. I think we need to continue to be prophetic voices today. Our good chapters are becoming more prophetic and outspoken. It is also changing the face of our worship. Some of our chapters, not all, are becoming more inclusive in terms of those who lead the worship. They are using ordained people for worship, those who have left the ministry, and the non-ordained, i.e., women. They are saying we will be an inclusive full church. We will say that now that you have removed us from the churches, we have taken off all restrictions and your silly rules. Some of our chapters are becoming extremely experimental. We have been forced into a militant stance. We would not have done this on our own had we not been forced.

There are days when I really hurt. During the "gay rights" battle I felt incredible betrayal by Bernardin. I left an interview with him with the sense that he would not involve himself in the issue. If he could not endorse the gay rights bill, at least he wouldn't say anything. When he came out against the bill I felt a personal betrayal since I thought he told me he wouldn't do that. Because this was such a public battle, I was taking on an institution that for years had been the center of my life. It was the hot days of July and August, and I was getting worn down. There were days when I would come home and couldn't do any of the many projects I had to do. I would literally come home from work and curl up on my couch in a fetal position and stay almost all night that way. I couldn't move. My life shattered in many ways. The only solace I got was from Dignity members around the country, who would send letters and cards. This was an incredibly immobilizing period in my life. Finally, one of the former chaplains helped me to pray the psalms, especially the ones about smashing your enemy and calling on God to smite them. We would read them and laugh, and in the process I rediscovered prayer and was able to come out of it. I was able to channel my anger and depression. I hope I will never have to experience that again.

I think things will get worse before they will get better. I think more chapters will be kicked out. I think there will be more retribution against priests who reach out to gay and lesbian people. Getting better means that women will be ordained, and that gay and lesbian relationships will be blessed. I think it will come, I'm not sure when. I think there will be a sexual revolution in the moral teaching of the church. I think the women's movement will be the major focal point in the future. I don't know if there will be a schism before we reach that point. I don't think all this will happen easily, which is unfortunate.

LARRY SULLIVAN

Larry is an educator in New York City. In addition to educational and political activities he is very involved in the Dignity organization.

I was born in New York City. When I was six months old my father died. My mother and father had both come from Ireland. We had no relatives in the city. Our nearest relative was a cousin in Boston. My mother was left alone with me, an infant, and my nine-year-old brother. As a child, I was shipped back to my grandparents and stayed in Ireland for fifteen years. By the time I came back here my mother was remarried, and I met both my younger step-brother and my older brother. I could really see the dichotomy between the Irish church, which is really conservative and rigid, and the American church.

I don't know if I can say when I knew when I was gay. I'm sure I was from the start. Our culture has made such hard lines between the sexes, that by the time people reach puberty there is usually conflict. Society is giving them one message and the internal self often gives them a different signal. The conflict can be astounding. I never had too much of that because I was pretty sheltered. I came back here in my last year of high school. I was not very athletic, not a very good student. If someone would have told me then that I would be an educator I would have laughed like hell.

I went into the military. In those days if you didn't have the money to go to college, you didn't go. My first real view of gay people was of those in the military who were caught in the act and were being transported out. They were put in the brig, then put on a bus to downtown Norfolk with a one-way ticket home, dressed in the most hideous outfit they could find. They were held up to public ridicule. Prior to going to the bus depot they were driven around the base by the Marine guards so everybody could jeer at them.

When I got out of the military I met an Irish girl and we got married. We had three kids. Today I have a twenty-four-year-old son, a nineteen-year-old son, and a twenty-three-year-old daughter. I am a grandfather three times. My two sons are living with me and my lover at the moment. I worked on the railroad, then as a police officer, then went into business for myself. I owned and operated five straight bars. Even when I was in law enforcement I could never figure out why I was a workaholic. I would work all day long, come home for dinner, then go out to work on remodelling a house I had bought. It never occurred to me that there was something lacking in my psyche.

I went to a meeting of the Ancient Order of Hibernians. There was a fellow there that I knew who was there with his son. The man was twelve years older than I, and the son was twelve years younger. The son was going to a nearby private college, living on campus. He came up to me and asked me to give him a ride to the college. All the signals were open. We got involved in this mad sexual experience. I was completely freaked out. I couldn't understand the magnetism of the situation. The next day I went down to where he was living and wanted to talk. We ended up in bed again. This led to a very hot and heavy romance. It got to be so intense and all-consuming that I knew there had to be a collision some place.

I didn't know what to do about it. I loved my wife and my kids, but I felt more fulfilled this way. That is contrary to everything I was ever taught. We were taught responsibility and sacrifice. In fact sacrifice was our middle name. All of a sudden I felt very guilty, not for the sex but because I was not doing what I should. This affair went on for about six months. He was a senior in college who was smoking marijuana and not doing his work. This annoyed the piss out of me. He had four incompletes. I loaned him fifteen hundred dollars so he could get a pair of glasses, some shoes, and a broken-down car so he could go to work and get on his feet. He was really a talented person but he didn't finish college. We were both trapped, he by marijuana and I by love.

He got sick so I moved him into our house until he got well. He got along famously with my wife. She was convinced that we were going to straighten him out. He was like a little brother. Now this really got stressful and confusing. While all this was going on, I saw that I was going to have to make some sort of choice in life. At the same time my brother who was working with me was stealing from the business. Here I was with three stresses going on at once, a torrid romance, a marriage going on the rocks, and my younger brother who was clipping from the cash register. I laid on the bed one day and said who needs all this crap. I might as well kill myself. I didn't know what to do or where to go. I didn't know any gay people per se. I have an uncle in New York who was always whispered about as being gay. I called him and asked if we could talk. As he was serving a cup of tea his hand started to shake. He said, "You are going through the same situation I have gone through." I made him admit he was gay. His advice was that I should go on being who I am and be quiet about it. Stay married and don't tell anyone and all will be fine. I decided I didn't want to grow old and be as lonely as he was. Here was an old man who was in the closet, and once in a while he would slip out then slip back in. Here I was with this big lust and a lot of internal confusion. I am basically an honest person and for me to live in a way that is dishonest was stressful.

I decided to go on a mini-vacation, a three-day drunk. I went upstate New York to a place near an aunt. I went to the early openers and the late closers. I was completely ossified. I fucked anything that moved. I called my aunt and she said, "Let's go for a ride in the country." This little old lady sitting behind the wheel of a pickup truck says, "What's wrong?" I laid it all out, told her everything. One of the qualities of our family is that we stick together in times of need. She just looked at me and said, "We love you, you have to do what is best for you, but you must remember that you have three kids and you have an obligation in life. Whatever you choose will be fine with us." I decided to sober up and come home.

Coming down the New York Thruway and looking at the Catskills, I made some decisions. I went to the place where my lover was working, took him aside and told him that I would not allow him to become an emotional or financial burden on me. If you can't clean up your act then you go your way and I'll go mine. He said, "You could never complete four years of college." I said, "You want to take a bet on that? I will go in September and register at the college you did not graduate from." I then went to my place of business and took my brother aside and said, "I'll give you three months to find a job and at that time I will buy you out."

I then went home and unpacked my bags and put the kettle on the stove. I asked my wife to sit down for a little chat. I laid it all out to her. Her response was, "You need help. I'll stick by you, and we will get you the help of a psychiatrist and everything will be wonderful." I said, "No, you don't understand. Everything is wonderful. I'm happy now that I can deal with me. I laid up in that room too many times thinking about killing myself." We tried to work it out for six months, then took a trial separation. At first there was an attempt by my wife's lawyer to use my gayness as a secret weapon to get whatever he wanted. When they found out that I wouldn't let them use it as a weapon, we worked out a fairly amiable settlement. The minute you buckle under to this secret weapon then your life becomes very constrained. I'm not proposing that we should walk around with signs on. But I don't think we should get caught in a situation where we have to be defensive about who we are.

When you are a gay father, I think you work harder at being a father. I came from a culture where the body space was always three feet away, and after the age of seven it was just a handshake. There was never a hug or wrestling on the floor. I try to be demonstrative to my kids. When I moved out on my own they came to visit on a regular basis. One day my oldest boy who was in the eighth grade at a Catholic school came to visit and he looked very down. I asked what was the matter. He said he wasn't allowed to go on a skiing trip with the class because the sister said he owed tuition. His mother had not paid the tuition money she received. I dressed down that sister for humiliating my son in front of his peers. I made her apologize to my son in front of the class and admit him to the skiing trip. I threatened to tear down the fucking school brick by brick if she didn't.

From the very start of this evolution I decided that I could not deal with the church. To me the church now became a structure that I couldn't deal with. The incident with the nun at school was the precipitating factor. I decided that I didn't need the church for any reason, so I stopped going. I was out of the church seven or eight years. I met somebody and we lived together. The relationship worked out pretty well. The kids called him "Mr. Mom."

A group of people asked me to join them at someone's house for a Mass. They were interested in starting a Dignity group. I thought they must be out of their minds. It's like jumping into the lion's den. They persisted, so I went. There were twenty-five gay guys sitting there; a table was set up with candles on it. The host was running around the house. I was sitting next to this guy with boots and a flannel shirt on, and I'm convinced that this whole thing is going to be a mockery. Any minute some pompous ass is going to walk in with a collar on and sit down and start waving his finger at everyone. This was the church I knew as a kid. The guy next to me in the boots finally introduces himself as the priest. He said, "There are a few things you must know from the start. I'm an alcoholic and I'm gay." The floor could have opened up and I would have fallen through it.

I hadn't been to church for about seven or eight years, and this liturgy was the finest, most spiritual event I ever experienced. The homily turned out to be a rap session that lasted for an hour and a half. I said to myself, if the Catholic church has changed that much then I'll give it another shot. If anything keeps me in the church now it is Dignity. They have given me my dignity as a person. I work on the gay hotline three nights a week that is run by Dignity in our county. There are times when you can walk away from that phone completely drained. On the other end of the line is a seventeen-year-old who wants to commit suicide. You might spend three hours on the phone talking him out of it, but you feel pretty satisfied when it is over.

In the meantime I had gone to college for four years. Then I went to graduate school, and ended up teaching at a Catholic high school. My lover is a teacher too. One day I stayed late after school, and as I was walking down the hall I ran into my first lover who was now doing custodial work at the school. He is the one who should have been behind the teacher's desk, and now he is pushing a broom. He was still as stoned as ever. I'm now working on my doctorate in educational administration.

I shared with each of my three children that I was gay at different times. A time presented itself unexpectedly when it was appropriate to tell each of them. They accepted it in a most beautiful way. My one son is nineteen now and he lives in my house with me and my lover. My brother's son also knows the situation and stays with us when he is in town. When this nephew first came to stay with us I decided to write to my brother and tell him the whole story so that he wouldn't at a later date try to accuse me of anything. I wrote an eleven-page letter to my brother saying that if he had any objections to his son staying with me he should mention them now. I had two envelopes on my desk, one to an aunt in London and the other to my brother. Lo and behold, I put the letter to my brother in the envelope to London and the other in the envelope to my brother.

After one of the boys took the mail to the post office, I realized that the envelope to London was much too heavy. Not to worry, there will not be enough postage on it and it will be sent back in the box tomorrow. Of all times for the post office to screw up it was this time. The letter went to London. Within a week I had a big brown envelope back from London with my letter inside. It had been opened and retaped, with a note from my aunt saying, "Apparently this letter was meant for your brother, I did not read it." I know my Aunt Mary, she would read the graffiti on the john walls. I photocopied the letter and sent it back to her and said, "If you didn't read it you might as well read it now." I never heard a word from my brother, but within a week I had another letter from London. My aunt said, "We don't know what the big hang-up is in the U.S. We have been here since 1935, and we have worked in the restaurant industry and always worked with gay people, they are some of our best friends. Any time you want to come here for a visit bring your friends with you, you are welcome."

I think the church is like a pendulum, it swings back and forth. It may take some time, but it will swing back. As long as we have the Polish prince sitting on the throne, I don't expect much to happen. I think we have gone through the era of conservatism. The poor American hierarchy are trying so hard to please him that when they shave in the morning they must not like the faces they are looking at. By the time the pendulum swings back there will be a whole new crew in there, probably more enlightened. They will have to say, we screwed up with Galileo and I guess we screwed up with the gay people too. What we have to do now is hang tough. They would love for us to go away; then they wouldn't have to deal with us. But we are the church and we are not going away. Psychologically I can agree with what the Cathedral Project people are doing. In principle I agree that they have the right to bring about that sort of notice. What I don't like is that they are tending to ruin the structure of the organization they belong to. If they are going to incur legal bills then they need to consult the whole constituency of Dignity. J.J. [Cardinal O'Connor] has lots of money and he can go to the deep pockets, local, regional, national. The Archdiocese of New York has a hell of a lot more money than we have.

We are in the position now that divorced Catholics were in thirty years ago. They couldn't be buried in consecrated ground, or have a funeral Mass. The Ratzinger letter caused a lot of ill will, hurt, confusion. If one looks at it from a sociological view it is a defense mechanism. Things were getting too close to the surface. They are dealing with a phoenix and they don't know it. They don't understand that we are not good little boys who are going to dance to their tune anymore.

As far as J.J. O'Connor is concerned, the poor man isn't really a pastor. He is a military man, a chain of command person. He is a good manager, but his stand on gays is stupid. We all know about Cardinal Spellman, and we know about many of the clergy. Whenever the church points a finger, she has to point it back at herself. While we are waiting for the pendulum to swing back to some normalcy, there will be two or three generations of gay people who will be mangled and alienated, who will be confused and hurt. What kind of theology and psychology is it that starts by degrading a person, then builds him up? We can stand here and be prophetic witnesses, but the generations coming along will be totally confused and alienated. To have this kind of theological hogwash in the midst of the health crisis sure doesn't help.

The name in this story has been changed to protect the privacy of the individual.

PAUL ALBERGO

Paul lives and works in Washington, D.C. He is the former president of the Dignity chapter in Washington.

I'm originally from Brooklyn, New York. A one hundred percent Italian family, so we are talking about the size of a small army. I went to eight years of Catholic grammar school, run by the Sisters of the Immaculate Heart of Mary. I went to a public high school, and then to college at Georgetown. Then I went to graduate school at Boston College. The choice of Georgetown as a Jesuit school wasn't all that important. It was the location. But once I got there I was enamored with the Jesuits and chose Boston College based on that wish to stay with a Jesuit school. I even toyed with the idea of becoming a Jesuit.

In graduate school I even went so far as to become a Jesuit candidate. I sat down with a priest who was a spiritual advisor. In the course of our discussion he knew that I was gay. He said he felt that the reason I wanted to become a priest was to run away from my sexuality. He said if that was the reason I was doing this he could not recommend me. He felt that anyone else who served as my spiritual advisor and with whom I was fully honest would come up with the same opinion. He went through this whole thing about celibacy being a gift. You offer your sexuality back to God. You have to honestly embrace it before you can give it up. His advice was for me to honestly embrace my sexuality, to accept who I was, and then if I wanted to be a priest to go through the process. So I went out and embraced my sexuality.

I was able to tell people I was gay, but was not able to act it out. What I was trying to do was avoid all the questions that would come up as a result of being gay. Becoming a priest would be a safe disguise. Certainly my parents would be thrilled. Many people think that by being celibate you don't have to worry about your sexuality, that you are a non-sexual being. I know now that it is just not true. But when you are just exploring it, that's what you think. You think that somehow when you get Holy Orders that whole side of you is just sort of given away. In a sense, that is what I was hoping for.

I knew I was gay when I was in high school. It was one of the factors that entered into my decision to go away to college rather than to stay at home. My parents could not understand that at all. First, they couldn't understand why anyone would want to leave their family and second, why anyone would want to leave New York. I knew I had to get away. It took me a while to verbalize to myself and to others that I was gay. I was very controlled in who I talked to. So it really wasn't until the point that this priest confronted me that I realized I was trying to run away. I was trying to hide and the church is a place to hide. At least it seems to a person on the outside that this is true.

I went to graduate school to get a Master's in history. I really didn't have any goals. My only goal was to graduate from college. My parents had lots of goals for me. They are very strong personalities. And as long as I was living at home it made sense to me to go through with their goals. When I got away I realized that I didn't have to do the things they wanted. They wanted me to be a doctor or lawyer, things like that. That's when I started to make decisions on my own. I finally decided to major in history. I got my college degree in history and toward the end of my senior year I thought, I don't know what I want to do, so I chose to go on to graduate school. Again I chose a Jesuit school because I wanted to stick with the Jesuits and it gave me a chance to begin thinking of becoming a Jesuit. The desire to become a priest was not career-motivated, it was just a way to avoid having to look for a job. My first year in graduate school is when I started working on the issue of my sexuality.

About that same time AIDS was just beginning to be talked about. People were recognizing that it was here and it was in the gay community. That's when *Newsweek* did two cover stories on AIDS. It was interesting, because on one side I was being told go ahead, go out and get your feet wet. On the other hand, all these other people were talking about being careful. Don't get your feet too wet. I look back and think that I was forced to approach it in a very healthy way. I tried to explore it in terms of interpersonal relationships. Up to that point I had never really met another gay person whom I went to and told I was gay. Most people I knew were straight friends of mine. And I did not know the few gay people I met were gay. As soon as I realized they were gay I did not pursue the relationship.

One of the first organizations I joined was Dignity in Boston. I should not say "joined"; I started going to some of their services. Boston College had a student organization, and I participated in that. That's really where my first exposure to gay people came. Although the group at Boston College did not profess to be a religious organization, just by the nature of the school, most of the people who belonged were Catholic. The Georgetown lawsuit had already begun, and we were watching it very carefully. During my first contact with Dignity two things were going on in my mind. To go from barely ever meeting gay people to walking into a room that was filled with gay people was really intimidating. They met in the basement of a Unitarian church in downtown Boston. At that time it bothered me not to meet in a Catholic facility, and not to participate fully in the church. As a result of those two things, I didn't really become involved in the chapter itself. I chose to stay with the people out at Boston College. I didn't really become involved with Dignity until I came to Washington.

For a while there was a period that I just didn't care about the church. I had been in choirs all my life, but for about a year I just stopped. I washed my hands of it. When I came to Washington I had a roommate whom I had met in Boston who took it all very seriously. He didn't care what anyone said, he went to Mass. He used to go to Dignity in Boston. When he came to Washington he got involved in the local chapter. Every Sunday night before he would leave for Mass he asked if I wanted to go. I said no, but he persisted. Every Sunday night he would ask. And I remember the first Sunday of Lent I finally said okay, I'll go. By this time I had become comfortable with gays since I belonged to a lot of political groups. I was no longer intimidated by large groups of gays. At this point I embraced who I was sexually and was comfortable with that.

So I went to Mass and it was a wonderful experience. I had never been in a religious service that had as much feeling as was there. It was the same feeling that was there in Boston, but I wasn't ready to receive it then. There were over two hundred people packed into this very small chapel on Georgetown University campus. What struck me the most, and I can remember it to this day because I used to sing in the choir and was choir leader for a while, was the fact that the congregation sang and that the choir director depended on the congregation to carry the melody so it wasn't necessary for the choir to do that, and you had all this harmony. This is unheard of in Catholic churches. The priest gave a wonderful sermon that seemed so applicable. Without even knowing what it was I was missing I knew that I had found what I was looking for, and that was a real sense of community. It's one thing to call yourself a lesbian and gay community, and it's another to experience what is community.

Here I was in an environment that was going to give me not only all the things I had before, but was in a community that would accept me fully as who I was. A community that I could genuinely become a part of. It was also a gay organization in which I didn't have to worry about being Catholic, because I find a lot of anti-Catholic feeling among many lesbian and gay community activists, mainly because they see what the hierarchy is doing to the church. But of course the hierarchy is no different from other leaders in society. There are very few people in leadership who are actually going out and embracing lesbians and gays. Homophobia exists within the church and elsewhere in society. But you can't explain that to someone from the outside who identifies the church with the hierarchy. Here was a place where I could be fully Catholic and fully gay. One Sunday Mass turned me around and I started to go regularly. Then a year later I ran for president.

My parents' approach to my gayness is denial. If we don't talk about it we don't have to deal with it. I had been involved in some organizations, one in particular was the national Lesbian and Gay Health Foundation. When they sponsored the national series of vigils on AIDS a couple of years ago, CNN was covering it, and as a representative of this organization they asked me to speak. I was interviewed, thinking that my parents would not see it because they did not have cable TV in Brooklyn. Cousins of mine saw it and were so excited that I was on TV that they videotaped it and gave a copy of the tape to my parents. There was no malicious intent, they were just excited that their cousin was on TV and wanted my parents to see it. My parents then called me. They were excited to see me on TV. My mother was kind of serious and said I should be careful. That was the last time we talked about any of it.

All my friends know and the people I work with know I am gay, including my employer. Last summer when Dignity was kicked out of the chapel of Georgetown and we went to St. Margaret's we got a lot of publicity. My name was in all the papers including the front page of the *Washington Post*, and my face was on the local news show so anyone who just knew me as an acquaintance knew everything about me after that. Actually I found it quite nice, because I didn't have to worry about anyone now knowing, which is especially nice at work. I know a lot of people who work for the government, especially the military, who are really afraid. You reach a point where you can't hide any more, you can't pretend. The kind of pressure that goes with pretending by lying just isn't worth it.

I think if I had to summarize my feeling about the church it's that I just don't care what the Pope or bishops say. When the Ratzinger letter on homosexuality came out I was put in a position where I was forced to share my opinion. I began to say it really doesn't matter. In the case of lesbians and gay people the church has made itself irrelevant. The frustrating thing about it all was not so much what they were saying but the fact that there were people who were very, very hurt by what they were doing. We have a chapter telephone line and people call. Every once in a while people call who are really hurt, and who hear what the church is saying and don't know how to justify what the church is teaching. Not everyone has been raised the way I have been, or had the opportunities I have had. And while it may be easy for me to pass some of this stuff off, others with a different upbringing find it difficult to understand that this is not Christ speaking, but people limited by their own prejudices and world view. They are allowing their prejudices to determine how they are going to lead the church.

Ultimately the Ratzinger letter was one of the most wonderful things that happened to Dignity. In many ways it was the last straw. A lot of people who really believed and wanted to be Catholic and participate in their parish became very disgusted. At that time more and more people began to come to Dignity. Our services began to go from around two hundred people to over three hundred. By coming out with these statements the church gave the press a chance to talk to us. People began to think about how silly some of the church rules are and the fact that something finally had to be done. Many who were sitting on the fence started to come out and work for change. I had this attitude of letting the whole thing go. I let the organization take my energy and never really paid any attention to what was going on inside me, until other Dignity chapters began to be kicked out of their various churches. Finally it was our turn to go, and you can imagine it was absolute bedlam trying to make the move. I was so involved with this that I didn't deal with any of my own issues.

Right in the middle of this a friend of mine was being ordained a priest in Boston. We went to college and sang in choir together. From his college years he knew that he wanted to be a priest, and he asked us to sing at his first Mass. After weeks of running around and worrying about a lot of things I went to the ordination. I had a great seat next to the sanctuary and could see everything. It was the section where all the priests were sitting. I was with a woman friend and I noticed how uncomfortable she was and I became more and more uncomfortable. I began to realize how horrible it was. Here we were surrounded by this wall of men. The emphasis by the Cardinal was on obedience. Do what I say, and go out and instruct the people on what we teach. What I kept hearing was this emphasis on obedience. I felt that I was not witnessing an ordination by an induction into a fraternity. Listening to this for about three hours, about how special they were and how select, I began to get angry. Angry because the Cardinal was saying how important he was and we must all listen. While I was thrilled that Mike had finally reached his dream, I was so angry. I was thinking, why is he so much better than me? At the same time I realized that next week was the last time we would be allowed to celebrate Mass in a Catholic chapel. What makes us as individuals so different from Mike? Is it because he is willing to go through all the pledging process that this fraternity has? On the plane trip home I was fuming because I was so disgusted.

I began to think, why should I go through all this? I kept thinking how wonderful St. Margaret's has been, the Episcopal parish where Dignity meets. The pastor there is a wonderful woman. I wondered why am I sticking through this. What's the point? It's all bullshit. We are playing a game of politics. We shouldn't be playing games when someone's spiritual life is at stake. Now it was genuine disgust for what was going on. It was not easy thinking about these things, since I have been involved in the church my whole life. I began to think that maybe I should resign my position as president or finish out my term and join an Episcopal parish. I went to Mass the following Sunday at St. Margaret's and had the same experience that I had before. There was the same spirit there, and all the people I knew said don't be a fool, this is what really matters. We have people who really care and are trying. People are there because they take it seriously. It dawned on me that I was not going to let Archbishop Hickey or Cardinal Law tell me what I can do. Because, as my mother says, they will change. Necessity brings about change. When reality finally hits them, when they are at a point where they can no longer deny reality, they will have to change. To me it doesn't matter what they say. They have made themselves irrelevant on the matters of gay issues.

I heard that we were getting kicked out of the Georgetown church on Tuesday. That following weekend my brother's son was being baptized. I had to fly up at four o'clock on Saturday to go to the christening. I couldn't pay any attention to what was going on because I had to worry about catching a plane to National Airport so I could be back to announce to the chapter that we were being kicked out of Georgetown. My brother's child was being welcomed into the church at a level that I did not feel welcomed.

Our catch phrase this year has been, we are the church. I think people genuinely believe that Christ is accepting them, that they are not being excluded. People are beginning to see that there is a difference between what the church is and the hierarchy. They are just one part of the church. I would say the real issue is not homophobia within the church, or anti-lesbian and gay feelings. The real problem is that we have a political structure in the church that does not lend itself to change. I think it would be wrong to think of the church as different from the rest of society. At least in the civil government we have a way to address our rights. There isn't that process in the church. What they have done is silence anyone who is not one of them. I think we are now seeing people who are tired of that structure. Instead of trying to speak through that structure they are creating organizations of their own. That's all Dignity is. It is not a teaching organization, nor a political organization, nor a militant organization. We are the voice of a people who come together to worship, to speak and to ask questions. We are creating our own church within the church. I think eventually there will be blending back. Those who stick through this nonsense obviously care enough that they are not going to break away.

The current situation is similar to what happened to Galileo. Galileo made popular and public new scientific views that threatened the authority of the church. How nice it would be if they could accept new knowledge and not see it as a threat but as advancement. I think the issue is not really homosexuality but power. I think it's just a matter of time, although it probably won't be in my lifetime that homosexuality will be fully embraced in the church. They don't want to give up power, so instead of making change they just suppress it. It was only after hundreds of years that Galileo was reinstated. That's what is happening with gays. It may take three hundred years before they fully understand and accept what we are saying. The issue is being talked about now, and once you talk about something it has to bring about enlightenment. As long as it is ignored and suppressed there can be no advancement. There needs to be a whole new approach to the discussion of sexuality in general. The church is very progressive on social and economic issues, but not on sexuality. Maybe the discussion on homosexuality will force the church to reassess how it looks at sex. More and more people are staying in the church and participating fully and not being driven away.

TOM MCLAUGHLIN

Tom is a banker in San Francisco. He has been actively involved in Dignity. He held several positions in the organization, including co-chair.

I'm forty-five years old. I'm a gay Catholic man. I was born in New York City. I'm one of five boys. My father and mother were born in Ireland. My two younger brothers are actually step-brothers; their mother was also born in Ireland. My mother was killed in an accident when I was very young. My father, who only went to the eighth grade in Ireland, sent five sons to Catholic colleges. Catholic education was a high value in our family. I liked the schools I was in, I liked the atmosphere. That's why I imagine I'm still a Catholic; it has been so ingrained in me. Am I still a Catholic? At the moment, yes.

Having finished college in the '60s, I know that almost all my graduating class stopped being Catholic. We were required to go to chapel on Monday night, but not required to go on Sunday, and nobody did. That didn't quite make sense. I did not go to Mass for years. But I always felt a closeness to the church. I always fell back into the church when I needed something, especially peace of mind. When I wanted comfort or spiritual time for myself I wound up in a Catholic church, but not on a Sunday. I didn't want to be there on Sunday because I didn't feel a part of the community. But I enjoyed going on a weekday.

My return to the church came in 1980, and that was through a Dignity advertisement. I had known about Dignity for a long time and I thought it was silly. I would laugh at them in the gay parade when they would be saying the Our Father. Their fervor was embarrassing. I had been reading their ads, then one Sunday I decided to try it out. I found immediate acceptance, and I have made my best friends in the city in the past seven years. They will be lifelong friends. It gave me

151

a sense of power that we could change what was going on, at least we thought we could. We are wondering now, however, with the Ratzinger letter and the way Dignity is being ousted around the country.

I knew that I was different when I was a kid, I just didn't know what it meant. When I was in high school I had my first sexual experience with a religious member of the faculty. One teacher would take me aside to discuss sexual things and ask if I was aroused, although nothing physical happened. I was not able to discuss this with anyone. Certainly nobody in my family would have believed it. My coming out sexually was not very romantic. I think it happened in a movie theater. I realized from this experience that there was an avenue for male sexual encounters.I was sixteen then and I've been going ever since. Of course it was always very quiet. I would sneak down to Broadway or Times Square. That's what one would do in New York. Of course it was always anonymous sex. I never shared a name or an address. I wasn't able to do this until I was in college.

I have never come out to my parents. We have never sat down and talked about my sexuality. I don't know if I'm doing them an injustice by saying that they are not able to handle it. I may be using that as an excuse, but I think they would rather not be confronted with it. All my brothers know that I am gay, and they probably have discussed it with my parents. I feel for their comfort that we don't have to discuss it. It has in no way stopped me from being outwardly gay. I have been on television and there is always the chance that they would see that. They are eighty years old and I can respect the fact that they don't want to openly discuss my orientation. I'm comfortable with my brothers and my nephews and nieces. They have been to Dignity Mass with me. I am out at the office and with all my friends. There is no one I know as a friend who doesn't know I'm gay. I don't advertise that I am gay, but there is no way that I would hide it. I moved from New York to San Francisco ten years ago. I requested a transfer from the bank I worked with in New York. There was an opening and I moved here. I hope to always live here.

I joined Dignity on Pentecost Sunday. I enjoy good music in church, and they have an unusual choir here. The liturgies are so beautiful. At first I chose to be nothing but a member. One night I was at a concert and I ran into a Sister of the Good Shepherd. She challenged me to stop sitting in the background and share my talents with the organization. Shortly after that there was a crisis in the chapter, and I stood up to point out the value of the organization and that this one crisis should not stymie us. From that day on I was involved. I went from the board of directors to secretary, to the national board of directors. Then I became co-chair of the chapter for two years.

The membership of Dignity is graying. One of the reasons this is happening is that twenty years ago it was able to attract people like me who went through ten or twelve or more years of Catholic education. Because there were so many of us, Dignity was able to appeal to these people. Today fewer and fewer people are going through the Catholic educational system. The Catholic Church is not part of their roots. I think those who joined Dignity and found a community and believed that the Gospel has freed them, will leave. I think we will see more of a solidarity with the Women's Church. This approach might well attract a different type of individual that we haven't reached before.

My response to the Ratzinger letter was shock and anger. I still don't understand why the church is hung up about gay people. There are so many other areas where the church needs to be involved and speak out: poverty, overpopulation, AIDS in Africa, and many other social issues. I just can't understand how the official church can say something like this when one considers the amount of homosexuality that touches the church. When they talk about intrinsic evil, they should look at the letter itself. It is evil. I was willing to stand up with those who would condemn this letter. I went to rallies. I participated in education for those who were confused and angry.

I believe that the Cathedral Project, which is a public protest during the church services at St. Patrick's Cathedral in New York, will come to Chicago and even to San Francisco. We have found an avenue where they are going to listen, because the church listens when there are tv cameras. We are going to win this war. I want my life affirmed by the Catholic Church. It might not happen while I am alive, but I do expect to see the church review all its teaching on sexuality, not just homosexuality. Some pastor asked what my beliefs were on homosexuality. I told him I had the same faith in the church's teaching on homosexuality that any senior in high school has on the teaching on masturbation. It doesn't affect me, or the adolescent, or the young couple who needs to practice birth control. The church does not really touch these people with its teaching on sexuality.

When church people study homosexuality they should listen to the stories of those who are homosexual. The bishops of California said in their pastoral letter that we can and need to learn from the lesbian and gay community how they have responded to the crisis of AIDS with love and compassion. They wouldn't have said this five years ago. We have done a wonderful service to the church and I think eventually we will be acknowledged for that. Five years ago they would not say gay, they would say homosexual. Now they say gay. Maybe there is hope.

I met my lover Ken at Dignity. I had known him three years before we began our relationship. I was on the board of directors with him for a period. We were friends and we liked each other but hadn't considered a relationship. Three years after I met him he became ill. He went into the hospital, and no one quite knew what was wrong with him. Finally he was diagnosed as having pneumocystis pneumonia, which is a diagnosis for AIDS. He was in the hospital over Thanksgiving. Sixty members of the chapter went to the hospital for Mass at the hospital chapel. This was a tremendous morale booster. It even made him feel well enough to ask the doctor to go home for Thanksgiving dinner. From that visit he said he would enjoy company in the hospital rather than phone calls. After he got out we had dinner together, and it developed into a relationship. I knew he was dying. But that didn't hinder our relationship.

It grew into a beautiful love story. It was very special for years. We decided early on that we didn't have time to waste being angry or fighting with each other, but that we would grow great memories. He had been a Franciscan seminarian for a few years and had a great desire to visit Assisi, Italy. So we spent Easter in Assisi. He always wanted to go to the Caribbean, and we went there. We had three really exciting years together. He was well during most of the time. He had a great love of life and wanted to do a lot with his life. I felt blessed being able to share that with him. I have good memories. He was an articulate spokesman for people with AIDS. He was on "60 Minutes." He was interviewed on several local television shows. He had a good relationship with the church, really with Jesus more than with the church. I was happy with the support we received at Dignity in that relationship. In the last few months of his life he needed someone to be with him constantly. There was always a member of Dignity when I couldn't be here. It really showed a community of love. He died December 8, 1986.

I think my energy in the future will go into the AIDS ministry. I have never been available for the training. I either have been out of the city or involved in something that prevented me from taking part in the training. I plan to get involved in the next training sessions.

TONY LAVECCIA

Tony works as a free-lance graphic designer in Washington, D.C. He is one of the founders of the Dignity chapter in Washington.

I was born in Brooklyn, New York, in 1936, of Italian parents. My father died when I was three. Raised by my mother and grandmother, my early life was nevertheless quite normal. I went to Catholic grammar school, and then to Brooklyn Tech high school. At Pratt Institute in Brooklyn, where I studied graphics design, I received a BFA degree. After graduation I worked for a while in New York and didn't like the rat race. If you know anything about the advertising game, you know it's a vicious business in New York. You work for an agency, but if the agency loses the account, everybody who services that account is fired automatically. That's the nature of the game. I had the opportunity to come to Washington in 1959.

I guess at that time I was aware of my homosexuality but I didn't act on it until I was about twenty-four years old, two years after I got to Washington. At the time there was a great deal of guilt involved. I went to confession but got the impression that what I did was not a sin. The priest told me to keep coming to confession, and that "we all have this problem."

People didn't talk about sex like they do today. There were no support groups at the time for gays and lesbians. It was an isolated existence then. I didn't feel very good about my sexuality. All information coming from the outside was very negative, different from the way it is now. When I engaged in sex it wasn't to form a relationship, but more one-night-only anonymous sex.

At the time I had a fetish for the military. There was a bar downtown that is no longer there where all the military hung out. It could also be a very dangerous place. Some people went there with the express intention to beat up faggots and rob them. In my early days I did have a few bad experiences. I was actually stabbed once. I took a person home who, it turned out, was setting me up. Two of his friends followed us home and broke into the apartment after we got there. A scuffle ensued, and if I had not resisted maybe I wouldn't have gotten stabbed. I can remember to this day saying the Hail Mary over and over because I thought I was gone. At first, being stunned, I didn't realize that I had been stabbed; then I saw blood running out of my stomach. I rushed over to the emergency room at the hospital. Fortunately, I was able to get to the hospital without any trouble. I had to have an exploratory. The intruders got off with what they wanted, my money and some other possessions. That was a very traumatic experience.

Because I didn't feel good about my sexuality I wasn't looking for a lasting relationship. It wasn't exactly a healthy attitude, it was more compulsive. The younger people today are more concerned about forming relationships, and that is more healthy than what was going on in the '50s and '60s. Most of the people I had sex with were very transient. They weren't the kind who offered a chance for developing a relationship. I met some people at that bar with whom I am still friends, so it had both negative and positive sides. I think the people today are lucky to have so many avenues other than the bars to meet people.

My life was pretty much a double life. You wouldn't dare come out at work if you wanted to keep your job. My relationship to the church was not too good at the time. I would go to Mass on Sunday only to realize that everything was geared to married couples and children. Single people didn't seem to matter, especially gays. There certainly wasn't any outreach to gay and lesbian people. People who were gay felt compelled to keep their sexuality hidden. What took me out of this rut was finding Dignity in 1972.

Dignity gave me a sense of community that I never had. We started with a small group of about twenty-four people at the George Washington University Newman Center. It was a small, well-knit group where everybody got along. It helped me get out of being narcissistic and got me interested in other people. I've been with Dignity since then, and it has been a very beneficial experience for me. It has helped me accept my sexuality as something positive rather than as the negative experience that the institutional church always taught.

Dignity has been my salvation. I can now accept my sexuality as an asset rather than an evil. I've been in Dignity for about sixteen years, and I never met one evil person. There are always those you don't get along with or disagree with, but the notion that gay people are inclined toward evil, which you find in the ridiculous and nonsensical Ratzinger letter, has not been my experience.

The Dignity group here has evolved from the original twenty-four people to the present membership of 320. We have a multitude of activities now. In the past it was strictly a Mass and social. We moved from George Washington University to Georgetown. Then this past year we got kicked out of St. William's Chapel by the new Cardinal Archbishop of Washington. I think it's interesting to note that Father Healy, the president of Georgetown, did not want to expel us. Apparently there are some Catholic clergy who disagree with the prevailing attitude towards gay and lesbian people.

My gripe with the institutional church is that they are not interested in gay people as people, but more concerned in upholding rules and regulations. They are trying to impose on people impossible restrictions. If on one hand they say it is all right to be gay but be celibate, I want to know why it is that gay people should have a special prescription for celibacy? Celibacy is not something that should be imposed, it should be freely chosen. We are born this way, and the church should accept the fact that we have a right to some kind of human interaction with people that is sexual, just as heterosexuals have that right. Why should we be denied just because we were born this way? The scriptural arguments that the hierarchy uses to condemn homosexuality are *not* convincing. They seem to me to be selective in how they interpret Scripture and tradition.

The Ratzinger letter was an unfortunate happening. It was a step backward. Before, they never talked about the homosexual tendency as being evil, now they call it evil. I think any gay or lesbian person who reads that filth, and that's what it is, would be greatly disturbed if he or she didn't have a positive self image. This letter has caused a lot of consternation and pain in the gay and lesbian community. I don't think there has been any document in recent church history that has caused as much anguish as this infamous letter. It infers that if you are gay or lesbian you have evil inclinations. I don't think I'm evil, or that God created me with evil inclinations. I'm no more evil than my heterosexual brothers and sisters. I have done some foolish and unwise things in my life, but they did not come from any evil inclination. Anyone who is gay or lesbian and has a positive self image has not taken the letter seriously.

The letter also indirectly promotes violence, by saying it is understandable that there are violent acts toward gay people. Those who tend to be uptight about gays take this as permission for an open season on gays, whether it be verbal or physical assault. The negative implications of the Ratzinger letter will unfortunately be felt for a long time.

Coming from the background that I had, where sexuality was never discussed, and homosexuality would be a mystery, I feel that there is no present need to upset my parents by telling them that I am gay. At age thirty-four the discussion of why I was not getting married ceased. I have no need to burden them with this issue. I have a good relationship with them. At work they knew I was gay. Now I work on a free-lance basis. I have never experienced any harassment about being gay during employment. Of course that may be due to the fact that there are a lot of gay and lesbian people in my profession.

I think today I have a much healthier attitude toward my sexuality. In the '60s I think I didn't like myself too much, or I wouldn't have engaged in such risky behavior. Today I think I have matured to the point where I don't do those things. While I may never have a lover, I do have many very good friends, both men and women. My life to this date has been a kind of reversal from a rather destructive early phase. I shudder when I look back on it; I feel lucky to be alive.

I still harbor a lot of anger and resentment toward the hierarchical church. I rarely go to regular parishes for Mass anymore. The only time I will do that is when I am home visiting family, or for a funeral or wedding. There is no place for me there, I can only experience community at Dignity. Dignity will go on with or without the approbation of the church. The institutional church preaches but doesn't produce a community that is warm, caring, and accepting of gay and lesbian people as they are. Dignity does that.

PEOPLE WITH AIDS

LOU TESCONI

*Lou is the director of Damien Ministries, a community of lay people
whose sole ministry is to people with AIDS, in Washington, D.C. He
is a lawyer by profession. He has AIDS.*

I grew up in rural Vermont. I went to Catholic school from kindergarten
through high school. I went to college, then to law school. I practiced
law for about ten years in New York and Houston. I decided about
three or four years ago that I wanted to pursue my studies for the
priesthood. So I sold everything, gave it all up, and came to Washington
to join the Carmelites. I was in my pre-novitiate year and was diagnosed
with AIDS. The next morning they told me I had to leave. They told
me I could remain as their guest until the end of the semester, but
beyond that I had to leave.

I was up against the wall. I couldn't return to my law practice
because I had sold it, and I agreed not to go back and compete with
anybody. I had no home to return to. I was in a city where I knew
no one. It was a major trauma. A couple of months later when I was
sitting around with nothing to do I found out that the archdiocese of
Washington was having a pastoral workshop on AIDS. I went, and in
the afternoon during a question and answer session I raised my hand
and identified myself. I indicated that I was diagnosed with AIDS and
asked to leave my community as a result. I wanted to know what the
archdiocese was prepared to do for people who were in the same
situation. I got a muddled answer, but was told that I would be called,
and I was. I went to speak with the priest who was then president of
the board of Catholic Charities. He asked what he could do for me.
I said I had a couple of desires that had not been changed by my
diagnosis. I want to live in community and I want to be a minister.
Since I couldn't do that in the Order I had chosen, I wanted to create
a community. He said that was a wonderful idea. You could have

picked me off the floor. We pulled together a group of people, about ten or twelve, who came together periodically. Last February 10 we opened Damien Ministries, which is a community of men and women whose sole ministry is to people with AIDS. It is currently a lay community. I don't know if we are going to bother climbing the canonical ladder. Frankly, I prefer at this point not to be under the thumb of Church authorities. Currently there are three members of the community. We are in the middle of an expansion, trying to find new quarters. We expect to be ten people before the end of the year. We operate two homes for people with AIDS in D.C. One is for women, the only one in the country. We have another for recovering drug addicts with AIDS. We do other kinds of ministry, personal outreach, retreats with people with AIDS and support groups. (Currently there are three homes in Washington, D.C., one in Joliet, Illinois, and one about to be established in New Jersey.)

I'm told that the archbishop is still angry with me for standing up that day and identifying myself and "washing my dirty linens" in public. We are independent of the archdiocese. It was Catholic Charities dollars that got us off the ground, although they now deny that. They agreed to pay the rent on the building for five months, after which we were on our own. Other donations come from religious orders, private individuals, and $75,000 from the government of D.C. On the other hand, we have a kind of working relationship with the archdiocese that we will not get in their way if they don't get in ours. They are happy to have us do the work because whenever it is identified in the media it comes out Catholic. So they look good. It's probably a good arrangement. It's a tough ministry to be in. It crosses so many of the issues the church is uptight about that our independence gives us a little more work room.

The drug addict and street prostitute have none or few services available to them. They are the people we serve. Unfortunately it is now a very trendy ministry. I get letters every day from all over the country from people who want to join us. We are looking for people who are committed to living in community and have an understanding of our ministry. We don't save souls; that's God's work. We try to walk their journey with them. We have had a priest join us but he left because he perceived it as a sacramental ministry. It was not that, so he left. Most of our people are not Catholic, and those that are, are mad at their church. This is hard fingernail sort of work.

A reporter has asked me, how come you have not lost your faith in all this? I gave a flippant answer at the time. I said, listen, when someone is about ready to leave this world you don't take chances. I'm not sure why I don't flip the church a bird. Mostly, because my relationship with God has very little to do with the church. My experience with people who have AIDS is that inevitably they reconcile with their God, but they don't reconcile with the church.

I was educated by traditional nuns. I come from a small family. My father was born in Italy. My mother was born here. My father was a factory worker, my mother a homemaker. It was a strict Catholic upbringing. When I was in high school I sent one of those business reply cards to a vocation director. One Saturday afternoon when I wasn't home he appeared on my doorstep. My mother fed him, of course, and told him they didn't want me as a candidate. He left and I never heard from him again. I bought into that, thinking that mother judged I wasn't fit to be a priest, so I shelved the idea. I decided to pursue law as a career. Through that period that followed, seventeen years, there was a piece of me that I couldn't find. So after seventeen years I thought, I don't want to be seventy and say I should have. So I gave it a try. Through most of that period I was away from the church, trying to find myself. It was a difficult period. It was the late '60s and '70s. As I look back on that time, I realize that all the money in the world, and I had lots of it, all the parties, all added together, didn't amount to anything. I have been in relationships with both women and men, and was not satisfied there. But I was satisfied with my decision to give it all up and enter religious life. At one time it was a toss-up between the Franciscans and Carmelites. I chose the Carmelites. I don't feel that it was a bad decision. I couldn't be doing what I'm doing now if all these things hadn't preceded it.

I don't know if there is any way to be told you are going to die, no matter what the circumstances, and find it easy. There is a part of me that understands the decision to tell me to leave the Order, but there is a part of me that is very angry with the decision. I told them that I was not necessarily interested in studying theology for four years, because I probably didn't have four years to live, but I'd be interested in living in one of their communities. When they said no, that's what I got angry about. I have heard from some community members that if they had to make the decision again, they would have made it differently. I'm at a point in my life when there's not a lot left, so I don't think I want to invest that energy in becoming part of a new community. My present community is very nurturing. If I had seven or eight years to live, it might be a different thing.

I knew when I was in high school that I was gay. For me it wasn't a problem of knowing, it was one of admitting. It took me a good ten years, until I was twenty-five years old, to admit it to myself. I felt very free and liberated when I was able to do this. On the other hand, by the decision I alienated myself from family and certain friends. Most of those relationships have been patched up since. It has caused me problems with my faith from the very beginning. On an intellectual level, I believe that sexuality is a gift from God, and I can't believe that God would give us this gift and not expect us to express it. On the feeling level, I have had people telling me all my life that it is wrong, that it is inherently evil. It's the feeling level that we operate on mostly. It induced lots and lots of guilt. What I believe on an intellectual level, my feelings don't buy. Being a lawyer, I like black and white answers, and this area leaves me confused.

About seven years ago my sister-in-law was in the process of divorcing my brother, and she decided one day that she was going to tell the family all the things about the family they never heard. One bit of that information was that I was gay. I had shared this with my brothers but not my parents. Initially I was very angry, but since then I have thanked her because it made my life a lot easier. It freed me and kept me from growing further apart from my parents. It would have made my AIDS diagnosis even worse. In retrospect, I'm glad it happened.

There's a lot of forgiving that has to happen that I haven't done yet. The first thing I have to do is forgive myself. It's tough work. The church has not been very helpful. The institution isn't budging on the gay issue, and I guess I don't expect it to. My experience with individual priests within the church is that they are as skeptical of the hierarchy as I am, and as a lot of people in the church are. There isn't any church that has really dealt very well with the issue. If and when they begin to listen to the psychological data available, the church will have to change its position. We don't know if we are born gay or learn it early in life. I know it's not a conscious free choice on the part of the person.

When I look at the Ratzinger letter I see it as just part of the same thing one would expect from Rome. It is needless and unnecessary. A lot of my friends are extremely angry over it. My attitude is, consider the source. They talk about ministry to gay people, there is very little of it going on. We have had to minister to ourselves. The church has become terribly misguided. It set up a government. It's obviously not what Jesus had in mind. There comes a time when I say, why fight the battle?

The irony for me is that Dignity is more traditional than most parishes. It seems to use a social situation for people to meet people, and it perverts the purpose of the Eucharistic celebration. As long as I have been in D.C. I have been identified with the AIDS epidemic. Everyone I know involves a business relationship, and that complicates things. In addition, we live where we work, which is extremely difficult. It's a compromise I've had to make. In the middle of all this I'm getting ready to die. That could come at any time. I could wake up tomorrow on my death bed.

I was talking to one of the members of my community the other night. He said, you haven't been engaging in denial, but you have been denying your feelings. Early on I think I just shut down my feelings, just turned them off. It's now starting to cause me problems. I sunk into a rather deep depression recently. I shut my feelings off when I was diagnosed almost two years ago. It's finally caught up with me two years later. I suppose a certain amount of denial is healthy. You really can't function if you focus constantly on the fact that you are going to die. It's difficult to let go of people. It will be difficult to let go of Damien Ministries. I've created the baby and I'm happy with it. But I'm getting used to the idea. Once I get back in touch with my emotions, there will be a lot of healing.

From a faith point of view, I believe that there has been a reason for my good health up to now, reasons for my joining the Carmelites, reasons for being thrown out. It's unnerving on the faith level to see things happen, things that can't be chalked up to coincidence. It is also very satisfying.

On an intellectual level, I have grown a lot. The one thing I have seen in this ministry is that the more you get into ministry, the more the walls between faiths crumble. Whether someone is Catholic, Protestant or Jewish is irrelevant. But until I get back in touch with my feelings, I am still incomplete. One of the toughest things about all this is that there are people who are acquaintances and close friends who have died. I stopped counting after a hundred. How much of that can any person go through? There isn't a bereavement group created that can deal with that kind of thing. In the middle of all this we see the government standing still, and the church as an institution shying away. Certain pockets of the church have done well with the issue.

Here in D.C., Mother Theresa was invited to open a hospice. Since then they have taken the attitude, we've done our part. As a matter of fact, Mother Theresa's place is catering to people who are in their last days, to whom the strict rules under which they live aren't important.

The place is run like a monastery. There is no TV, you can't go out after a certain hour, you can only have visitors on a limited basis. The attitude is, if you want to live in our convent you can, but you have to live by our rules. They are filling a need, but when they opened, some church people thought that it was going to be the salvation of all the people who are homeless and have AIDS.

At Damien Ministries we guarantee people a place to live until they die. We set the homes up as independent living situations, so that while they are able to care for themselves they do. When they can't care for themselves and need hospitalization, we facilitate that. We can provide home care, but not nursing care. We don't charge for our services at all. We hope to open two more homes this year, and we expect them to be full in short order.

One of our intentions when we opened was to be a place where priests and religious with AIDS could come. That hasn't happened for a lot of reasons. Communities by and large are taking care of their own. For some reason the disease has not spread among diocesan priests but it is rampant among the religious orders. The problem is not going away. When I was interviewed for the religious community, I told them up front who I was, that I had a past, and that I wasn't going back into the closet for anyone. I was not going to wear my sexuality on my sleeve, but the person I was would not change. They were very comfortable with that, and I was comfortable with it. My estimate is that at least fifty percent of the religious are gay.

I don't think the church is going to change soon. Faith is like a package deal, once you buy into it you automatically buy into a lot of baggage. The progress for gays depends on where the AIDS issue goes. Too many people have linked gays with the AIDS issue. Until we get beyond that we will be stuck; in fact we have already regressed a little. There is a lot of hate out there, because people are blaming it on gay people. There are a lot of horror stories. I had someone call me two weeks ago from Connecticut who was diagnosed with AIDS. He was told by his Catholic pastor that he was no longer welcome in the parish. Until we get beyond that fear, there will be little progress.

The book *And the Band Played On* by Randy Shilts shows where the government really dropped the ball because of the people who were victimized by this disease. In 1976 twenty-six American Legion members contracted a disease, and the government really moved in on it. Within a year they had discovered the cause and the treatment. If AIDS had attacked Legionnaires instead of gays, the government's response would have been a lot different. Gays, drug addicts, and prostitutes are on the fringes of society, always have been. They are considered expendable elements of the population. Until that changes, there will be little progress.

JOHN O'LEARY

John died in early November 1990, after working with a gay rights organization and engaging in political lobbying. He had a law degree from the University of Minnesota.

I am the oldest of six children in a very conservative Irish Catholic family near Boston. My parents still don't eat meat on Friday. They prefer the Mass in Latin. They are very active with the Catholic schools. I went to sixteen years of Catholic schools. I went to a Catholic grade and high school, then to a Catholic college. After that I took a year off, then went to law school at the University of Minnesota. Part of my reason for going to the Catholic college was that I received a scholarship from the Knights of Columbus, called Pro Deo et Pro Patria, a four-year scholarship.

When I was in elementary and high school, I was involved in what most other kids were. I was an altar boy, I studied Latin, I was a delegate to the Catholic Youth Council when I was in high school. I listened to my parents and really didn't doubt their views, which were pretty conservative. During college I became more lax in attending Mass regularly.

As far as my sexual orientation goes, it seems that a lot of people realize which sex they are attracted to around puberty. For me it happened later, after I was in college. I went through high school without any tensions or problems. I was successful in high school. I was involved with the yearbook, the newspaper, and student government. When I got to college, toward the end of my freshman year I started to realize that I was attracted to guys. I recognized that the girls I liked, I liked because I knew them. This was also true with guys, except that I noticed that there were some guys on campus that I thought I would like to meet. I didn't know them, so it couldn't be personality that attracted me but rather their physical appearance. There were no girls I wanted to meet just because I was attracted to them. I got the first inkling that I might be attracted to guys, but I felt this was a terrible thing, so I admitted that maybe I was bisexual.

During the next couple of years it became more apparent to me that I was attracted to the same sex and had no particular attraction to females. It took me a long time before I was able to say to myself in the quiet of my own mind, I am gay. It was a huge step just to admit that to myself. After that I relegated it to the back burner. That was one part of me, but it was a part I was not going to tell anyone about. I planned to get married and have a lot of children. I remember thinking that this is terrible that I am homosexual because I had an ideal view of what marriage would be. It would be a perfect partnership between me and my wife, and this is something I couldn't tell her. I figured I couldn't tell anyone, it is so terrible. If I were ever to whisper it to someone it would be long after my parents were dead so they would have no chance of hearing about it.

I don't consciously remember any sort of negative teaching coming from my parents or the church or school about homosexuality. I think I picked it up by osmosis from my parents. Even when I realized in college that I was homosexual I didn't want it, and I thought maybe I could change it. When I would masturbate I would think of girls. It didn't help. Women have as much sexual excitement for me as a turtle. So what I would do was think of some guy I had just seen on campus or on tv and then masturbate until the point of orgasm. Then I would start to think of girls when it was impossible to stop the process, thinking that this is my own little therapy that might help me in some way. Despite the fact that most normal college students were doing this at least once a day, it was really a very repressed and back burner type of thing for me. It stayed pretty well buried.

In my senior year in college there was a group of gays that applied for official recognition as a gay group on campus. I was news editor of the student paper and had to write stories about the gay group. The editorial board wrote editorials in favor of the group. I was gratified to see all the support that was there. No one had any inkling about me. I didn't know any of the gay students. This kind of stirred up the waters for me. It was difficult not to think about myself. Also, at that time, a friend of mine told me that he was bisexual. This was the first person who had ever done this, and it got me thinking also.

There was a pressure cooker going on in me. Everywhere I turned there was some stimulus. The resident director of my dorm, a priest, "came out" in an interview in the daily paper. The very thing I didn't want to think about was the thing I thought about most. I felt that I had everything going for me except this one thing that I could not even whisper to someone. My fantasy was that if I told someone they would come after me with a net like I was a butterfly.

When I came back for my last semester in senior year, I remember the day very clearly, January 25, 1979. I woke up that morning and it was like any other morning. That afternoon my best friend called. He was resident assistant and lived by himself in another hall. On impulse I said, "Can I come over to see you? I have something to tell you." I went over, sat on his bed, and wasn't sure I could say what I knew I had to say. It was a big gamble, but I trusted him. So I decided, just like when I was a kid and jumped into the cold pool, to count to three and plunge in. I counted to three and said, "I am gay." He knew I had never had sex with anyone. He was doubtful that I was gay because I hadn't had sex. He tried to fix me up with a girl so I could have sex and find out for sure. He was trying to keep me from making a wrong choice if I really wasn't gay.

That was such a turning point in my life. Before I told him I could keep putting it on the back burner. Once I told him I could never again go back to earlier times. It was hard to get to that point because everyone assumes that you are heterosexual until you are able to admit the opposite. This was such a relief, because everything else in my life was wonderful except this secret. When my friend accepted me as someone he cared about no matter what my sexual orientation, it was such a wonderful experience. When I realized that I could control this information and not have to tell my parents, this was also helpful in coming out.

A couple of days later I told another friend, and then another. Each of them accepted me as I was, much to my relief. I've heard of other people committing suicide when they realized they were homosexual. I can understand the pressure they were under. I think what kept me going was that deep in myself I knew that I was a good person. That can be credited to my parents, to the way they gave us each a sense of personal value. When I told my parents that I was gay, I explained to them that their training helped me get through that crisis.

I probably told fifty or sixty people that I was gay that last semester before I graduated from college. I had not had sex with anyone. I originally assumed I would not have sex until I got married. It didn't dawn on me till later why it was so easy to be a good Catholic boy. Other guys were having sex with their girlfriends, and I assumed that they were exaggerating. I only later realized why it was easy for me to not have sex before marriage. I modified my views a little about people having sex before marriage, because some of my best friends were doing it and I knew they were good people. That was the kind of thinking I had when I came out on January 25, 1979.

I felt that before I had sex with a guy I would want to fall in love first. However, now my thinking was in a process of change. My friend said I should go to bed with somebody, male or female, before I tell everyone I was gay. I was pretty sure that I was gay, and I was feeling all right about it. I felt it was important to tell my friends, people who liked and respected me, that I was gay, because at some future time when they are faced with gay issues in a referendum or with other people, I didn't want them to think of gay people in the abstract. I wanted them to think of their college friend John O'Leary. I still had not been to a gay bar or involved in any gay groups.

I considered talking to a priest. There were two priests on campus that I thought about. One was the resident director of my dorm who had come out, or I could talk to another priest who was a psychologist. He was more conservative on the gay issue. So I decided to talk to both of them. The gay priest was great. He helped me think through my plans to get married. He made sense to me, and I realized he was right. The priest psychologist tried to convince me that I was not gay. I didn't fit the image. He said, "You don't have the 'aura' of a homosexual." He said, "I don't think anyone can know he is homosexual without having sex with anyone." I challenged him that no one, homo- or heterosexual, would know his orientation until after he was married or had sex with someone. He admitted the good logic in my position. After that the discussion ended.

Around this time I met a guy in the fraternity I belonged to. I got vibes that he was gay. I was powerfully attracted to him. There was going to be a fraternity party, and I decided that this would be a good occasion to have sex. On Monday of that week, I asked my roommate if he could go and stay with his girlfriend on Friday night. He was very excited; he said, "Is that going to be the night?" Everybody on my floor in the dorm heard about it and was helpful. One guy donated his bong toward that effort. Everybody knew that Friday was the night that something was going to happen for John. I went to the party and said to Mike, "Would you like to come back to my room after the party to smoke a joint or listen to music?" He agreed. We went to the dorm. Mike and I had sex. That's all it really was. He didn't show any affection and he left right after it was over. I was really disappointed. It confirmed my original feelings that I didn't want to go to bed with someone until I loved him. Apparently Mike was pretty experienced in sexual matters, as I found out later from some friends. I enjoyed it immensely and it helped confirm to me that I was gay.

Here I was, twenty-two years old, and it was the first time that I had ever been naked with anyone. Physically it felt fine, but it didn't mentally. I couldn't sleep that night. At four in the morning I was in the laundry washing the sheets. This happened in March, and I didn't go to bed with anyone again until I graduated from college.

Between my first sexual encounter and graduation I read every article about gay civil rights and other gay issues. I should have been studying for exams, but I spent most of my time in the library reading about Anita Bryant and skimmed what books I could about gay issues. I soon discovered that there were a lot of gay bars, and also a rainbow of gay organizations. I heard about Dignity, but avoided it while I was still in college. The first Sunday after graduation I went to Dignity for the first time. It was wonderful. Here was a group of people who were basically like me, with the same kind of background. I went every Sunday until I went to law school a year and a half later.

I met a guy named Ron that summer through a gay youth group that he was counseling. We were attracted to one another and started dating in July. He was planning, like I was, to go to law school after a year off. He went to law school in 1980 and hated it, so he dropped out and came back home in November. During all that time we were still in a relationship and being monogamous. We got an apartment together in January of 1980. I wanted to go to law school and Ron wanted to become a doctor. We tried to find a university that had both a law school and a school of medicine. We applied to about six places and got into the University of Minnesota. The first summer we came back to home, and I got a job as an intern with a gay rights organization. Ron got a job at a medical center. Our relationship sort of deteriorated sometime in the summer of 1981. We went to a counselor at the university, but each of us was growing in different directions. We broke up in the summer of 1982. We see each other every now and then.

Over the years I have developed some very definite ideas about the church and the hierarchy. As I became imbued with the spirit of gay civil rights and more aware of sexism and feminism, I started to realize that the structure of the Catholic Church is all wrong. With all authority at the top, it is too much like the kingdoms of the middle ages. When Cardinal O'Connor disagreed with Geraldine Ferraro when she was running for vice president I thought, what right does he have to say anything to her? He was described as her spiritual leader and she had not one word to say about his selection. Until the structure of the church changes, I don't want to be part of it. I feel that Dignity serves a good purpose, because it is a bit of thorn in the side of the hierarchy.

A year ago, I discovered that I have been exposed to the AIDS virus. I'm HIV positive. I was very depressed for six weeks after finding out about that. In the intervening year I have been monitoring my immune system for my T-cells. Just last Tuesday I got the test results; they had gone below 200, which is the point where doctors recommend that you get on AZT even though there are no symptoms. I was home this weekend and told my parents and my brothers and sisters that I am HIV positive and that my T-cell count is going down. It was in January of this year that my younger brother told me he has AIDS. He has since told all the family. He is married. Naturally my family was very upset to be told about me, but they were very supportive. It was extremely difficult to tell my parents, but I feel a little relief now that I have.

As far as the Catholic Church goes, I don't think about it a lot. Some of the recent developments, especially the Ratzinger letter, I see as ridiculous. I was planning to have children either through adoption or through a surrogate mother. The church also seems to make this a moral evil. It condemns procreation without sex, and sex without procreation. I think there is too much fixation on sex; you never hear comments about stealing, lying, or killing, which I think are the big three. I think the fixation is due to celibate old men who don't know what they are talking about.

I plan to go back to Dignity, mostly because of the supportive community. Now that I am HIV positive I want to see more of my family and friends. I'm dealing more realistically with my own mortality. I'm faced with the possibility of dying in the next few years, perhaps dying a terrible death. I've always felt comfortable with the idea of getting old and dying, but the threat coming this early, at age thirty-one, was not expected. I am at peace with myself, and with the idea of dying sooner than I expected. I'm doing everything I can to prevent it, and I'm trying to keep a positive attitude through mental imaging and other routines. At this time I'm not really looking to the Catholic Church for spiritual nourishment. Perhaps I'll change later.

The name in this story has been changed to protect the privacy of the individual.

COUPLES

JIMMY KENNEDY and
DERRICK A. TYNAN-CONNOLLY

Jimmy and Derrick live in San Francisco. Jimmy is twenty-five years old. He will be attending school at the American Conservatory Theater, in a three-year Master's program. Derrick is twenty-four years old. He is planning to go to school at San Francisco State University to get his credentials for teaching high school.

Jimmy: I was born in San Francisco. My great-grandparents bought this house in 1917, so we are kind of rooted here. I am the middle of seven children. I went to parochial school and to a Jesuit high school where my father teaches. After high school I went to Stanford for my freshman year of college, and during that year I decided to enter the Jesuits. It was there that Derrick and I met. We entered in August and by December we had fallen in love. As things unfolded, we feel lucky in our process of coming out: we have had people with us all the way helping us work this out. There was always a supportive person, asking questions and challenging us, but always giving a lot of love and support. We have been a rock of support to one another through a process of confusion and doubt.

Derrick: I was born and raised in Los Angeles. Both my parents and my sister were born in Ireland, with a strong Catholic background. They moved here in 1963, and I was born in 1964. I went through Catholic grammar school and a Jesuit high school. During my last couple of years of high school there was something inside me causing me distress. I wasn't quite sure what it was. I think deep down it was the issue of homosexuality, but at that point I wasn't ready to deal with that. So I started thinking about the Jesuits, how they lived their lives, and I respected them. I thought that would be a good life for me. I entered the same year as Jimmy.

Neither of us had confronted our homosexuality. As we became friends it was a very unspoken thing. Neither of us thought of broaching the subject of the possibility that we were gay. As the months went on our friendship became closer and closer. The Jesuit novitiate was in an atmosphere of beauty and peace, in the hills above Santa Barbara. It's a beautiful place, with hundreds of acres, a view of the ocean, beach house and all. We were removed from society and family and friends with tons of free time to spend with one another. There was no responsibility, no car insurance or bills. A lot of time to play. No one was telling us that intimacy between two men was bad, in fact it was encouraged. This was your family that you were to get to know.

I had felt a special attraction to Jimmy as a friend because we had a lot in common. It still was not a sexual thing—I was not aware of sexual feelings toward him. What it turned into was a real infatuation. It wasn't until January that we were head over heels in love. Even then when it became a physical relationship we couldn't admit that we were gay. It was physical, but we rationalized that it happened because we were in this closed society with all men, and I'm just in love with *one* man. I don't feel that way about *all* men. We stayed in the community until the end of 1983. Jimmy left in November and I in December of 1983.

Obviously we were torn both ways. We would like to have stayed, but this lifestyle supposedly is not acceptable in the Catholic clergy. What confused the situation was that there were older men in the community who made passes. There were very vibrant sexual things going on. Within my first few weeks there someone made a pass at me. I reacted with fear. I'm eighteen years old, this is the last thing in the world I expected in this place. I thought when I cam here I wouldn't have to deal with sexual things. I thought well, I'm a Jesuit now, I can just forget about my sexuality, it's not an issue anymore. I'm a good person, I can do good work.

In my relationship with Jimmy, we became friends first, and the friendship just followed a natural progression of deepening of intimacy and sharing until it became physical. But even at the beginning, though I knew something so based on love and affection couldn't be bad, our process of fully accepting our gayness has just happened in the last couple of years. After we left the novitiate we gave each other space to date women and see where that would go. We had a number of long separations. He was here in San Francisco and I was in Spain for a semester. He was in El Salvador for a while. But all these separations just kept leading us back to one another. We realized that this was the person I want to spend my life with. How can I contemplate dating someone else when my heart is with him? The difficult part of the whole thing was the way my parents dealt with it. There has been complete non-acceptance of our relationship even to this day, which is five and a half years later. June 20, 1987, we celebrated our wedding. We wrote the vows for ourselves. All the family members were invited. A lot of Jimmy's family was there and a lot of our good friends.

My parents and brother and sister did not attend the wedding. My parents treat Jimmy as if he were a non-existent person. Originally when Jimmy was just a friend they loved him and brought him gifts from Ireland. When they were faced with our real relationship a wall went up. They don't want to hear his name, they don't want to talk to him or see him, he is not welcome in their home. Supposedly I'm welcome in their home if I go alone and not talk about Jimmy and play the "straight charade" with them. I haven't done this in a long time. There is little reason to go there when they don't accept the most significant part of my life. Some of it may be based on their religious upbringing, but I don't think that's the major part of it. They even said it's not that the Catholic Church is against homosexuality; it seems to be more the societal issues. I'm grateful that Jimmy's parents have been so accepting. I don't feel as isolated from a family environment as I might feel otherwise. I'm hopeful that the love Jimmy and I share will someday get through to my dad and mom.

Jimmy: I feel that I'm a schismatic Catholic. I have a lot of attachment to the Catholic symbols and liturgy, but I can't feel part of it with the position it takes on homosexuality. When one day the church does embrace homosexuals and women as equals, then I might come back. But I don't expect that to happen in my lifetime.

Derrick: When we talk about our personal relationship with God, at some point every individual has to make a decision when to embark on that relationship with God. The church may be able to help some people to a certain point, but at some time one has to say, leave church behind, leave dogmas behind, and personally embark on that journey with God. Although I don't go to Mass anymore or pray as long as I did in the novitiate, I feel that I am a much more spiritual and whole person since having come out of the closet. The spirit of the Gospels is to create wholeness and make people whole again. For years my faith wasn't making me whole, but keeping me divided. When I accepted my gayness fully I felt the beginning of wholeness and completeness. I never felt that before as a practicing member of the church. When Jimmy and I talk about the Gospel passages, we think how in Latin America the Gospel has been interpreted for the oppressed people in terms of liberation theology; we find that it is equally liberating for us as gay people to read the Gospel from the perspective of the gay person. Jesus was a sensitive and sensual man. Heterosexuals simply assume that Jesus was straight. Yet he was more fully human, as we see in his relationship with John. They have tried to "create" Jesus in their image; but it is people who are created in the image and likeness of God. Thus my sexuality is a reflection of that image and one I am thankful for.

A passage that I never understood before was the one where Jesus said I have not come to bring peace. I will cause division, father against son, mother against daughter. Before it never made sense, now I know what it means. Being truthful with my parents and telling them who I am has not brought us peace, but has caused extreme division in the family. It makes me angry. I struggle between wanting to be patient with them and give them time, and growing more impatient and wanting to reprimand them for their behavior. If I had treated people in a bigoted way when I was a kid because of the color of their skin or where they were from, I would have been reprimanded by my parents. Here they are, usually the most hospitable, generous and kind people in the world, and they treat the person who is the most important person in my life as if he didn't exist. I have spent the last five and a half years of my life with Jimmy, building a relationship, and have committed my life to him. Here we have a relationship that is really working based on trust, faithfulness, and commitment, and they can see it as evil or bad. They would "accept" us if we lived in the closet, if we never mentioned that we were a couple. I keep telling them when they say they love me that they don't love me but rather an image in their mind who I should be. I told them that person doesn't exist.

At the end of my junior year in college I told them I was gay. Jimmy was coming back to Stanford for the senior year, and we decided to move in together for our last year in college. I decided I had better tell my parents in advance because they were helping out financially, and I figured if they were to withdraw their support there would be time for me to make other arrangements. Despite their inability to support me emotionally, they continued to show their love with financial support during the coming year. I am hopeful that some day they will be able

to share in our happiness as well. Jimmy and I had some real eye
openings, and one day we said, what the hell are we doing. I love you,
you love me, and we want to spend our lives together, who cares what
people think, let's just do it. We went to talk to Jimmy's family together.
I knew with my parents we could not talk face to face. We tried before
and immediately there was no listening. There was lecturing, raised
voices, crying, and nothing got said. So I finally decided to write them
a letter, a fifteen-page letter explaining how much I loved them, and
what good and supportive parents they had been. I talked about the
last few years, when I felt that the relationship had ended for me, that
there was no communication. I have been unable to share with them
who I really was and the important things in my life. I said I was telling
them this because I would like to have that relationship with them
again. I sent them the letter on Tuesday, and they called and said they
would be here Saturday morning. My dad's first statement was, "Is
there anything we can say to talk you out of this?" I said no. Then
they tried everything. We went through guilt, then to family obligations,
and the suggestion that I should sacrifice my personal happiness for
the sake of the family. It would be better for me if I went through life
as a single man, rather than have somebody in my life. I said, "Are
you serious? Would you rather have me go through life never having
loved anyone or be loved by someone just to spare the family
embarrassment?" My dad said no, we don't want that. But from there
the willingness to talk and discuss the issue is very limited. They keep
saying, we don't want to change our minds. We've read the books you
have given us, this is the way we feel.

Jimmy: It's interesting that in the fifteen-page letter that Derrick wrote
to his parents, the one thing that gave them hope was a short phrase
that a priest suggested that we insert. It said that we will be together
"for the foreseeable future." I had asked a Jesuit friend if he had any
advice on how to come out to our parents. He thought that mentioning
that our commitment was life-long was perhaps too much too soon.
Soften it, he said, by saying foreseeable future. Immediately Derrick's
parents picked up on that phrase and said how can you say that this
relationship is like ours or any other married couple's? Even you do
not think it will last forever. You say it is for the foreseeable future,
do you call that commitment? Needless to say, that is the last time we
asked a closeted person for out-of-the-closet advice. Another difference
among our parents was that because we were going to school here in
northern California, my parents had the chance to see us together a lot

more than Derrick's parents who were away from us the whole time. The time they did see us was when we were so obviously in love that they didn't have to guess much. They saw it as disaster down the road. Whereas, my parents saw us at birthdays and family get-togethers. They loved Derrick very much before I had come out to them. I think my dad considered Derrick another son. My grandmother was our biggest supporter and closest mutual friend. She loves Derrick very, very much.

For me, coming out to my family was more than just admitting I was gay, but also sharing that Derrick and I were lovers. That's why I thought it was important for him to be there when I shared this with my parents. My mom is uncanny in her intuitions, so I think she knew. My dad was reading a book and kept his face down and listened and nodded his head. He said, "Well, whatever makes you two happy, I guess that's fine." On the whole, my brothers and sisters have been very supportive. Whereas Derrick's parents are very outspoken, mine are more quiet. I don't always know their doubts and questions. I try to encourage them to voice their concerns. But from every visible signal I can get, they are very supportive. My sister and brother-in-law, my grandmother, and my mother came to our wedding ceremony. The rest of my family came to the party afterward. My grandmother was like our "Best Person." A Jesuit friend gave a beautiful Irish blessing at the end. All in all, my family has really been great to us.

Derrick: We were still going to Mass when the Pope's letter came out on the "Pastoral Care of Homosexuals." That was the straw that broke the camel's back. I was so pissed off. We had been rationalizing for a while that it's just the hierarchy and they are not the church. What was more disturbing was the deafening silence of the hierarchy and clergy. We know so many clergy, especially Jesuits, who are homosexual, and all in the closet. None of these people whom we admired for so long spoke out about that atrocious letter. There is an underlying hypocrisy here. The worst part of the letter is the tacit approval of violence toward gay people. What I consider "immoral" is that the Jesuit high school and university that I attended continue to graduate so many homophobic people when there is the potential for these priests who are in the closet to teach the truth about homosexuality. They are followers of Jesus. Jesus was nailed to the cross for speaking the truth. How can they be silent when gay people are being persecuted?

Jimmy: Once again we saw the act of rationalization exercised in full force. We had a copy of the letter and read it. Then we heard clergy interpret it as if it didn't say what it said. Because of their silence they are accomplices to the violence that results. If the clergy were to get into their pulpits and say, as Catholics you can't have homosexual relations, then I would feel, okay I have a choice, I can leave the church. But the church is not content to teach its own people only; it enters the public forum and tries to impose its teaching on others. Every time a gay civil rights bill comes up in this country, at the forefront of the opposition is the Catholic church. There seems to be a lack of compassion and understanding.

When you think of all the things in the world the church could be fighting against, why are they fighting this issue? Why are they fighting intimate relationships founded in love? I can see the church speaking out against promiscuity, but why the attack on relationships based on love, when there are so many true evils in the world? It seems that they are threatened. Our experience of thirteen months in the novitiate affected our perception of the church. We had a great love for the church. But now my experience is that they are the pharisees of today.

Derrick: I can only imagine what it would have been like when I was young and struggling with my sexual identity, if one of the many homosexual teachers I had would have had the courage to be out of the closet. This would have had a tremendous effect on my life as a young man, and my acceptance of who I am. I hope as a teacher I can be a role model for gay and straight kids to live lives of dignity and integrity.

Jimmy: We only had negative models when we were young. Our hope is that good will come out of positive examples of gay love. Maybe more priests and nuns have to be kicked out for being homosexual. Once you know and love and trust someone, it doesn't make any difference what their sexual orientation is. They could say, "Father Joe is a great guy, he is the most compassionate person I know. His openness about being gay does not change my regard for him." We see the need for these positive examples today, not only from clergy but from teachers and counselors. If there is anything that is going to change the homophobia in the world today, the hope lies in the young people. We need to let others know that gay people can be happy and live fulfilled lives with wonderful relationships. To see them as not evil, intrinsically or otherwise.

Derrick: We are both members of the Harvey Milk Lesbian and Gay Democratic Club. Jimmy delivers food to people with AIDS. In the fall I'll be speaking in public high schools with a program called "Demystifying Homosexuality," sponsored by Community United Against Violence. I think where we do the most for gay people is just being open. I see the tremendous effect it has on the people at work for me to be an openly gay person, and to have a picture of Jimmy on my wall, and bring him to Christmas parties and picnics. A friend at work just got back from Denver from a wedding. He told me how people ask if he ever saw a fag in San Francisco. He said, first of all the word is gay, not fag. I don't like the word fag. And the guy who sits next to me at work is married to a man and he is a fine person. Then he explained why he wasn't afraid of getting AIDS by being close to gay people. He told me that if he had never met me, the fag remark would have passed right over his head. So I think my greatest contribution is to be open about who I am. It is our responsibility to make this world a better place for the children coming after us. A lot of gay kids commit suicide or hate themselves because the feelings they have are condemned by everybody around them: family, society, and churches. They feel alone, frightened, and ashamed. *This* is sinful. If at the end of my life I have not helped make this society more accepting and tolerant for these kids, *that* will be my shame.

Editor's note: Since this interview, Derrick has begun a process of reconciliation with his family, which he describes in these words.

Last November my dad wrote me a letter expressing my parents' desire for reconciliation. They were not sure how this might happen, but they were open to suggestions. I responded eagerly and asked them to welcome both Jimmy and me into their home. On Christmas day my mom called and asked if Jimmy and I would like to come down to Los Angeles to their home on our birthday weekend (mine is February 3 and Jimmy's is February 6). We went down and had a great time, even with the uncomfortableness that will obviously take time to get over. But we're on a roll! My parents have been up to our place to visit at the eighty-eighth birthday party we threw for Jimmy's grandmother at the beginning of June, and we went down there again for my mom's birthday at the end of June. I think this is something a lot of young gay people and heterosexual people need to hear—all people really need to hear the message of reconciliation.

MAUREEN HICKEY and NANCY SWISTEK

Maureen and Nancy live in a committed monogamous relationship near Chicago. They both work in printing-related businesses.

Maureen: I went to a Catholic grammar school and a Catholic all-girls high school. It was some time during high school that I began to realize that I was different, although I didn't really know what that meant. Being in an all-girls school has advantages in terms of being allowed to show affection for one another. Life was really easy for me in high school. After high school I went to college for a couple of years. It was then that I realized that I was gay. I had some problems with the church, but I was so happy realizing that I was gay that if the church said I was wrong, I still knew that I was right. I just kind of left the church and said, let them think and believe what they want. I knew they were wrong. I never doubted God's love for me.

Years later I met Dignity and found that I was not alone in this situation. It was good to find other people who felt the same as I did. I didn't have a lot of trauma dealing with being gay. I was always sure that this is who I am and that it must be right. I've had it relatively easy. The only boys I liked were the softer, nicer boys. But my heart always raced when I was around women.

I fell in love for the first time when I was nineteen. I really knew and accepted that I was gay. That was a wonderful experience. The only problem with this relationship was that the other woman didn't think she was gay. We got involved in intimate things, but she would always panic and say this is not what we want. So we tried to go straight, we would double date. But I was more interested in what she was doing, and I finally realized that this dating is not what I wanted, it was not me. If I wanted to be happy, I had to follow who I was

185

and what that meant. I quit college and went to work. That made life
easier.

I moved out of the house when I was twenty-three. My mother
thought that was too young to move out. I used to go back to visit
every Friday afternoon. One Friday we were sitting around the table
and my father made a comment about Liberace being a faggot. I said,
"So what? What difference does that make?" My father looked at me
and said, "Maureen, your mother wouldn't know if she were sitting
next to a gay person." My mother was sitting next to me. I looked at
him and he said, "I think it's best that we keep it that way." We
changed the subject. So I knew that my dad was aware, but I never
talked to him about it.

I don't know if my mother knows. She couldn't handle it if I told
her. She would be more comfortable denying it. She always hated any
women I was close to, even my best friends. We survived on mutual
dislike for many years. Actually it was Nancy, my lover, who got me
and my mother back together again.

When my father was very sick, my brother and I flew to Florida
to visit him. I decided that I was going to come out to my brother.
On the plane I told him I was gay. He said, "Yes, I've known that
since you were twelve years old." My other brother is very chauvinistic.
When I told him, the first thing he did was go to a priest to see if
there was something the family did wrong. We haven't gotten along
since then. When I was in Florida with my older brother, he took me
to a car wash where all the workers were lesbian. He thought it was
wonderful.

I have been involved in relationships with four women. Nancy and
I have been together eleven years. It's a nice relationship. We are closer
now than we were when we first met. Nancy's father lives with us.
He doesn't know, and yet he does. He considers me his other daughter.
In some ways I'm closer to him than Nancy. I yell and scream at him,
and take him shopping, and confide in him. He is a very special man.
He doesn't question. To him lesbians are those very masculine bull-
dykes, and since we don't fit that category he won't experience us as
lesbian. It's easier for him.

I didn't go to church for about ten years. When I met Nancy she
was going to Dignity in Chicago. As our relationship developed I got
more involved in Dignity. We would come into the city almost every
Sunday, but it is a very long ride, thirty-four miles one way. We then
got involved in the DuPage chapter of Dignity. Nancy was president
for two terms. That made me the first lady. We have been active there

for four and a half years. Nancy is more involved in the political aspect of Dignity and I'm more involved in the social part.

Nancy: I went to a Catholic grammar school and a Catholic all-girls high school. At the end of my junior year I entered the convent. I spent ten years in the convent and made perpetual vows. I was dispensed from my vows in 1969. All this time I did not know I was gay, but I knew I was different. As a kid I was a goody-two-shoes. I still am. If I were in the Garden of Eden, we wouldn't be in this mess. I always do what I'm told. I was a tom-boy and didn't like to be with the girls. In high school I started to feel the pressure. All the girls were concerned about dating, but my relationship with boys was to be on their baseball team. When that was over, I didn't want to be with them.

I was involved with the Legion of Mary. I was a class officer, and very popular. I hung around with the cheerleaders and when they would want to be with the football players I would leave. I liked being with the cheerleaders. I didn't know what all this meant. I just felt comfortable this way. I usually hung around with older girls. Most of them went to the convent. So in my junior year I would spend every weekend with them at the convent. I really liked it there. I also realized that I wouldn't have to date, or be concerned about the senior prom. One day my homeroom teacher said, "You have a vocation." That really surprised me because I was not very religious. She invited me to attend her final vows ceremony. At that event I had this feeling that I really belonged there. And so I joined.

During the time I was in the convent I enjoyed it very much, but I didn't know that I was gay. Somewhere around my eighth year one of the sisters actively sought me out and we became particular friends. There was a lot of hugging and kissing. I felt guilty because of this, even though I was enjoying it. I still didn't see this as homosexual behavior. We carried on like this for about two years. My superior was having an affair with another sister at the time. She knew that I knew about her, so she had me transferred. These two years were very difficult on me so I decided to leave.

I continued to stay in the church. I really didn't have any trouble with the church. It is only recently that I have begun to question things. About a year or two after I left the convent I met a guy at work who was gay. He asked me out on a Friday. After I said yes, I was petrified. I was twenty-seven years old and scared to death about the date. Ten minutes before he arrived I had this revelation that he was gay. I don't know where this came from. As we were driving he said, "There is something I have to tell you. I am gay." I said, "I know that." From then on I was at ease with him. He took me to gay bars. I still had not admitted to myself that I was gay, even though he tried to tell me I was.

My concept of lesbians was what my father told me, that lesbians were women who dressed like men. I didn't have that concept of myself, so I decided I was not lesbian. I hung around this gay man for years and the result was that I knew a lot of gay guys but no women. He kept telling me to go meet women. So one day after work I went to a lesbian bar. After one evening there I realized that I don't like drinking: I don't like the bar scene, therefore I can't be gay.

I didn't know where I fit. It seemed like the whole world was a play and everyone had a script for me. I didn't feel in step with things. Somehow I got hold of the gay publication in Chicago and spotted an ad for Dignity. I decided to give it a try. I can remember my first visit—I almost cried through the whole Mass. I felt like I just came home. It was a peaceful and friendly place to be. After that I went every week. Through that contact I met a friend who owned a bar, and although I don't like the bar scene, I would go there every Friday and help her clean glasses and organize things. It was at a party in this bar that I met Maureen.

Within the year we moved in together. She had a house and I had a condo. We decided that it can't be your house or my house, so we sold both and bought our house. At this point we stopped going to Dignity. There were political reasons why we stepped out. I continue to go to Mass, but it is beginning to mean less to me, because as a female it doesn't reflect me in any way. This is something that has begun to bother me in the last couple of years. I was never a separatist, but all I experience at church is men. Even in Dignity I feel that most of the men don't really understand my feelings. They can't see it from my point of view, or why I am unhappy in this structure. We dropped out of Dignity for several years, although I espouse the purpose of Dignity.

We eventually got involved in the DuPage chapter. A man and I went to see the bishop to explain what we were all about. The bishop told us he doesn't agree with us, but he respects our sincerity and good faith. He suggested that we would have Mass once a month. We had permission to have any priest in the diocese to have Mass for us. We continued to remain in low profile. The bishop had a Mass for the group and told them that he loved them and would do whatever he could, but that he could not sanction the group. That was three years ago. During my term of office I wrote to him often, keeping him informed about our activities. In view of how different bishops are reacting to Dignity, we are fortunate.

Maureen: When we read the Ratzinger letter, we found it hard to accept that he can really believe what he wrote. The tragedy is that he is highly educated and highly placed, and yet can make the kind of statements he did. I don't know where the church is going, the upper hierarchy. It seems like a men's club where members are so taken up with who they are that they have lost the rest of us. I am offended not only as a gay person, but as a woman and a Catholic. When they talk about women on the altar it reminds me of the myths we heard as kids about not letting the host touch your teeth, and other unimportant things like that. I don't want to wait for the change, I want it to happen now.

I wonder what the future will bring. Are we strong enough to break away from the church and still be united? I don't have the faintest idea. We need to get together with our people to find out where they are. Nancy wants to "walk," she wants to leave church property. If a large number of the membership wants to stay, then we have to decide what we will do. I think I'm in the frightened group now. To me the worst scenario would be not being able to get a priest, and having to go to the Episcopal Church with an Episcopal priest.

Nancy: The church has a tendency to control and keep you in one place. I see value in stepping away, it gives us a new freedom. The bishop really doesn't have any power over us. We chose to give him that power. I think this is true throughout the church, the people in the pews have given him this power. We don't need his permission to be who we are. We can always go to other places for worship.

BILL KNOX and JOHN BRADY

Bill and John live in a committed monogamous relationship on the west coast. Bill works for a pharmaceutical house. John is a college administrator.

Bill: I was born and raised in the midwest. I have two younger sisters and a brother. My mother has always been very involved in the Catholic Church, both on the parish level and the diocesan level. My father was not Catholic, but was willing to let us be raised in a Catholic background. I went to a Catholic grade school for eight years, with very good grades. I did not go to a Catholic high school, and this was by design. My father was a mortgage banker and knew the priests at the local Catholic high school. He had numerous loans to them for their buildings, and wanted nothing to do with them from an educational standpoint. My two sisters went to the local girls' academy, but he would not let my brother or me attend the Catholic boys' school. During that time I still remained attached to the parish through their outreach program to high school students.

I attended a state university and became involved in the Newman Center there. I was fairly active there for five years. I would never say that I was an orthodox Catholic, but I certainly identified myself as being Catholic, and I still do. It was after earning my undergraduate degree that I went to Boulder, Colorado. I started the process of coming out. That was my basic reason for moving to Boulder, to come out. I needed to deal with that away from my home town. Boulder seemed like a good place to do this. I used graduate school as a pretense to leave family and friends and job. That didn't require any explanation.

In Boulder I became involved with the Newman Center, but I was not "out" as a gay man. I was really looking for an affirming environment, and initially didn't believe I would find that in the Catholic Church. I looked at the Unitarian Church and found an affirming place that helped me through that process of maintaining a religious belief system. The pastor of that church encouraged me to deal with the people at the Newman Center in terms of being gay and to complete the process of leaving the church if in fact that was the direction I was to go. He felt that there would be a strong chance that I could find a place in the Catholic Church where I could be comfortable. So it was through the Unitarian pastor in Boulder that I moved back into Catholicism, to the Newman Center. I found them to be quite supportive. It was through the Newman Center that I was introduced to Dignity. Dignity had just had its first convention in Los Angeles, with write-ups in the *National Catholic Reporter* and other places.

I was asked to represent the collective university ministries at a conference on gay ministry at Bergamo Center in Dayton, Ohio. I spent a week there with about fifty people, who ranged from theologians to gay activists, to people in pastoral roles. I met people from National Dignity there, and when I naively asked why there was no chapter in Colorado, they responded, wonderful, why don't you go back and start one? I worked with some people at the Newman Center and began the Colorado Chapter of Dignity. For a significant period of time that became the thrust of my view of Catholicism. During this process I found myself developing a view of Catholicism that was less traditional and certainly more mature as contrasted with the schoolboy image that had been imprinted on me.

The rest of the process really became one of believing in myself as a person and that I in fact have the ability to make decisions about my life. I was taking responsibility for both my physical and spiritual growth. While I still believe in the traditional values of the church, I also believe that I have the right and responsibility to myself to understand those values and to relate them to the world as I know it. For me that has meant leaving the hierarchical church in favor of the communal church. We are the church. My view of the church focuses on that. In Colorado we were able to put on retreats for Dignity people and other gays. We were able to bring in people like Bob Nugent, Richard Woods, and John McNeil. In that process I was able to see myself as a gay man and an active Catholic. When John and I moved to our place together in Colorado we became involved with a local parish. It was a very open community that was willing to accept us as two men who were in a relationship. They allowed us to become integrated into the community there. We were involved in liturgy planning.

When we moved to the west coast we found the quality of liturgy lacking; it didn't exist in fact. We spent a number of months going from parish to parish trying to find anyplace where we felt comfortable. We wanted a parish environment to belong to. Spirituality for us transcended a gay situation, and we didn't want to belong exclusively to Dignity. Eventually we found our little neighborhood parish tucked in the hill around the corner to be a good place to be. We are now very involved in the parish. We are both on the liturgy planning team, we lead small group discussions, we are ministers of the Word, and we are ministers of the cup. The parish priests and sisters know that we are in a relationship. It is not an issue.

Our basic philosophy is that we believe in the worth of the person more than in any preconceived moralistic approach to life. We are strong believers that the hierarchical church is dying and will continue to die. New communities are evolving which literally preach and live the Gospel, and who call ministers from their midst. There seems to be evidence that there is a split beginning in the church. Within the church it is difficult to find a nurturing environment as compared to the legalistic environment.

I've been very fortunate with regard to my family. I spent a number of years hiding from them after coming out. I got tired of phone calls and letters about the weather and school. After a few years of that and not talking about all the experiences I was going through coming to terms with being gay, I could no longer not talk about it. So I came out to my parents. My mother was surprised and shocked, but was willing to learn what it meant. My father went through a period of coming close to total rejection. He and I spent the better part of a year in which we did not talk. When I would call home, I knew that he was on the line because I could hear the click of the other telephone, but there was no communication. We worked through that, and by the time I met John, my father and I were at least in a position where we could talk. We didn't talk about religion, politics, or my lifestyle as a gay man, but about life in general. When John and I had our commitment celebration we invited my parents. They declined, but did come out a couple of weeks later and spent a very good time with us. Just before I came out to my parents I came out to the rest of my family, my brothers and sisters. My father died shortly after our commitment celebration. I feel blessed that he and I were on positive terms—open terms—when he died. John is considered a member of the family, and we both participate in family events, such as christening of nieces and nephews. We feel very fortunate. My mother is comfortable enough to complain when her doctor made a negative gay joke in her presence. She was incensed that he was so insensitive.

My coming out process was painful because of all the baggage I brought along from the traditional Catholic education. I didn't necessarily buy into the baggage, but needed it to be okay for me to reject it. That is what the experience with the Unitarians gave me. They empowered me to say, I can reject that part of my background and training, to believe in myself and still be okay. The most painful part of coming out for me was the lack of dealing with my family, and the lack of having support from them during that process.

I had sexual experiences with men three years before I came out, but they were infrequent and under miserable circumstances. I guess I don't consider that as part of my coming out process. I see that as the time when I asked if I could be gay. The first experiences I had were extremely miserable. It was unfortunate that I did not have a supportive environment when my struggle began.

John: I come from a very strong Catholic background, both parents being very religious. I went through eight years of Catholic elementary school, four years of Catholic high school, four years at a conservative Catholic college, and two years of Catholic graduate school. So I've had about all the Catholic education and background that I care to have.

I began the coming out process in my late twenties. One of the things that was going on that made the coming out process possible, although not easy, was going to a university to pursue a doctorate. When I was there a number of things happened. One, I was taking courses in the psychology department in counseling. I was associating with people who were very tolerant of different lifestyles. Two, I was going to classes where these kinds of issues were being discussed and we were trying to focus on what we could do as counselors to help any person we worked with to realize himself or herself to the fullest. That included sexuality. Also, I associated myself with the Newman Center at that university. I found a couple of priests there who, when I would discuss my sexuality, didn't become alarmed or offended. They were very supportive. I felt that I had "permission" to explore that person that I really was. I'm not sure that there was explicit "permission," but I had the feeling that it happened.

I was at the point where I realized that, hey, kiddo, you are a gay man and it's about time you start dealing with this issue. I had a few infrequent sexual experiences that were not positive. I can remember driving to another city to go to a gay bar, because I wouldn't go to one in the city where I lived. I met a couple of people who told me about a man I should meet who lived in the same city where I lived. I did call him, and he was the first gay man who became a significant contact in my life. We had a short relationship. I felt so good in that period of time about that relationship, a feeling that it was right. This added to the support I was getting at Newman Center, and the things going on in the classroom made it all come together. It made my being a gay man possible.

The other good thing that happened at that time was that I was beginning to be able to reject a lot of the rigid, conservative Catholic approaches that I had been taught. A lot of moral theology that I had been taught no longer made sense. I had the opportunity to explore not only my sexuality, but also my own spiritual development at the same time. I would look back at that point of association with the Newman Center as a time when I began my mature Christian life, and began to develop a different kind of conscience. I was assuming a responsibility for what I was going to do, even to deviate from the traditional Catholic norms.

That's also the time that I made connection with Dignity. I was associated with Dignity for about two years before leaving for Colorado. That's where Bill and I connected. We met in May, 1978, at a Dignity retreat. Probably the good thing about meeting someone on retreat is that in that context you are discussing your value system. You wouldn't be discussing these things if you met in a bar or even over dinner. We were talking about things that were intensely personal and very spiritual. We were going together for months when we realized that we knew a lot of significant things about one another, but we didn't know the superficial things that most people find out immediately.

I was also fortunate when I arrived in Colorado and associated myself with the university parish. There I encountered a wonderful priest who gave me "permission" to continue to explore my sexuality. It was with this priest that Bill and I did our Pre-Cana training in working out our relationship. There were positive things that occurred for me in a short period of time that allowed me to make a radical shift toward positive growth and development.

I was in my late twenties when I came out. At the time I was coming out my dad died, so I didn't have to deal with him on this issue. After my dad's death, my mom's health went into immediate decline and she died a couple of years later. It was neither appropriate nor necessary for me to involve them in that process.

Bill: The current developments in the church, i.e., the Ratzinger letter, I see as an effort of a church that is struggling to regain power and authority, and in a sense almost becoming desperate. It's trying to use legalistic means to enforce a position that no longer can be supported theologically and spiritually. The church may have made some progress in the area of sexuality, but certainly not on the gay issue. In describing what that is going to mean to gay men and women, I have a mixed response. Many of us have come to terms with being gay and Catholic and have moved beyond the legalistic church. I think that as Dignity chapters are forced out of the church, we are going to see a strengthening of Dignity. Those people are going to remain involved because of the depth of their belief. Those who have not integrated the two are going to want to stay in the church building.

In a way I appreciate what is happening in some cities where the church is officially supporting a Mass for the gay community. Even though I may not agree with all the overtones of their supporting that Mass, I think that for a number of people that will be important. For me, I don't care where I celebrate liturgy. I'm there for what happens in the community and don't care where we are. I think the whole event is forcing Dignity to move to another level or stage. I think the change will be good. What most concerns me about the Ratzinger letter is the approval of gay bashing, physical and verbal violence against gay men and lesbians. It is unconscionable that Rome would come out with that position, and the American bishops have not taken it apart.

John: I would probably go a little further than Bill went in terms of the hierarchical church. He spoke as if this change will probably happen. I'm not sure it hasn't already happened and just hasn't been acknowledged by most people. We don't feel that we are operating outside the structure. Even though we may believe differently than some of the people who share the community with us, we are as much a part of the community as they are. The Pope knows a lot more theology than I know, he has a lot more authority in the church than I do, but we really are equal members of this church. I'm as much a part as he is. Most of us have the feeling that this is a Pope who does not listen. I have a distrust of anyone who feels so right that he cannot listen to someone who disagrees with him.

Bill: I feel sad that the process of discernment that took place at Vatican II seems to be ending. The present Pope has effectively done away with that process. Many of the things that are happening now will have lasting effects, and will not disappear in our lifetime even if we got a new Pope soon. The pain that is being thrust upon us now will not soon disappear. The church is losing much of its lifeblood. That makes me sad, because I believe in the church, in its power and its community. I see a significant loss taking place as many of us are saying that we are church, and if the hierarchical church doesn't accept that, it is their loss.

The names in this story have been changed to protect the privacy of the individuals.

NICKIE VALDEZ and DEBORA MEYERS

Nickie and Debora have been living together as lovers for the past two and a half years. Nickie is a carpenter by profession. She is one of the original founders of the Dignity chapter in San Antonio, Texas. Debora is a physical therapist.

Nickie: I was born into a Mexican-American family. This culture of course is tied in with the Catholic Church, at least it was when I was young. I went to public schools; then in junior high school I decided to go into the convent. I was in the convent for two and a half years. I finished my postulancy and novitiate. When I entered I was told that I was the child of a non-legitimate Catholic marriage, so that I might not be permitted to continue. When it was time to take my first vows they sought a dispensation, and it was not granted. This was in 1957. After that I went back to school and graduated from high school. Then I went to college for a while. I eventually got involved with the carpentry trade and became a carpenter by profession and also a picture framer.

Prior to going into the convent I was aware of my homosexuality. Of course, now I see that part of the attraction of going to the convent was being with those women. I had not yet named this tendency, but was aware that I could probably suppress these feelings by entering the convent. In this way I didn't have to deal with sexuality. After I left the convent and went back to school I began to realize and admit what my sexual orientation was. During my senior year in high school I was able to call myself gay, and I sought out friends who were gay. After graduation I realized that I could not stay at home because my family would not approve of my lifestyle. At that time I was not involved in church attendance. During the 1970s I got involved with the gay community in San Antonio. Things were just beginning to develop in the gay community. I got very involved in the free clinic and worked the switchboard. I also was involved in many of the gay social events, the gay pride parade and other conferences. During the bicentennial year San Antonio was given a government grant to put on a conference on gay life. We were able to draw big names to give talks, and we drew attendance from all over Texas and around the nation. Soon after that I started getting involved with a small group who were looking for some spiritual connection in our lives. We started meeting in our homes about once a month to discuss spiritual matters and to pray together. Then one member of the group mentioned that there was a Catholic group called Dignity. We investigated it through the national Dignity office. They told us we could have our own chapter if we could get ten people to join. We began to gather membership to get our charter. We met in homes every month until we found a chapel at St. Phillip's, which is a college. One of the nuns there was very supportive and allowed us to use their facility. The archbishop at that time was very anti-gay, and he forced the nun to ask us to leave. After that we disbanded for a time. Meanwhile, some of us decided to continue, so we sought out a priest who was sympathetic and allowed us to use his chapel. The archbishop died around this time, so he was no longer an obstacle. The new archbishop has maintained a kind of peaceful coexistence.

Several years later we decided to find a parish, which we were able to do. After a time a new pastor was appointed and he just threw us out without any explanation. When we moved to another parish some of the people at the former parish called members of our new parish and made crazy accusations about us. We eventually were asked to leave there, and ended up at the parish where we now attend. We've been there for about three years.

I don't know that I am very hung up on the church *per se*. I do believe in Jesus and his teachings. More gay people need to know that they are accepted by God, even if the church seems to not accept them. That's the reason I'm involved in Dignity. I don't need the church to know that I am okay spiritually, but I want to keep working in the structure as long as I can. I want to help others find what I have found.

I believe that Cardinal Ratzinger is misinformed, or if he is informed about gay life, his position is a political one. If he handled this issue honestly, it would mean that a lot of church teachings would have to change, and that would constitute a loss of power. I feel a responsibility to show them that they don't have to be afraid of losing power. I believe that the teachings of Jesus are very clear, and that the position of the church on women is not the teaching of Jesus. I have said at one time that there was no place for me in the church. But now I see a difference between the church and some of the teachers in the church. I have been able to separate the two. I belong to the church, and I won't solve anything by walking away. I feel a responsibility to try to do what I can do to make some change.

Debora: I was in parochial school until the fourth grade. My mother was Catholic and my father was a Baptist who became a convert when I was about nine years old. My mother is from Spain and she had difficulty teaching us in English, which I think accounts for the fact that we didn't have a really strict interpretation of Catholicism. We moved after my fourth year in a Catholic school, and then I went to public school. I had a good experience in CCD during those years. I went to a small Presbyterian college where I received a good liberal arts education. It was there that I became aware of my sexuality, and I started coming out. It was difficult for me to come out because I was surrounded by and influenced by people who were religiously very conservative.

When I moved back to San Antonio my mother found out that I was gay by going through my possessions. The terrible thing was the way she handled it. She didn't say anything to me but confronted my lover and told her to get out of my life. She also told her that she didn't want me to know about her contact with my lover. Of course my lover told me, and that's how the process of coming out to my family began. This was difficult for me, but it had a good effect in that it helped me grow up, to get on my own sooner than I would have. It was a sudden breaking of the family tie rather than a gradual one. Now my mother speaks to me but refuses to acknowledge my lifestyle or accept it. She has difficulty calling me; I have to call her. It's a very strained relationship.

I got involved with Dignity as a consequence of my mother's discovery of my homosexuality. I found out about it through a young adult minister at my parish who referred me to Dignity. It made me feel accepted and aware that there were other people like me who have gone through similar experiences. The church to me is the people, not the institution. Regardless of what the institution's teaching is, it won't mean anything if people don't appropriate it. I never thought about leaving the church. I have never stopped attending regularly. It fulfills a need for me and I enjoy it.

I have never felt not wanted in the church until the Ratzinger letter came out. I guess I knew the church's teaching on homosexuality, but I guess I chose not to look at it or take it personally. I always felt accepted in the church, and never expected someone to be at the door to take my ticket. If I felt accepted by God, what difference did it make? I guess my family gave me the sense that it was okay to be different, especially my father, who was brought up in a strict Baptist background. From him I got the sense that it was not necessary that everybody be the same. When the Ratzinger letter came out I wondered how people could be so cruel. How can people who are supposed to be peaceful say it is acceptable to expect violence against gay people? I feel comfortable where I am now. I am staying in the church because I can't help change it by leaving.

Nickie: Our Dignity group was founded by three women and one man. From the beginning we were using inclusive language and concerned about women's issues. Our active membership is about half women and half men. I think the only chapter that has as many women as we have is Boston. The key is that from the beginning we were involving women and conscious of their presence and their needs.

My former relationship lasted fourteen years. We parented a child in that relationship. He is the biological son of my former lover, but I am considered a parent. Now that she and I both have other lovers we all parent this boy. We all help pay for his education and his other needs. He is sixteen. We all love him very much. He seems comfortable to come to any of us for help.

Spirituality is what I'm looking for. I could probably find it in a lot of places, even Buddhism, but I'm Catholic. I think the Catholic Church, of all the religions I have observed and been involved with, has the most room for dialogue. Even though there are doors closing, I believe there is always someone who is willing to listen and offer alternative ways of dealing with any issue.

TOM KAUN and
KEVIN CALEGARI

Tom and Kevin live in a committed monogamous relationship in San Francisco. Tom is a teacher. Kevin works for the University of San Francisco. Kevin was a spokesperson for the Catholic gay community on the NBC program on Catholics in America, in preparation for Pope John Paul II's visit to the U.S. in 1987.

Tom: I had twelve years of Catholic education. Then I joined a religious teaching order for eight years. That involved my college years, a year of novitiate, and three years of teaching. Then I left the order. I was late in coming out in that I was not sexually active until I was in college. My Catholic upbringing was influenced by the B.V.M. Sisters from Iowa and the Irish Brothers of St. Patrick. In my early twenties I became aware that I was gay. My struggle with the church has more to do with its whole position on sexuality than with homosexuality.

My first sexual experience was with someone in the Order, a person who taught me when I was in high school. When I left the order I was struggling with sexuality in general. I had a relationship with a woman for a while, even though I was becoming more aware of myself as a gay person. This relationship didn't work out, obviously. Then I fell in love with a man and that relationship lasted about five and a half years.

After I left the order I did not go to church regularly. Then I found Dignity. My first encounter with Dignity turned me off because of the negative attitude of some of the men toward a woman speaker. Later a friend invited me back and I then went regularly. I have been involved with Dignity fairly intensely since then.

I have one brother and three sisters. One of my sisters is gay. I came out gradually to my family. The first person I came out to was my brother. He was very accepting. I wrote to my sister and told her about my lover. She said, that is interesting because I also have come to realize that I am gay. I went into therapy and it was during that time that I decided to come out to my mother. She had kind of suspected it by the time I told her. Since then I have told my other two sisters. I delayed telling my dad until I moved to San Francisco. I told him about Kevin. When he came to visit the next summer he didn't say a thing to me, although he did go to a family Mass at Dignity. As he was leaving he said he was glad I told him.

Because of my religious education I had a lot of guilt over masturbation and sex in general. But at some point I must have made a decision that sex is good. I had made a decision when I was ready for final vows that I would do my best to be celibate. I never had a chance to test that since I left before vows. What is really significant to me is the idea of relationship. Once I was able to accept myself as lovable and loving, I could feel good about myself. It took long years to get there. I think this is where the church failed me. It didn't teach me self-worth, but the opposite.

It's not so important to me personally where the church is. I experience frustration more because it oppresses those who can't free themselves from the church's grip. The church's sexual teachings are so irrelevant that I don't listen. Even though there is a lot of discussion by theologians, I don't expect any great change in my lifetime. That's why I think it is important that in Dignity we develop our own strengths and our own community, because there is no one to do it for us. I appreciate the catholicity of the church, I like the connection with people throughout the world struggling with the same issues we are. I'd like to maintain that as long as I can.

Kevin: I'm a native of San Francisco, one of the few. I'm a son of the church, coming from an Italian family. I have just one sister. I went to a Catholic school. I was an altar boy. It was a requirement of the pastor in order to play sports; you had to be an altar boy. All the others were altar boys in order to play sports; I was the only one who did it voluntarily. My family culture is very ethnic, northern Italian. It is warm, engaging, and very affectionate.

Strange as it may seem living in San Francisco, I had to go to Europe in order to come out. There were too many psychological barriers to do that at home. An anecdote that summarizes my religious education about sex is this: when I was in the eighth grade the pastor took the boys aside to explain the birds and the bees. He had been a military chaplain for years. He was telling some story about an airman who was treated badly by his comrades and was discharged. He stopped and said, "And that, my boys, is God's lesson to us. Never shave off your pubic hair. God put in there for a reason." Imagine telling this to a group of thirteen year olds, none of whom had any pubic hair anyway? It didn't register, but later when I look at it I appreciate that I had as few scars as I did from all the misinformation from the church regarding sex.

I had bought into the ideology that no sex is better than any sex. There was something about it that wasn't good. In order to be sure, I would go the path of celibacy. Until late adolescence I was a holier-than-thou kind of person. I had relationships in high school with women. One particularly was a very cerebral relationship that continued after we graduated. I went to Stanford and she went to Santa Clara. She kept corresponding with me, although I kind of forgot about her. I immersed myself in the Great Books program, so I was challenged early in college to look at all my traditions. I realized by the end of my first year that I believed in everything that Sister taught me but for totally different reasons. For the first time my faith was examined and critiqued. I decided to stay part of my tradition, but not merely to give mindless obedience to it. I'm part of a tradition to which I will contribute as I pass it on.

I decided to do my honors thesis on Augustine. I took his work entitled "De Nupsiis et Concupicentiis" ("Marriage and Concupiscence"). Of all his works this is the sickest. He completely succumbed to his Manichaean roots and said there is no cure for sex. The title of my paper was "De Nuptiis et Concupicentiis; Augustine's Cure for Terminal Illness." For him, sex was a terminal illness. This paper came after my coming out.

About a year later I was living in the dorm and my roommate was a very attractive person. At the same time I found myself attracted to his girlfriend who lived next door. We became a happy threesome for a while. I was fascinated by this, although there wasn't anything sexual involved on my part. My hormones started to act up. Up to this time I had done a marvelous job of being intellectual and cutting off this part of myself. As their relationship grew more intense I was left out and began to feel very lonely. One day I found myself saying to my best friend, "I love you." He said, "I love you too, Kevin." Then I said, "No, you don't hear what I'm saying. I love you." He finally caught on to what I was saying, and his response was very affirming. He said it was okay for me to feel that way although he didn't feel the same about me. I'm lucky it happened this way. It could have been more traumatic.

I went to Europe in my junior year and that's when all hell broke loose. I had to leave my roots in San Francisco to get back to my roots in Europe in order to get the perspective to come out. I still had a bifurcation of sexuality and spirituality. I had to put one part aside, my spirituality, in order to investigate my sexuality. I went to Rome for six months, for one term. My first experience was when I was coming out of the Vatican gift shop. I had to go to the bathroom. There I encountered a tall blonde German who was obviously soliciting me. I was scandalized and mortified. I ran out into the piazza, then stopped and turned around and waited for him to come out. He never did. Then the guilt started. I think I said a whole decade of the rosary at every altar in St. Peter's Basilica trying to get over this.

My favorite spot in Rome wasn't St. Peter's but St. Clement's. It is a basilica on top of a basilica on top of a temple to Mithras, a popular god in late antiquity. This church and its foundations symbolizes the ongoing tradition of which I am a part. Each of these different layers represents a different spirituality, yet all are part of a common tradition, and I am part of it. It challenged me to think about what am I going to pass on.

My first sexual experience was on a trip to Amsterdam. I then developed a relationship with one of my teachers in England when I was at Oxford. It was like *Brideshead Revisited*—it was all very elegant and English. The man I was having the relationship with was an Oscar Wilde scholar.

In my senior year when I returned to California I began to work seriously on dealing with my sexuality. I knew I had to deal with it honestly and completely. It's been a challenge and a joy. A priest at the Newman Center helped me begin to deal with it. I've been working on this process for eight years now.

I've been very involved with Dignity. I've been on the Board for many years. I've been a national delegate. The last four years I've been in the Task Force on Sexual Ethics. We are developing a pastoral statement we hope to have available for our next convention.

Coming out to my family was not easy. I felt the need to be explicit and forthright. When I came back from Europe I invited them to my apartment for dinner, and told them I was gay. It was pretty traumatic for several years. Only recently things have improved.

Tom: Kevin's relationship with his family has changed radically, especially with his mother. Since they didn't know gay people, or any of Kevin's friends, they were skeptical. Now that they have a better acquaintance with me and others they totally accept us.

Kevin: In my former job I was transferred to Hawaii. That occurred shortly after Tom moved in with me. I was very unhappy in the job and I missed Tom very much and was very lonely. It was also at that time that I was diagnosed as having ARC. So I quit that job and came home. It was important for me to come back to my primary community. I am in good health. The diagnosis was two and a half years ago, but at the time I was scared and didn't know what could happen. Since then I have been diagnosed with AIDS. I had been carrying that secret until about six months ago, and I then shared that with my new boss. He has been wonderful. I felt the need to tell him because there are days when I need to be away from work, either for doctor's appointments or because psychologically I need some time away. My health remains good and, for the most part, my spirits are high.

I was on national television prior to the Pope's visit. I was on the NBC program hosted by Maria Shriver. I was a spokesperson for the Catholic gay community. I was largely responsible for giving a Catholicism 101 course to the producer of the program. I encouraged her to get a picture of the Catholic Church in America other than a monolith, a group of mindless masses. Show local communities as being different. I decided at that point I had a message, and I didn't care about the consequences. It all worked out well, there was no problem at work.

The next stage of my spiritual development, and Tom's too, is coming to grips with a new mode of oppression. Whereas we have been very involved in Dignity and know the value it has been for both of us, we are moving from a passive stance to a more active one. Maybe it is better said that we are more active than reactive. We have moved from an appeal for acceptance to a demand for acceptance. We are moving even beyond that insofar as we know that acceptance comes from within, rather than some outside party conferring acceptance. That's what's happening in our lives, and that's what's happening in Dignity. There is no longer a need to look to the church for acceptance, or look to the magisterium for validation. We will no longer play games of bargaining or negotiation. I feel strongly that we can stand on our own two feet and that we bear the Gospel of Jesus Christ as much as anyone else in the church. I'm confident that what we are about is good.

We may have to create a community if the conflict becomes too great with the institutional church. Maybe now is the time to look for ways to create new communities that supply what Dignity has always been, an alternative, dynamic, grassroots community. We can do this without being bitter. We have benefited from this approach and we would like to see it continue. We are going to be Catholic no matter where we go, even if we join the Lutherans or Episcopalians. Our concern now is how we continue to learn as this process unfolds, and how we can become stronger and more effective teachers.

Tom: Our Dignity group wrote an extensive letter in response to the Ratzinger letter. We were accused by the local gay press of being in complicity with the letter because of our silence. Dignity is seen as associating with the enemy. We find ourselves always being on the defensive in regard to the church vis à vis the gay community. We see good things coming from the church, as well as the disastrous things like Ratzinger's letter. We were forced into taking a stand. The letter is so outrageous that it is difficult to respond to it point by point. This letter never would have come out if it had not been for Dignity. It was obviously aimed at Dignity. So what we are really dealing with here is a political issue. In another sense, it is probably a good thing. We at least are getting some attention, some reaction from the church. This is the first salvo from the other side.

My biggest desire for myself is to get more in contact with other people who are oppressed. For example, the whole issue of the oppression of women is a struggle which we are just beginning to understand. The linkages between homophobia and misogyny, between the struggles of women and of gay people, are becoming more apparent. We're dealing with the same oppression here.

Kevin: If I leave Dignity it will be to find more connections between our situation and other oppressed people. I find myself moving into alternative church experiences where these new ministries are developing.

JIM REVAK and
MICHAEL CONLEY

Michael and Jim live in a committed monogamous relationship in San Diego. Michael works for Lambda Legal Defense, a national legal rights organization that defends the civil rights of lesbians and gay men. Jim is a computer typographer and designer.

Jim: My family came from two religious backgrounds. On my father's side they were Roman Catholic, of the Byzantine Rite. My mother's side was Lutheran. In the beginning I was actually raised to some extent in both traditions. I would go to my mother's church for bible school. Then a little later I would also go for religious instruction at my father's church. It was comprised of a great number of Hungarian immigrants and people who were first generation Americans. This was in New Jersey. My father went to church every week. I was baptized in the Catholic Church. I have been exposed to both traditions, but I preferred the Catholic tradition more. It was the sacramental ministry that attracted me as opposed to the Lutheran, which emphasized the Word of God. For a long time I was very pious in my own way. I did all the things that were expected.

What caused my crisis was not being gay *per se*. My sexuality was repressed for a long time. What began to give me serious doubts, believe it or not, was *Humanae Vitae*. I was still in my teens, but I had a grasp of the enormity of this decision and how it shook the church from top to bottom. I could not for the life of me see what was wrong with artificial birth control. This so boggled my mind that I began to examine the whole concept of magisterium and papal infallibility. I really delved into it, and came to the conclusion that I couldn't believe it. I couldn't accept the magisterium as it was traditionally, conservatively taught. That was my real break from the

church. I also could not accept the church's teaching on masturbation.
No matter how much I tried to grasp it, no matter how guilty I felt
for years, I came to realize that this really didn't make sense to me.

This break from the church went on for years. For most of those
years I was a very spiritual person. I drew a lot of strength from eastern
religions, although not getting too involved with them. I even went
through a brief period when I doubted the existence of God. Then I
learned of Dignity during the early '70s. By this point I was coming
out. It was a difficult period. I wasn't getting along with my parents.
There was a period when I felt terribly guilty about being gay. Then
I started to go to some consciousness-raising groups, and some campus
organizations which I joined. I went to a workshop presented by a
couple of priests who were affiliated with Dignity during a gay
convention on our campus at Rutgers University. I thought this was
nonsense. I couldn't see how you could be gay and Catholic at the same
time. Then a few years ago I decided I wanted to meet people, men
I could potentially date. I was getting serious about getting involved
in a relationship rather than one night stands. The decision was also
hastened by the growing AIDS crisis.

I started going to Dignity. They had socials and liturgies here in
New York. They were very well attended, hundreds every week. I
found it difficult at first to meet people, because I joined Dignity at
a different time than Michael did. By the time I joined it was a huge
organization. I experienced it as impersonal. Very few people knew
everyone else. Then I started meeting friends like Michael. This was
a supportive environment. It was a chance to get to know people, not
like the bars. There wasn't this tremendous pressure to physically impress
others, or to go to bed immediately with them. It was a different and
a good experience. Michael and I dated and fell in love. We have been
lovers for four years. Without Dignity that would have been impossible.
I owe a lot to the movement. I'm glad it exists, and I'm proud to be
a member.

I found that I grew spiritually in different ways. For the first time
I began to realize that maybe it flies in the face of tradition but it is
possible to be both gay and Catholic. I began to listen to the sermons
and it began to make a lot of sense. I began to read Scripture, I began
to identify with a Christian tradition for the first time in years. I read
Fr. McNeil's book, which is now banned but widely read and I think
well-written. I accepted a lot of what he said, and after thinking it over
and examining it with an adult mind, I felt that you could be gay and
Catholic. I have formed my own conscience, and it has been a valuable

experience for me. This has made me more spiritual, and a better Catholic.

The so-called "Halloween" letter of Ratzinger was a terrible thing. The people who wrote it don't know what they are talking about. I think there is a long struggle ahead of us. I think the church will eventually change, although it is very slow. The church is changing. Anyone who looks at it historically knows that. My basic feeling is that I am part of the Catholic tradition, and I have just as much right to call myself Catholic as a Pope, a Cardinal, or a Bishop does. I may dissent on certain matters. Sometimes it makes me angry, but I really look toward Christ as my example, and at the Gospel as my primary teacher. I weigh what the hierarchy has to say but ultimately I have to come to peace with myself. I live with the fact that there is a hierarchy that doesn't particularly like me as a gay person.

Michael: I was born in a small town in Kansas and lived there until I was ten. Both my parents were and still are very religious Roman Catholics. Until I was in high school, I cannot ever remember missing Mass on Sunday.

I went to Catholic school all through grade school and one year of high school. When we moved to the east coast during my second year of high school, I attended public school and took CCD classes on Sundays.

And then when I was a freshman in college, I had a spiritual crisis that came about because of my interest in history. As a youngster, I was deeply religious and torn apart by the idea that my friends who were not Catholic would not go to heaven. In my history and philosophy courses in college, I began to learn that the Catholic Church is built upon a lot of traditions—some of which grew out of mythological and pagan legends and rituals.

What caused my crisis was the realization that what I had blindly believed all my life until then was not as ideologically pure as I had thought. Indeed, what I had believed was based in part upon rituals that I had been brought up to believe could not be questioned.

I don't fret so much about the mysteries that I accepted so easily as a youngster. But the spiritual crisis remains with me to some extent even to this day. I am more religious now than I was before joining Dignity, but a lot of the doubts from my days as a student have stayed with me—not in a way that makes me an atheist, but in a way that keeps me healthily skeptical.

After college, I worked a couple of years before moving to New

York ten years ago to attend graduate school at Columbia. For the first couple of years, I socialized with people at school and, later, in bars. I "came out" at this time, and had my first relationship.

That relationship broke up after a year. I began meeting people in bars. This was before AIDS, of course. It wasn't terrible, but it wasn't great either. Most of these were one night stands, and I found myself sleeping with men before a friendship had a chance to begin. They were very nice men, but after a while I realized that I wasn't meeting the kinds of people I wanted to meet. I was meeting one night stands in bars. I was meeting men who couldn't make a commitment to getting together for the weekend, much less for a relationship. And the breakthrough was in realizing that I was not the one who was unable to make a commitment. It was just my responsibility to do something to change it.

In a rare fit of self-analysis, I tried to figure out what I was looking for: I was looking for people who had had the same interests as I had. Since half of New York City at times seems like it is gay, I quickly decided I had to be more discerning than just that.

And then I realized that what I really wanted to meet were people who had had the same experiences as I, and who shared the same values. Although I had not been to church in over eight years at this point, I still knew my roots were Catholic and I instinctively suspected that I would find something in common with gay Catholics.

I decided to look up a group I had heard about several months before—Dignity. That was, simply put, one of the two or three major events in my adult life. It changed my life profoundly. I doubt whether I would be in my present job, in my relationship with Jim, or would have told my parents I was gay had I not gone to Dignity.

The minute I walked into Dignity New York, I realized that this was what I had been looking for since college. I met people with the same interests, the same values and—most important for me—I didn't feel that I had to sleep with anyone to be sure I would see them again. That might sound pitiful, perhaps, but I suspect it happens to more people—straight and gay—than one would suspect.

I met people that first night that I still know as close friends. My first year in Dignity I went to dances, worked on a musical revue, and joined committees. I was very lucky to get a second chance to experience the social life I never had in high school.

My nine years in Dignity New York would read like someone's resumé: board member, newsletter editor, and national convention director. In addition, Jim and I have been given many wonderful opportunities by the officers of the organization to write brochures and advertising—things that have helped me professionally.

Six months after I joined Dignity, I came out to my parents. This was another plus factor. I would never have expected what followed to happen. My friends had given me a lot of advice: "tell them," "don't tell them." I went home the first Christmas after joining Dignity wanting to tell them, but not knowing how. I told them that I had started going back to church. They were very happy about that. They wanted to know which church and I casually mentioned that there was a church in the Village that was for single people so they have a chance to meet each other. My folks were very happy that I was meeting people, but wondered why I went to a church so far from my apartment.

So I told them about Dignity, and it was one of the hardest things I've ever done. My father had always told us that there was nothing we could ever do that would cause them to hate us. This was in the back of my mind. They were stunned, but quiet when I told them. We didn't speak about it much that weekend.

Because I was living in New York and they had retired to Florida, we didn't see each other for the next two years. During that time, we spoke about Dignity and about being gay over the phone and that helped. A couple of Christmases later when I went to visit them, everything was different. My father treated me much better than I could ever recall and we had a long discussion about being gay. He acknowledged he had often wondered about me, and now felt bad. I told him there was no reason to feel bad, because I was happy.

I remember the night I met Jim. We saw each other distantly for several months, but it wasn't until later that we started hanging around each other after the social. Then we started dating. It was completely different from anything I had experienced before in terms of relationships. Before I had slept with guys and then tried to find out if there was any basis for a relationship later. But Jim and I knew each other for six months before we slept together. We've been together now for over four years.

I didn't go through the same struggle that Jim did about trying to reconcile being gay with being Catholic. For me, it was a struggle to reconcile being a Catholic, period. I came out later than Jim, and with relatively little guilt because I had all the guilt when I was younger.

People like John McNeill have helped me in this and other areas. I think John is a real hero as far as movements go. He has changed an entire movement's thinking about what is valid for gay people. I know John, and I'm proud to think of him as a friend. He has suffered terribly for what he has done.

I think the Catholic Church is going to change, but unfortunately it probably won't be in our lifetime. It will have to change in many ways. For example, it is inevitable that they will ordain women. Before I joined Dignity, I wasn't aware of how women are put down in the church as second-class citizens. Before 1982, I thought that talk about women being ordained was tantamount to high treason! But the church has already changed: priests were allowed to marry until the fifth century. So there is obviously flexibility, but not under the current pope.

I think it is more than coincidence that Pope John Paul II and Reagan came in at the same time. I once hoped that they would go out at the same time. The pendulum is going to swing again. Pope Paul VI looks better every day. He really carried out a lot of the reforms from Vatican II. He dealt with people like Cardinal Cooke did: with benign neglect. We could use some of that now.

I had hopes when Cardinal O'Connor was appointed. But now I see him as someone who loves to stand on ceremony. He was a Navy chaplain for twenty-five years, and within eight months went from the Navy to Scranton, Pennsylvania to head the preeminent archdiocese in the American Catholic Church. He owes everything to the Pope and will follow the party line. I once went to one of his Masses at the cathedral and it revolted me to be in the same room with him. He spouts all these pious beliefs such as "there can be no love without justice," but he just doesn't practice what he preaches.

Jim: I have difficulties with him because I don't like the way he comes across in the media. He's too quick on the trigger. Anything he says off the top of his head is read all over. I would like to see him think before he speaks. The issue over the American bishops' statement on AIDS is another example of his knee-jerk reaction. He has actively gone after gay people. If he had wanted to resist, he would not have had to throw Dignity out of St. Francis, where we had been meeting for years. What it says is, it is open season on gay people. He doesn't talk to people for input. He has the answers.

I stay with the church because of the need for a community with which to celebrate. I have hope that the church will eventually change. If gay people never fought back we would be nowhere. We would still be hiding in the closet. We have to stay and tell people who we are, and not be ashamed of ourselves. This does nobody any good, neither the gays nor the church.

Michael: I approach it in a more secular way. I was baptized in this church in the same way as the Pope and O'Connor. This is my church also. I don't think for one minute that I can win out over them on quoting Scripture, but I'm just as much a member of this church as they are. The church will change. The movement of history is inevitable. Gay people have an enormous amount to offer the church. I think gay people in general are more compassionate. They are significant contributors in every culture. Staying and fighting for what we believe in is going to make the church better. We are all part of the church—the hierarchy doesn't own it for themselves. One group cannot exist without the other.

Once upon a time Dignity did not exist, and many people felt guilty just being who they were. People committed suicide over it. As someone who came up through the ranks and who has benefited enormously by having a group like Dignity to help me, I want to be sure that the organization stays around and survives and grows for the sake of others. When that young man, young woman realizes that they are attracted to the same sex and feel guilty and dirty for it, I want to be sure there will be an alternative for them. I don't want them to have to listen to the claptrap that tells them they are disordered.

It's hard to be optimistic sometimes. But the tides of history are with us. A quarter of a century ago black people fought for their rights. Gay people will be next.

STAYING IN THE CHURCH/
LEAVING THE CHURCH

GERALD ALLEN

Gerald is a health services professional in Washington, D.C. He manages a clinic for sexually-transmitted diseases. He is married and the father of two sons.

It is interesting to me how I have arrived where I am today. I think the thing that is helpful to me is that I regard myself as an unfinished work. I am still evolving and growing emotionally and spiritually, in terms of my relationship with the world, with significant others and with professional life. I suspect that my background is a little unique. I come from a family of ten children. I'm the youngest. My mother was married to two brothers. The first six children are half brothers and sisters to me. Then my uncle died, and she married the younger brother, who was my father. About three months after I was born my mother died. I am from southern Maryland and among the black families children were never allowed to become wards of the state or be moved from their families. We were distributed among aunts and uncles.

I thrived and prospered. I went to Catholic schools and was with nuns and priests. I came early to recognize that the church was my key to survival and to thriving socially, and toward upward mobility, although no one knew what that meant then. I got the message that the key to success was doing what was expected of me, and doing it consistently and reliably. It worked for me. My parents were functionally illiterate. I taught my father how to read when I was about nine. But they were bound and determined that I was going to get an education, and that I was not going to be held from school to do the crops on the farm. They had to do battle with the landlord because I was not in the fields. I suspected that the landlord was threatened by me because I was talking about a world out there that was beyond the county I lived in. I never missed a day of school from elementary school through high school, not one day. It was clear to me that my parents expected me to do well, and I did well.

It was the same for the church. I got A's in school. I was an altar boy *par excellence*. I was a liturgist and was master of ceremonies for big events. I was active in CSMC (Catholic Students Mission Crusade), Holy Name Society, Boys Club, and 4H Club. I did what the family expected of me and did it well. I did what the church expected of me and did it well. My payoff was that I had *carte blanche* with the community.

I went into the military to make it a career. Eventually I was expected to marry and raise a family, and I did so. I was very much in love with the woman to whom I have now been married for twenty-five years. My youngest son is with the Navy on an aircraft carrier. I was almost twenty-seven when I married. Most of my classmates were married before they were twenty-one. I didn't get to go to college in the traditional way. I was working at my education for a long time.

I often think the compulsive activity that I was engaged in, and trying to do all things well, was probably suppressed sexual drive. It was never in my awareness. I had teenage post-pubertal experiences, out-behind-the-barn kinds of things, the post-skinny dip playing around. But those things didn't bother me. As I think of them today there was nothing special about them. They were biological passages. There was nothing to suggest to me that there was anything going on with me until after I was married. I had enough social and sexual contact that I should have recognized something. It was a few years after marriage that I experienced that there was something missing. I wasn't dissatisfied with married life, but I sensed something was missing. I slowly came to the realization what it was. I don't remember what the keys were that helped clear up the message. I was active athletically, I was competitive with men, so I had always been around groups of men. I did quite a bit of time overseas in the Navy. When I was in Spain some of that confusion started to bubble up. I was agitated and disturbed. At some point I became aware that I was interested in the men who were around me at a level that was greater than ordinary social exchange. I did a lot of observing of myself and my feelings. I looked back on all past experiences. Then I started to read things of a gay nature. At some point it dawned on me that a large component was sexual.

At first I rationalized that I was lonely for companionship, and that I was looking for adult males to replace the adult males of my family. It didn't take me long to realize that wasn't the real issue. It was around 1968 and there was a lot going on. The Navy was receiving its first draftees. The volunteers came out of a similar mold, lower to middle class, patriotic and focused, and driven by goals. The draftees were older, irreverent, undisciplined, and seemed to have no concern for the things we valued. They thumbed their noses at the Navy regulations. Their behavior made me question a lot of things I never questioned before. That's when I was exposed to more homosexual men than ever before. Up until that time there was always just the barracks talk. Some of these men were comfortable with homosexuality. It was all new for me. I was disturbed, but kept it to myself. I was around thirty years old at the time. When I was in San Diego about three years later I experienced the roaring in my head. I finally found out about the bars and the whole gay world, I finally acted on it. I did all my research on what places were available and acceptable. Let's face it, I don't fit in every situation. I'm black and I'm big. I took an afternoon off from work. By going during the day I thought I wouldn't look like an utter fool because there wouldn't be anyone there. I went, and was surprised at how welcome I felt. There was a real sense of relief that there were other people out there like me. I started to get a lot of parent messages about "thou shalt not," and "beware," and all of that. Here I was, a married man with two children.

Once I had clarified who I was, I started to deny it. I processed all this for a long time. I felt that the institutions I depended on in the past were not going to be there for me. I was on the horns of a dilemma, realizing that I wasn't responsible for who I was. I have a suspicion that if I had come to terms with my homosexuality before I was married, I probably would have been fairly comfortable with it. The thing that concerned me was my family, my obligations, my commitment.

I kept the secret from my wife from 1971 until 1985. There are a couple of things that made it possible. I remained very, very busy. I completed my undergraduate work in 1975 going to classes nights and weekends. I worked on my Master's degree, in school four nights a week and two weekends a month. I completed that in 1980. My wife took over running the house and taking care of the children. I was back into sublimation, which isn't all bad. The other saving feature was that I moved into a relationship with one man. That kept me from cruising and that frantic search. I was secure in this relationship. There was time that I spent with him. Eventually the pressure of leading the dual life became too much, especially after I finished graduate school. My wife started to home in on what was going on. She brought up the topic about a week before I planned to tell her. Scary as that was, we survived the initial stages, and she began to ask questions of other women and do some reading. I think things are okay today. I had joined a gay married men's group. I was getting a lot of help and support from the group, from people in the same situation. Many wives of gay husbands say that they can somehow deal with a relationship with another man, but couldn't deal with it if there were another woman involved. However, some women feel frustrated because they can't deal with the competition from another man.

I am happy in my work. It's exactly what I want to be doing at this particular time. Socially I have two social sets. I'm a member of my neighborhood community, and I have a good deal of activity in the gay community, mostly because of my job. I identify myself as a health services professional, working mostly with gay men who have sexually-transmitted diseases. People can conclude what they want. Nobody has ever challenged me or asked if I was gay. I do presentations as a professional in some very conservative areas, and nobody has ever asked me anything inappropriate.

I have a very interesting relationship with the church. It's never quite settled, I have my ups and downs. That was true before I came to admit that I was gay. About every five years I would have a falling out with the church. I would find something to be angry about with the church. I would pull back, and stop going to church for months, at one time for a year. That has stopped happening. I still have a lot of issues with the church, but I haven't backed away for the last fifteen years. I suppose I'm growing up. Now my level of discomfort is with the conservatism and unwillingness to deal with the real lives of people. I'm more upset with the church's treatment of women than I am with any other issue. That's the issue they are least likely to give on. I'm also uncomfortable with its treatment of homosexuals and other stigmatized people. Here I am a member in very good standing in the parish. I'm a lector and vice president of the parish council. It is very likely that I will be nominated for president of parish council next year. It's a real struggle with me to decide what to do. Would it be hypocritical for me to take that position when I am at variance with some of the church's teachings? The wrestling match that is going on between Dignity and the bishops is of concern to me.

I'm just beginning to get a grip on the greater implications of my sexuality. Coming to an awareness of being gay was a major piece of work. I think that I have long ago given up that image of church I had as an altar boy. Being gay and married makes me struggle over how to play out my role as husband, as Catholic, as a gay man. I can honestly say that I have dealt with the guilt I once experienced. I have to deal with two people with whom I am emotionally involved. My wife and my lover are good friends. The two of them have helped me solve some of my own problems.

We lost our oldest son about sixteen months ago. He was hit by a truck on his way to work. I don't know if he suspected that I was gay or not. I think I could have told him because we were becoming closer in the last few years. He went through the drug route and had rough teenage years. But he was coming around to the bright side. I have always been prepared to discuss it with both boys if they asked questions. We have always operated on the assumption that if they are ready to ask the question, they are ready for an answer to the question. If my other son asks, I'm ready to discuss it, but I don't feel any obligation to discuss my private life with him.

I happen to be Catholic, but I'm also black. For black people it is a cultural given that we should get sustenance and nurturance from the churches. That is always there for us. When I see things like the Ratzinger letter I really feel hurt, because the church is denying the reality of its members. The thing I know with scientific certitude is that nobody chooses his or her sexual orientation. I truly believe that, and I am comfortable with that knowledge. I am puzzled by this document. I think at the very least the church could be compassionate. Christ did not allow them to stone the woman. Those who are making these decisions are old men who are not married. They do not have families, or pay mortgages. There seems to be a real gulf between them and where the people are. It's very painful when my church does not support me as I am. Some people say, why don't you get out? My stubbornness moves in and says, I'll be damned if they are going to run me off. I cannot have an effect on the house if I'm not of the house.

The name in this story has been changed to protect the privacy of the individual.

LAURIE BROWN

Laurie is a physician assistant in Detroit. She chooses to work with the poor and underprivileged.

I'm the fourth of five children. I have a half-brother who is younger than I. My father was a congregationalist who converted to Catholicism. My mother was an Irish Catholic, born and raised in Ireland. She died at my birth. She felt that if she died in childbirth she would have done her duty. She should not have had more children because of her heart, but here I am. Two years after that my father remarried, and I grew up thinking this woman was my mother. She had one child, a boy, who is also gay.

I went to parochial schools for the first eight years in Cleveland. I went to a private Catholic girls high school. It was a fairly standard school, but on the more progressive side in regard to teaching religion. It was about midway through high school that I started to question things. In both grade and high school I was exposed to some social action projects. It has had an influence on my life. That's why I choose now to work with the poor. I was one of the few who spoke out against the Vietnam war. I got good grades all through high school. There was a strong academic influence in my family. We learned to deal a lot with our brains, but not much with our feelings.

By the time I got to high school I was beginning to become rebellious, although quietly rebellious. It was due in part to the fact that my stepmother was a very rigid person. I used some drugs, and I would fool around in class rather than do my work. My grades went down some, but I was always able to keep up. It was about my sophomore year that I became aware that I had feelings for women, but I was not clear what these feelings were. I just felt very close to certain women. I grew up with my best friend who was my age. We used to fool around and do some sexual experimentation. I enjoyed it, but didn't know what it meant. When she got a boyfriend I do remember getting jealous. So I decided to get a boyfriend too. Through high school I was close to women. I had a big sister who was assigned to me. I really liked her. She was special. I wrote her a song, since I was into playing my guitar and writing songs at that time. In my sophomore year I had what I think was my first crush on another girl. We hung around and smoked pot and stared into each others' eyes, but never did anything sexual. We never even discussed it. She and her family were transferred out of the city.

There was an English teacher with whom I got pretty close. She was Jewish and not really accepted, and I was a rebel, so we got along well. I talked to her a lot and I felt attracted to her. I remember at a school dance when she was a chaperon and she danced with her husband, I got these sudden sexual feelings. I had no idea where that came from. I immediately tried to squash it. I was also close to another teacher who was a nun. She and I still correspond. She was living in an apartment with another student, and when she left the convent she continued to live with this other women. I'm convinced that she is gay, although we have never talked about it. We only talk about it indirectly. She knows about me but is careful talking about herself.

I dated guys and got sexually involved. I was trying my best to do what I was supposed to do. There was one guy that I was involved with who I really liked. I realized later that all the qualities I liked in him are the qualities I liked in his mother. He was a gentle, literary, intellectual person. He went away to school and our relationship broke off. I tried to get involved with other guys, but it didn't work.

When I graduated from high school I got a scholarship to go to a university out of state. I was glad to get away from the family. My older sister stayed home and it made her nuts. My first year away was very exciting. It was okay to be openly intellectual, which wasn't true at my high school. In other ways it was a difficult adjustment. My roommate was a completely radical Californian. I was unsure about how to deal with relationships with men. I got close to some other people who were there on scholarships. I also got close to another female student and the two of us ended up going out with the same guy, who dumped both of us. We spent one afternoon holding hands and declaring that we would never let another guy come between us again. I meant it. I think she did too in some way. When we went home for the summer it was a very teary departure. I was beginning to be aware that maybe I was lesbian.

My roommate had come out three months before. Earlier in the year we went to a talk on lesbianism. I said about myself, well, I guess this is possible. I got introduced to some of my roommate's very radical friends who talked about lesbianism. I was struggling with these feelings, at the same time trying to do what I was expected to do, date guys. I was trying to prove to myself that I wasn't gay. It felt horrible. On the way home that summer I was reading the *Diary* of Anais Nin. That summer I was trying to figure it all out. I would drive down to the gay bars, and drive around, but not go in for fear of being discovered. Also at the time my drug use increased because I wasn't dealing with all this and because of the tension in the family. I was starting to process it all. When I was on vacation with my family and another couple I talked with this other woman. When she started to ask questions about my ideas and other things I told her I was a lesbian. That was the first person that I said it to.

Right after that I went back to school. I was very unsettled because I really didn't now where I was with my sexuality. I had a relationship with a man during the summer and while it wasn't too bad, it did present me with difficulties. At the same time I was working as a bank teller and fell madly in love with the manager who was this gorgeous, tall, blond German woman. When I went back to school and started to think about all this I got pretty freaked out. When I met my friend from the previous year whom I had a crush on, I started to tell her what I had been through. She told me that she too had thought about the fact that maybe she was lesbian, but decided she wasn't. So I had to struggle with what this meant to me. I also decided that I had to deal with my drug use. I decided to stop cold turkey, which was not a good idea.

I was very depressed after this. I felt very lonely, and knew that I was lesbian. The person I was in love with didn't want any part of it. It all came crushing in on me. I was very depressed and attempted suicide. I was very close to being successful. I don't remember being found but apparently I wandered out of my room into the corridor and passed out in the lounge area. I was on the respirator for two days. I remember waking up and the intern hovering over me asked why I did it. I said that I was bisexual. He was very supportive and said he went through some of that when he was my age and that it was not that unusual.

I was hospitalized for a while after that episode. My parents were pretty upset. My stepmother had figured it out. I think she had read some of my diaries. I told her, yes, that I thought I was what she expected. She didn't deal with it very well. After I got out of the hospital I started to get involved with some groups who would be supportive of who I was. It helped me to integrate the various parts of me.

When I went back to school the finances became a problem. The family was in a financial situation that didn't allow them to help. I also had a hospital bill to pay. So I got a full-time job in the library and continued to go to school at night. I did that for three years. During that time I began to integrate what it meant to be lesbian. I first started with a group who were heavy in the separatist movement and found that didn't fit for me. Then I started going to the bars. That went on for a while and I got into some relationships that were okay, but not satisfying. I got involved with the gay switchboard and some other things. What helped me put it together again was church-related things. I went to MCC church and found some people who helped me integrate my sexuality. I eventually drifted away, and then became involved with Dignity. That gave me some focus and a way to get back to the church, but it wasn't working. Once I went to Mass at the Newman Center at the local university, and the sermon was about homosexuals being the same as animals. I walked out. Dignity helped finish the process that had begun at MCC. Although my theology was probably far different from the theology of the Catholic Church, the sense of community and spirituality were helpful to me.

At that time I was involved in a relationship with a woman a little older than I. We were living together. That was the first time I lived with one of my lovers. We were together about two years when she fell in love and left me. It was painful but I got through it. I was involved in another love affair that lasted about three and a half years. During that time I finished school with a degree in biology and psychology. I got a job in Detroit as a physician assistant, and she did not want to move up here with me. Not only did she not want to move, but she was involved with someone else. That was pretty painful. Again the old issue of drug use came up. I also realized that at times I drank too much. I also jumped into a relationship that was not good for me. We fought constantly. I started to see a therapist and started to go to Alcoholics Anonymous. Shortly after that I went to a professional conference in Denver. There I met Mary who is my current partner.

I went from involvement in Dignity to finding my spirituality through the twelve steps of AA, to joining the Unitarian Church where I find acceptance and meaning. My stepmother is shocked at this, and my father is more accepting. He came from a congregationalist background which is somewhat similar. My brothers and sisters are sort of in and out of church. None of them is deeply involved in anything religious. My brother who is gay has AIDS. He lives in Hartford. He is also a recovering alcoholic. We have become close because we have been able to share these common issues. When he called up my stepmother to tell her about having AIDS, he asked her to call me and tell me. I got the next plane to Hartford to be with him.

Although I'm not involved with the Catholic Church any more, I still keep up with what is happening. I appreciate what I have received. I would like to be able to fight for the rights of gays and lesbians but I don't have the energy to expend. It doesn't fit for me, but I admire those who do try to make changes. I don't want the bastards to take over, but I also don't want to spend all my life fighting when there are so many other good things to do. It was a hard decision to leave the church. I still feel pulled. I received my whole concept of social justice from the church, and most of my life and work is based on that. I get my meaning from what I do in all my life rather than going to church. I'm ambivalent about the Catholic Church. It has oppressed me as a woman and as a lesbian, but there is also something good about it.

The name in this story has been changed to protect the privacy of the individual.

JOE MCGUIRE

Joe lives in a committed monogamous relationship in Austin, Texas.
He works as a probation officer for the county.

I was raised in a very conservative and midwestern Irish Catholic family
in Cleveland, Ohio. My father was a self-educated man. He was a
merchant marine engineer, and consequently he was gone nine months
of the year most of my years of growing up. I didn't get to know him
until later. Mom ruled the house with a very strong hand. She had three
sons and no daughters. They were very religious people, and I've always
appreciated that about them. They were the biggest influence on my
life in terms of religion. A sister of my mother who is an Ursuline nun
also had an influence on all the family.

My mother was persuaded by her sister the nun that if she had
safe delivery of her children, she would name them Mary after the
Blessed Virgin. So my name is Joseph Mary McGuire. My twin brother
also had the middle name Mary, which he had changed at age sixteen
to Michael. I only use the initial M., but all my friends know my name
and that I am proud of it.

When I got to grade school I developed a special relationship with
a nun who taught me in the third grade. We remained very close until
her death, which occurred when I graduated from high school. She was
always ahead of her time. Although she died in 1965, I could see her
now, if she were alive, being a very progressive person. Her blood
sister who was also a nun in the same community became a close friend
also. All these people were influential in my religious upbringing.

I went through Catholic grade school, high school and college. The
high school was run by the Holy Cross brothers. I received an academic
scholarship to their school here in Austin, St. Edward's University.
This was from 1965 to 1969, when all the changes were occurring in
the church.

I think that was the right timing for me, because I didn't realize that I was gay until after I graduated from college. I had good theology courses that made us question some of our conservative thinking. I was able to put the whole thing together without throwing out the baby with the bathwater like a lot of my friends did. I have a friend, with whom I taught high school after I graduated, who always said that the church would be all right if they could deal realistically with sexuality. He was a former Jesuit. I see what he means when I think of the subject of homosexuality.

When I realized that I was gay, I was able to accept it because I felt that God created me in that way. The irony of it was, that of all the people I knew, the gays were the most talented and sensitive ones. I saw something unique about that group of people, and so that which I discovered about myself, I didn't consider anathema. I was discovering something that I was proud to belong to. I suppose my personality helped to integrate the do's and don'ts of society. I'm a private person to the extent that I don't carry placards or go to demonstrations, although I'm supportive of the movement by other means. I have never had the need to seek acceptance in the public arena. I was able to separate my homosexuality from the jobs I have had as a high school teacher, administrative hearings officer, and probation officer. I taught theology and English in Florida. When I realized that I didn't like teaching, I quit and came back to the Austin area.

I have always been active in my church. When I came here I became affiliated with the Catholic Center at the University of Texas. It's the most vibrant community in the area. I believe that my religion is an integral part of me. Two and a half years ago an elderly great aunt became critically ill in Florida, and she had no one. I loved her very much, so I offered to bring her here for the last fifteen months of her life. This was a fantastically religious and growing experience.

About a year and a half ago, a brother of Holy Cross was taking a leave of absence from his community. He was a very good friend of mine. I had known him for twenty years. He was gay. We would read the leading progressive Catholic papers and discuss the issues. We were both concerned about the Pope's visit and the image of the church he was portraying, especially his critical role in regard to gays in the church. This friend decided to write to the Pope and ask him to stay home. He showed me the letter he wrote, and I thought it was good. The next day he died of a heart attack. I waited until his death notice was published, and put it in the mail with his letter to the Pope. I also wrote a note to the Pope. I basically said that with all the turmoil in the American church, and with his ideas, nothing positive could be accomplished by his visit and it would only serve to increase the turmoil. That was a pretty strong statement for me to make, considering my upbringing. We got an answer from Archbishop Laghi, the Apostolic Pronuncio. The answer was to Mark's letter, not mine. It stated, "His Holiness has noted his feelings." After I wrote the letter to the Pope asking him to stay home, the backdrop for his special altar in San Antonio collapsed. I said to myself, "Well, maybe the Lord was trying to tell him something."

When I left teaching I took a job with an insurance company as temporary employment. I wanted to get something in the line of social services. I then also had to declare my true religious feelings as a conscientious objector to the Vietnam war, and all wars. I took a job with the Texas Rehabilitation Commission. I was with them thirteen years as a hearings officer. When I took my aunt in to live with me, I was ready for a change. My lover Ken and I have been together for over five years. He comes from a Catholic family too. He helped me take care of my great aunt. I love him very much and am very proud of our relationship. After my aunt died I took a position of adult probation officer, and I like my work.

I don't remember a lot of guilt in dealing with my homosexuality. A lot of the courses in college helped me deal more realistically with guilt and its accompaniments. They helped me put most of these things in perspective. I tried to keep my gayness from my family. Finally, after ten years, I decided that I should not keep this from them, especially when there were a lot of questions about dating and marriage. So I told them, without too disastrous results. Today, at age forty-one, there are some family members I have never told. One is my mother's oldest sister, Rosalie, who will be eighty-four this year. She is a very special lady and I love her immensely. While we never discussed the issue, I feel that she knows, and that it is okay with her not to discuss it. There are a few other members that I have not told. However, my parents, brothers and favorite cousins all know. They still love me and have accepted who I am.

I'm not an angry person, but here's how I handle what is going on in the church today regarding its view on homosexuality. Cardinal Ratzinger is not Jesus Christ, nor is John Paul II. They are men like me who have views, but I do not accept their views. I see them as men who are very fallible, and on this issue I believe they are misinformed. Some day the church will change its official position. The real church that exists on the day-to-day basis does not operate from the position about which Ratzinger wrote. I don't feel less a part of the church because of Ratzinger's letter. I feel my relationship with my God is much more spiritual, and the position of Vatican II affirmed that mature people who inform their conscience and live by their conscience are doing the virtuous thing. I think the mission of the church is a very needed one in today's world. The sacramental life of the church is important to me. The church is much larger than one cardinal or a Pope who will pass away in time.

I had a guidance counselor in high school who helped me get the scholarship to St. Edward's. I also qualified for a scholarship to Notre Dame, but he saw the value in me getting further away from home. He always teased me every time we met with the same question, "Who are you dating, when are you getting married?" He was one of the people I never told I was gay. About seven years ago he visited Austin and St. Edward's to bring some students down. I invited him to my home for dinner. I knew he would ask the old question about who I was dating, so I was prepared this time to tell him the truth. When I did tell him, he said, "Well, I wondered when you were going to tell me." He then said, "You know what? I'm gay too." He said he knew I was gay in high school, and that was one of the reasons he wanted me to get out of that household situation and get to Texas where I could learn who Joe McGuire is. He had never discussed homosexuality with me or made demonstrations or passes. All I knew was that he was a kind and loving person and he thought a lot of me.

Many of my friends are in religious life. Many others left as an aftermath of Vatican II. They have been significant people in my life. I had thought about religious life, but I was pretty strong willed and I didn't think it was fair to require celibacy of priests. I had a few other strong feelings that kept me from buying into the party line in all these things.

I feel that the AIDS epidemic is a real tragedy. I have had many friends die of it. I stopped counting at twenty-five. I think the religious "right" are unfortunately spreading fears and lies about it. If anything good has come of it, I think it would be the stability and commitment that has moved into the gay lifestyle. It's a shame it took a tragedy to do this.

I feel good about being able to see the larger picture, and I'm very satisfied with my life. I'm very happy with what I'm doing now. I'm supervising a caseload of about a hundred and sixty probationers, and feel that I'm able to help them. I'm amazed at how many people have not been able to put together their lives after having gotten into trouble. There is usually an underlying problem that surfaces when I talk with them. My whole philosophy is putting Christian principles to work. I don't discuss religion with them, I'm not an evangelist. I just try to put into practice what I believe and have been taught by the great persons who have touched my life.

CATHY HOHL

Cathy graduated from a women's college in the spring of 1988. She wrote her senior paper on the topic, "Homosexuality and the Catholic Church."

A lesbian identity for me has been something very recent. I really started to claim it this year, and have been struggling with it about a year and a half.

I have a strong Catholic background. I didn't go to Catholic school until high school. I was sent to CCD during grade school and that was a good experience. The emphasis was on the God of love, rather than on a God of fear or judgment. We went to church each Sunday as a family, in fact we were the only people on our block that went to church. I always felt as though that made my family different somehow— set apart from the neighbors. Not that I thought we were better or more moral, but rather that we had to "play" by a different set of life rules than they did. Somewhere between CCD and Sunday homilies I learned that there were specific ways of being—things that one did or did not do—because one was Catholic. I vividly remember thinking that premarital sex, getting a divorce, or breaking a religious vow were sins from which one could not recover. That is, if one committed them, his or her life would somehow be forever marred.

When it was time for high school my parents insisted that I go to a Catholic school. I had been in public school previously and I was very apprehensive about going to Catholic school. I had images of uniforms, saddle shoes, and manic nuns with rulers. Although the uniform and the saddle shoes did come to pass, my experience of the sisters was very far from that of strict disciplinarians. In time I grew very close to them.

For a lot of students in high school the big issues were dating and proms and sexuality. For me they were not issues. I think it was an asexual time in my life. I enjoyed sports and I enjoyed my studies. I spent a lot of free time with the sisters. By the time I was a junior I was really close to one sister who went to the missions. She took me to their college. At that time I was thinking about becoming a sister. Some of my friends would ask me how I could embrace the celibate lifestyle of a vowed religious. For me that was not an issue because I didn't see that as giving anything up. I spent my senior year of high school thinking about becoming a sister. I was offered a very good scholarship to their college and that is what I used as my reason for why I was going to a school so far away. A lot of people didn't understand why I wanted to go there when I didn't even know what I wanted to major in. I never really leveled with any of them. My heart was really dragging me there because that is the motherhouse of the sisters.

I accepted the scholarship and went to college. My first two years I studied a lot, got involved in campus ministry, and in social justice groups—the Peacemakers and the World Hunger Coalition. My employer in campus ministry was a sister and she would take me to special events and social occasions with the sisters. I felt very comfortable there. If someone would have asked me to enter at that point I think I would have. I was pulled toward ministry, and toward reading the gospel radically, and standing up for social justice issues. It seemed to me that these women were living all that.

I wanted to join them in their ministries, in their option for the poor, and most of all, in their community living. To me community living was attractive because I did not want to get married, but I certainly did not want to live alone.

My junior year of college was really a transitional year for me. It was a difficult academic year. I had a lot of classes in my major with a demanding amount of papers to write. I tended to pull back from my friends and spend a lot of time in the library to get my work done. By November I had just about lost all my friends because nobody wanted to be around me. I would get moody because all I was doing was studying without any recreation. A couple of friends approached me and said, you really should talk to someone because you are not the Cathy we know. I turned to a friend who is a very wise woman and we would meet frequently. She helped me look at my relationship with my mom and why I was so intense on getting good grades. Second semester she raised the issue of sexuality. It was an area that I had never thought about. I never thought in terms of straight or gay, especially about myself. It was through these conversations that I realized sexuality had never been an issue in my life.

These conversations led me to think about why being a sister would have been acceptable for me. I had never been sexually attracted to men, so I thought that my interest in ministry predisposed me to a life of celibacy. What I did not realize at the time was that my interest in becoming a sister was really the awakening of my lesbian identity. I was attracted to this group of women for their strength of character, their integrity, their passion for justice and their ability to really care for each member of their congregation. The thought of living intimately, but not sexually, with these women was a plus because of the support and love, rather than a minus because of the vow of celibacy. Then a friend challenged me to take a closer examination of my most intimate relationships. For the first time I realized that all of my most intimate relationships, with one or two exceptions, were with women. Initially I said, so what? I'm attracted to their inner beauty. When I finally let my guard down and was honest with myself, I had to admit that I could also be sexually attracted to some of these people. That was a very difficult step and admission and I know that I could never have made it without the support of good friends. For me, there was nothing in my life that offered a lesbian identity as a possibility. When I realized that I was not attracted to men and marriage, then I figured that celibacy must be the road for me. I am very grateful to those people who enabled me to consider the possibility of loving women. I see that offer as a gift, a gift which no one else had offered me, a gift that proved to be very liberating.

I started to do some reading, and started to pay attention to places where I felt most comfortable. When I started to observe who I was attracted to, I realized that I didn't have any answer to my many questions. I just had to let them be. I stopped trying to force myself into a specific sexual identity. When I let go of it a little, it was an identity that was more easy to accept as I went along. If someone asked me today, I would say that I am a lesbian, although it is an identity that I am slowly growing into. What is most important to me is to fall in love with a person's heart, not their sexual identity.

Our campus ministry was supportive of gay people and prophetic in terms of social justice issues. Just having people around the staff who weren't condemning gay people and talking in homilies about marginal people, was a positive thing for me, and I'm sure for others. Some people felt our campus ministry was radical. It depends on how you define Catholic. I consider our case history a credit to the Catholic

Church. When campus ministry co-sponsored the gay and lesbian student group for a poetry reading, the whole campus was in an uproar. So I think I have been encouraged to a positive self respect for my own identity.

Anybody at my college who is perceptive probably knows now that I am gay, because of my senior thesis. In the beginning of the semester when people would ask what my paper was about, I'd say theology. Then I got to the point where I'd say ethics, then sexual ethics. Then I finally told people that I'm doing my paper on homosexuality. For me that was a journey. I had about fifteen friends who were really close, and for them this was not an issue of condemnation but one of social justice. It was basically a non-issue to them whether or not I was gay. We spent many hours in our cafeteria talking about the attitudes of people on our campus toward gays and lesbians. At the same time the sociology department brought in speakers to talk about homosexuality and AIDS. I think that all of these programs challenged the students' negative attitudes about gay people and encouraged them to develop more accepting attitudes.

I was disappointed with the faculty at the time of the defense of my paper. I poured an incredible amount of energy into it. It was supposed to be a twenty-five page paper. I ended with sixty-five pages. It was frustrating because they asked questions that danced around the issue. At the end of an hour-and-a-half defense, we had never said "gay" or "lesbian" or "homosexual," except once. How can we talk about this topic and not use the words? My friends and I were laughing, but we were really crying, because nothing really happened. Most of the questions were methodological. We never talked about my last chapter where I encouraged the Catholic Church to move forward. The faculty talked about how I could rewrite the paper. I didn't want to rewrite, I wanted to talk about what I wrote. We never really touched the issue of the Catholic Church's teachings about homosexuality.

I could finally see a purpose in my efforts when a friend came to me and said, "Cathy, we've been friends for four years and there's something I have never told you." She admitted that she was a lesbian and had been in a relationship for the past year. She had a hard time dealing with it, and was not able to tell anyone. She said, "I can tell you." This made all my struggles with the paper worthwhile.

One of the hardest parts of writing my senior thesis was that my mother did not know that I was working on it and that my father did not know the "real" reasons that I chose that topic. I decided not to tell my mother because I knew that she was not very open about the topic of homosexuality and especially in the context of religious beliefs. Also, I assumed that if she knew I was working on this topic, she might begin to put a few pieces together about me. I was not ready or willing to come out to her, so I kept my paper from her. My dad, however, knew that writing a senior thesis was a requirement and so he asked me what I intended to write on. At first I was going to say something vague like ethics, but I decided to tell him the truth. He was immediately at peace with my answer because he agreed that gay people were not being ministered to as all people should be. He could see my paper as a legitimate issue of justice in regard to the Catholic Church and society in general. He never once led me to believe that he saw my paper topic as a reflection of my personal life. That is, he saw my paper as an objective topic, rather than subjective. Though it is true that my paper is written from an objective standpoint, my reasons for choosing the topic were subjective. I needed to really search out the haunting questions about what Scripture had to say, what moral theologians had to say, as well as what Catholic doctrine and current feminist thought had to say. The paper was a journey for me. I was able to answer my questions, to squelch a few anxieties and above all to celebrate the gay experience and to be proud of the individual and collective contributions of gay people. What was difficult was that I could not share my work with my parents. My mother never knew that I had this enormous project weighing on me and could not understand why I was never in my room when she called or why I did not go out socially more often. I wish I could have told here that I wasn't a "library nerd," but that I was excited about my work. The hardest part was when I finished the paper and I was invited by my college's women's studies department to deliver the paper at the annual Intercollegiate Women's Studies Conference. This was a very happy achievement for me and I wish that I could have shared it with my parents. I thought to myself, if this paper had been on any other topic my parents would have been proud, but as it was I had to hide the whole occasion.

Being a woman in the church is so different from being a man, because there are so many ministries closed off to me just because I'm a woman. That makes me question the whole structure of the church. The Ratzinger letter is just one problem I have with the church. During the time that I was researching and writing, I went to meetings of gay and lesbian Catholics. I began to notice that there were two distinct groups of gay Catholics: (1) those who just want to be accepted and belong; (2) and those who challenge the church on their teachings and beliefs. I also noticed that there tended to be more men than women in the first group and more women than men in the second. As I thought about this, those proportions began to make sense. In most cases, but certainly not all, men feel more at home and at ease in the Catholic church because they are not alienated by the language, the images of God, and their ability to be ministers and leaders. But, if a man is gay, then he is alienated and the issue for him is the church's nonacceptance of a homosexual lifestyle. For women, however, the issue of homosexuality is just one example of how women feel alienated in most Catholic environments. Hence, women have to deal with being gay, but more especially with being a woman. Women see that the church has to be reorganized on more than just this one issue.

* * * * *

At the conclusion of her sixty-five-page senior paper, Cathy makes the following remarks: "Some readers might be surprised that my reflections on a re-constructive theology of homosexuality do not solely concern sexuality, as would be expected. This is because I view homosexuality as an orientation which influences and shapes *all* of one's life experiences, not only one's sexual experiences. Therefore, I believe that a re-constructive theology of homosexuality ought to comment on the lesbian and gay experience, rather than solely their sexual experience. That is, how do gay men and women, because they perceive and experience the world differently, open up new horizons for the formation of theology? What are the new images of God or new religious symbols which would arise from dialogue with the gay community? What can gay men and lesbian women teach us about the sacramental nature of our religion? Seeking answers to these questions, as well as exploring similar ones, would be to formulate a theology which views homosexuality as a life orientation, rather than solely a sexual orientation. Indeed, such a theology would promote a portrait of gay women and men as integrated, whole individuals, rather than one-sided sexual beings."

The name in this story has been changed to protect the privacy of the individual.

* * * * *

These observations from a young woman in her final year of college exemplify what can be learned from people who have traditionally been excluded from the church's deliberations on theological matters. The lesbian and gay experience has much to contribute to the ongoing theological reflection on the issue of homosexuality. Theology cannot be formulated in a vacuum. To remain a living force in the world, it must reflect on the experience of all *people in light of Scripture and the* whole *tradition of the church. This cannot be done by shutting out the voices of lesbian and gay Catholics. It will only begin to happen when we allow these people to speak about their personal histories, their struggles to find God in their lives and in their church. In other words, we must listen to their stories.*

APPENDIX

A Condensed Version of:
Letter to the Bishops of the
Catholic Church on the Pastoral Care of Homosexual Persons
Joseph Cardinal Ratzinger

1. The issue of homosexuality and the moral evaluation of homosexual acts have increasingly become a matter of public debate, even in Catholic circles. Since this debate often advances arguments and makes assertions inconsistent with the teaching of the Catholic Church, it is quite rightly a cause for concern to all engaged in the pastoral ministry, and this congregation had judged it to be of sufficiently grave and widespread importance to address the bishops of the Catholic Church this letter on the pastoral care of homosexual persons.

. . . .

3. Explicit treatment of the problem was given in this congregation's "Declaration on Certain Questions Concerning Sexual Ethics" of December 29, 1975. That document stressed the duty of trying to understand the homosexual condition and noted that culpability for homosexual acts should only be judged with prudence. At the same time the congregation took note of the distinction commonly drawn between the homosexual condition or tendency and individual homosexual actions. These were described as deprived of their essential and indispensable finality, as being "intrinsically disordered" and able in no case to be approved of (cf. No. 8).

In the discussion which followed the publication of the declaration, however, an overly benign interpretation was given to the homosexual condition itself, some going so far as to call it neutral or even good. Although the particular inclination of the homosexual person is not a sin, *it is a more or less strong tendency ordered toward an intrinsic moral evil and thus the inclination itself must be seen as an objective disorder.* [Italics added.]

247

Therefore special concern and pastoral attention should be directed toward those who have this condition, lest they be led to believe that the living out of this orientation in homosexual activity is a morally acceptable option. It is not.

. . . .

8. . . . Nevertheless, increasing numbers of people today, even within the church, are bringing enormous pressure to bear on the church to accept the homosexual condition as though it were not disordered and to condone homosexual activity. Those within the church who argue in this fashion often have close ties with those with similar views outside it. These latter groups are guided by a vision opposed to the truth about the human person, which is fully disclosed in the mystery of Christ. They reflect, even if not entirely consciously, a materialistic ideology which denies the transcendent nature of the human person as well as the supernatural vocation of every individual.

The church's minister must ensure that homosexual persons in their care will not be mislead by this point of view, so profoundly opposed to the teaching of the church. But the risk is great, and there are many who seek to create confusion regarding the church's position and then to use that confusion to their own advantage.

9. The movement within the church takes the form of pressure groups of various names and sizes, attempts to give the impression that it represents all homosexual persons who are Catholics. As a matter of fact, its membership is by and large restricted to those who either ignore the teaching of the church or seek somehow to undermine it. It brings together under the aegis of Catholicism homosexual persons who have no intentions of abandoning their homosexual behavior. One tactic used is to protest that any and all criticism of or reservations about homosexual people, their activity and lifestyle are simply diverse forms of unjust discrimination.

There is an effort in some countries to manipulate the church by gaining the often well-intentioned support of her pastors with a view to changing civil statutes and laws. This is done in order to conform to these pressure groups' concept that homosexuality is at least a completely harmless, if not an entirely good, thing. Even when the practice of homosexuality may seriously threaten the lives and well-being of a large number of people, its advocates remain undeterred and refuse to consider the magnitude of the risks involved.

10. It is deplorable that homosexual persons have been and are the object of violent malice in speech or in action. Such treatment deserves condemnation from the church's pastors wherever it occurs. It reveals a kind of disregard for others which endangers the most fundamental principles of a healthy society. The intrinsic dignity of each person must always be respected in word, in action and in law.

But the proper reaction to crimes committed against homosexual persons should not be to claim that the homosexual condition is not disordered. When such a claim is made and when homosexual activity is consequently condoned or when civil legislation is introduced to protect behavior to which no one had any conceivable right, *neither the church nor society at large should be surprised when other distorted notions and practices gain ground, and irrational and violent reactions increase.* [Italics added.]

. . . .

15. We encourage the bishops, then, to provide pastoral care in full accord with the teaching of the church for homosexual persons of their dioceses. *No authentic pastoral program will include organizations in which homosexual persons associate with each other without clearly stating that homosexual activity is immoral. A truly pastoral approach will appreciate the need for homosexual persons to avoid the near occasions of sin.* [Italics added.]

. . . .

17. . . . All support should be withdrawn from any organizations which seek to undermine the teaching of the church, which are ambiguous about it or which neglect it entirely. Such support or even the semblance of such support can be gravely misinterpreted. Special attention should be given to the practice of scheduling religious services and to the use of church buildings by these groups including the facilities of Catholic schools and colleges. To some, such permission to use church property may seem only just and charitable; but in reality it is contradictory to the purpose for which these institutions were founded, it is misleading and often scandalous.

DATE DUE

HIGHSMITH 45-220